Interaction and Language Learning

Edited by Jill Burton and Charles Clennell

Case Studies in TESOL Practice Series

Jill Burton, Series Editor

Teachers of English to Speakers of Other Languages, Inc.

Typeset in Berkeley and Belwe
by Capitol Communication Systems, Inc., Crofton, Maryland USA
Printed by Kirby Lithographic Company, Inc., Arlington, Virginia USA
Indexed by Coughlin Indexing Services, Annapolis, Maryland USA

Teachers of English to Speakers of Other Languages, Inc.
700 South Washington Street, Suite 200
Alexandria, Virginia 22314 USA
Tel 703-836-0774 • Fax 703-836-6447 • E-mail info@tesol.org • http://www.tesol.org/

Director of Communications and Marketing: Helen Kornblum
Managing Editor: Marilyn Kupetz
Additional Reader: Ellen Garshick
Cover Design: Capitol Communication Systems, Inc.

Chapter 2, Appendix B, from *Study speaking* (pp. 8 and 46), by T. Lynch & K. Anderson, 1992, Cambridge: Cambridge University Press. Copyright © (1992) by Cambridge University Press. Reprinted with permission from Cambridge University Press.

Chapter 7, Example 4, from *Use of English in teaching* (pp. 26, 69), by A. Brown, 1997, Singapore: Prentice Hall. Copyright © (1997) by Prentice Hall. Reprinted with permission from Prentice Hall.

Chapter 7, Table 1, from *Clear speech from the start* (pp. 44–45) by J. Gilbert, 2001, Cambridge: Cambridge University Press. Copyright © (2001) by Cambridge University Press. Reprinted with permission from Cambridge University Press.

Chapter 10, Figure 1, from *"I see what you mean." Using spoken discourse in the classroom: A handbook for teachers*, by A. Burns, H. Joyce, and S. Gollin, 1996, Sydney, Australia: National Centre for English Language Teaching and Research. Copyright © (1996) by Macquarie University. Reprinted with permission from National Centre for English Language Teaching and Research (NCELTR).

Chapter 10, Example 1, from *Hello Australia*, by Department of Immigration and Ethnic Affairs, 1986, Canberra, Australia: Department of Immigration and Ethnic Affairs. Copyright © (1998) by Macquarie University. Reprinted with permission from National Centre for English Language Teaching and Research (NCELTR).

Chapter 12, Examples 5–7, from *Perspectives on Fluency*, by H. Riggenbach, 2000, Ann Arbor: University of Michigan Press. Copyright © (2000) by University of Michigan Press. Reprinted with permission.

Every effort has been made to contact the copyright holders for permission to reprint borrowed material. We regret any oversights that may have occurred and will rectify them in future printings of this work.

ISBN 1931185050
Library of Congress Control No. 2002109051

Table of Contents

Acknowledgments

We would particularly like to thank Marilyn Kupetz, Ellen Garshick, and Carla Heath for their guidance and insights during the production of this volume. There has been enjoyable interaction—and much valuable language learning.

Series Editor's Preface

The Case Studies in TESOL Practice series offers innovative and effective examples of practice from the point of view of the practitioner. The series brings together from around the world communities of practitioners who have reflected and written on particular aspects of their teaching. Each volume in the series covers one specialized teaching focus.

◈ CASE STUDIES

Why a TESOL series focusing on case studies of teaching practice?

Much has been written about case studies and where they fit in a mainstream research tradition (e.g., Nunan, 1992; Stake, 1995; Yin, 1994). Perhaps more important, case studies publicly recognize the value of teachers' reflection on their practice and also constitute a new form of teacher research—or teacher valuing. Case studies support teachers in valuing the uniqueness of their classes, learning from them, and showing how their experience and knowledge can be made accessible to other practitioners in simple but disciplined ways. They are particularly suited to practitioners who want to understand and solve teaching problems in their own contexts.

These case studies are written by practitioners who are able to portray real experience by providing detailed descriptions of teaching practice. These qualities invest the cases with teacher credibility and make them convincing and professionally interesting. The cases also represent multiple views and offer immediate solutions, thus providing perspective on the issues and examples of useful approaches. Informative by nature, they can provide an initial database for further, sustained research. Accessible to wider audiences than many traditional research reports, however, case studies have democratic appeal.

◈ HOW THIS SERIES CAN BE USED

The case studies lend themselves to pre- and in-service teacher education. Because the context of each case is described in detail, it is easy for readers to compare the cases with and evaluate them against their own circumstances. To respond to the wide range of settings in which TESOL functions, cases have been selected from diverse EFL and ESL settings around the world.

The 12 or so case studies in each volume are easy to follow. Teacher writers describe their teaching context and analyze its distinctive features: the particular demands of their context, the issues they have encountered, how they have effectively addressed the issues, and what they have learned. Each case study also offers readers practical suggestions—developed from teaching experience—to adapt and apply to their own teaching.

Already in published or in preparation are volumes on

- academic writing programs
- action research
- assessment practices
- bilingual education
- community partnerships
- content-based language instruction
- distance learning
- English for specific purposes
- gender and TESOL
- grammar teaching in teacher education
- intensive English programs
- international teaching assistants
- journal writing
- literature in language teaching and learning
- mainstreaming
- teacher education
- teaching English as a foreign language in primary schools
- teaching English from a global perspective
- teaching English to the world
- technology in the classroom

◈ THIS VOLUME

In this volume, the insights and uses of interaction for the ESOL classroom are examined. The studies make clear that interaction is a central means of language learning—as both content in the classroom and structure in the curriculum.

Jill Burton
University of South Australia, Adelaide

CHAPTER 1

Interaction as the Way and Means of Language Learning

Jill Burton and Charles Clennell

Interaction is the pivot on which language learning turns. How people interact, how context affects interaction, the shifting status and importance of discourse(s)—these and other aspects of interaction are of central interest to TESOL practitioners. This volume celebrates interaction as a central source of and opportunity for course content and structure.

Because of the range of connections among the topics investigated in the chapters in this volume, and their intricacy, we have organized them under three broad, encompassing frames of reference; the frames are by no means mutually exclusive, however. The first half of the volume contains a variety of classroom-based case studies on interaction; the second half profiles two of the concerns that language teachers are increasingly acknowledging and seek to address. These are the increasing prominence of English as an international language (EIL) and its implications for language learners, and, secondly, how to use native-speaker (NS) and learner interaction in the classroom as a means of learning; though maybe different in emphasis, these two concerns are not unconnected.

As would be expected, a number of continuing, central themes are reexamined in the chapters in this book. Communication is featured in studies that investigate

- potential points of communicative breakdown and miscommunication (chapters 6, 7, and 11)
- intelligibility and comprehensibility (chapters 4, 6, 7, 8, 11, and 12)
- communication management strategies (chapters 2, 3, 5, 11, and 12)
- pragmatics together with the construction and negotiation of meaning (chapters 2, 6, and 12)

Language acquisition is investigated via

- interlanguage (chapters 3 and 5)
- learning strategies (chapters 5, 11, and 12)
- learner task work (chapters 2, 5, 11, and 12)
- interactional modifications and adjustments (chapters 4, 6, 7, 9, and 11)
- learner motivation and persistence (chapters 5 and 11)
- pronunciation and intonation (chapters 6, 7, 8, 9, and 12)

The role of English, and, therefore, its importance or impact on learners' lives is addressed in studies that look at

- EIL (chapter 7)
- knower status in interactional episodes (chapters 3, 6, and 8)
- being a nonnative speaker (chapters 8, 9, and 11)
- the role of NSs in the classroom (chapters 2 and 11)

Whereas all chapters cover the teaching of spoken discourse, its use, nature, and roles are featured in subject-specific studies on

- aspects of technical and nontechnical language (chapter 11)
- teacher education (chapter 10)
- classroom discourse (chapters 4, 5, 11, and 12)
- learner language and learning language (chapters 2, 3, 8, and 9)
- authenticity (chapters 10 and 11)

Discourse analysis as a research tool underpins every chapter. For all analysts (teachers, learners, and teacher educators), discourse analysis is a means of learning about their own language competence as well as that of others. In unique ways, the authors employ a range of methods, including

- systemic functional analysis (chapters 6, 9, and 10)
- conversational analysis (chapters 2, 3, 4, 11, and 12)
- speech act analysis (chapter 5)
- genre and register analysis (chapters 3, 10, and 11)
- lexical analysis (chapter 6)
- pronunciation and intonation analysis (chapters 6, 7, and 8)

The implications of interaction research studies for language teaching are comprehensively discussed in chapter 10 and central to chapters 11 and 12, which focus on units of work that coincidentally feature learners as discourse analysts of their own language input. In addition, the first and last cases (chapters 2 and 12) examine specific examples of speaking courses—their approaches, materials, and learner participation—that were designed to promote learner interaction.

Where might studies of the kind in this book lead? The authors make a number of suggestions that, taken together, could form a sequence of principles for language teaching:

1. Teach strategically: Develop learners' awareness of how discourse is organized and managed, how to improve communication by making effective language choices, and how to use circumstances and language as tools for language learning.

2. Use language as a means of teaching: In and outside the classroom, learners can record and analyze language use—their own and others'.

3. Teach learners how to record and analyze discourse, including their own output: Show them first how to transcribe; next discuss with them how

transcription systems are in themselves interpretations of discourse; then have them analyze transcript extracts.

4. Teach learners to discriminate and compare different meanings and effects: Have learners compare different speakers' output on the same tasks, the different kinds of language that different tasks generate, and the effects of different circumstances on the same communication goal.

5. Teach learners to value linguistic and cultural diversity within their own learning environments: Show them how to adapt and accommodate the rich linguistic and cultural resources that they and other learners bring with them to the classroom.

These recommendations for a discourse-based approach to teaching language have implications for course materials. The authors in this volume offer suggestions here, too, on

- classroom tasks and how they can be structured to stimulate language output that students can analyze and use as a model for their own production

- text and task authenticity and how classroom activities can be made meaningful, purposeful, and motivating to learners

- learners as learning resources and how learners' own language output can become a source of learning for themselves and others

- comprehensibility and accommodation and how working to identify an international phonological core can support learners to become mutually intelligible and articulate users of English in international contexts

- cultural sensitivity and how classroom tasks that involve analyzing discourse can encourage interaction that values difference and open-endedness

- ethical practice and how pedagogic activities can stimulate understanding of others' vulnerability in using a nonnative language to express themselves and thus limit marginalization

Finally, collaboration is the other central theme linking the research practices, teaching activities, and language learning processes examined in this book. The connections among the approaches and goals throughout this volume, and the ways in which participants in these studies have worked together to uncover shared understanding, confirm once again the value of collaborative research and reflective practice in TESOL. Quite simply, recognizing the importance of interaction as a language teaching tool is an effective way for TESOL practitioners to approach studying and sharing language practice.

❖ CONTRIBUTORS

Jill Burton is associate professor of applied linguistics at the University of South Australia, in Adelaide, where she teaches and supervises postgraduate work in discourse analysis and language curriculum. She has published on these topics and edited a number of publications on TESOL. Her current research interests include how learners can, as analysts of their own discourse, become more effective language users.

Charles Clennell is an adjunct senior lecturer in TESOL at the Underdale Campus of the University of South Australia, in Adelaide. He has contributed to the TESOL master's program over a number of years in the fields of phonology, discourse analysis, and interlanguage studies and has published a number of papers in TESOL journals on learner language, prosody, and the grammar of spoken discourse in English language teaching.

PART 1

Researching Interaction

CHAPTER 2

Learner/Nonteacher Interactions: The Contribution of a Course Assistant to English for Academic Purposes Speaking Classes

Tony Lynch and Kenneth Anderson

❖ INTRODUCTION

This is a case study of innovative practice in a presessional English for academic purposes (EAP) program. The innovation is the introduction of a nonteaching course assistant to work alongside the class teachers, in order to increase the students' opportunities for native-English-speaker/nonnative-English-speaker (NS/NNS) inter- action. Analysis of classroom recordings from one type of speaking class and of students' postcourse evaluations suggests that the availability of this additional NS led to NS/NNS interactions that were quantitatively and qualitatively different from those among the students and their teachers.

❖ CONTEXT

Speaking is one of four main strands taught in the full-time summer EAP program run by the University of Edinburgh's Institute for Applied Language Studies. The principal aims of the program are to raise students' overall English proficiency to the point where they can cope with the linguistic demands of academic study and to extend their study skills. The program is divided into three 3-week courses and one 4-week course, as shown in Figure 1.

The program is designed for students preparing for degree courses in British universities or colleges. It attracts participants from around the world, but in recent years, the majority have been East Asians, who have tended to be less proficient in listening to and speaking English than in reading and writing it. Many have had little exposure to the natural speech of NSs and need to improve their fluency and confidence in spoken interaction. Furthermore, they may never previously have been in situations in which their English pronunciation presents a problem for their interlocutors, so they need to develop strategies to make themselves more clearly understood. Sociopragmatically, too, many find that British people are less tolerant of silence in conversation and may interpret their quietness as diffidence, lack of interest or ideas, or incomprehension. So a main aim of the speaking strand in the program is to bring students' competence in the spoken medium more into line with their written-medium skills.

Grouping	*By Language Level*									*By Subject*			
COURSE	1			2			3			4			
Week	1	2	3	4	5	6	7	8	9	10	11	12	13
WRITING	Academic writing/grammar						Integrated language skills work (listening, reading, note-taking, summary and essay writing) on three topics			Research skills/ language practice in classes grouped by subject area. Microprojects; academic writing; extensive reading; videos; lectures; library work; word processing			
LISTENING	Lecture listening/ note-taking												
READING	Vocabulary and reading												
SPEAKING	Accuracy: Information tasks Fluency: Scenarios						Seminar presentation skills			Seminar participation skills			
INDIVIDUAL STUDY	Self-access work under tutorial guidance, focusing on language learning strategies, and self-assessment; based on study room materials/facilities, including microprojects									Library research project and tutorials			
LECTURES	Two optional weekly lectures (Social and Lecture Program)												

FIGURE 1. Institute for Applied Language Studies Summer English for Academic Purposes Program

The speaking strand features materials (Lynch & Anderson, 1992) in three genres of oral communication, requiring attention to different aspects of successful speaking:

1. Information tasks concentrate on improving the clarity of the spoken message.

2. Scenarios focus on the flexibility with which students react in situations where they need to persuade someone to accept their point of view.

3. Seminar skills work sharpens the effectiveness of students' contributions to academic discussions, in which they participate either as main speaker or as a member of the audience.

Each genre involves preparation, performance, and feedback. We attach particular importance to feedback, believing that adult learners make the most improvement when active practice is combined with the chance to reflect on and evaluate their performance. Our experience is that EAP students especially benefit from instruction with an explicit metacommunicative orientation, involving analysis and comparison of performances on communication tasks. As Kramsch (1985) put it, "If many of the difficulties encountered by learners are interactional in nature, explicit attention to interaction processes should be the first step in learning to construct discourse" (p. 180). Consciousness-raising is therefore an important aspect of the speaking strand.

◈ DESCRIPTION

The Course Assistant

The EAP program ran as shown in Figure 1 for a number or years. In postprogram evaluations, some students had expressed a desire to increase their opportunities to speak English and suggested we should take on an additional NS for that purpose. Some stressed that this person should not be a teacher but rather what they called a "normal" NS, who could offer speaking practice to supplement the types of interaction already available in speaking classes. In 1996, we decided to take up the suggestion by employing a NS course assistant (CA) to act as a conversational partner outside class and also as a participant in speaking classes. It is this innovation that forms the focus for this case study.

The theoretical grounds for assuming that a second NS would enhance classroom interaction came from work such as that of Swain (1995) and Pica, Lincoln-Porter, Paninos, and Linnell (1996), who suggest that although learner-to-learner talk in the classroom provides a useful platform for negotiation of meaning, formal improvements to students' own output are more likely to arise in interaction with a competent speaker of the second language (L2), who pushes the learners to greater accuracy. The availability of two NSs in the classroom ought, therefore, to be better than one because it potentially doubles the opportunities for pushed interaction. There were also obvious advantages for our students in terms of their understanding of NS speech because many of them—especially those from East Asia—are unfamiliar with the British varieties of spoken English that they will encounter during their academic studies in the United Kingdom.

The EAP CA we appointed for summer 1996 (who subsequently returned for the following 3 summers) was a 20-year-old female Scottish undergraduate studying for a modern languages degree. Her contribution to the students' oral skills development took three forms:

1. She participated in each class's information task and scenario lessons.

2. She talked to the students during the class's weekly review.

3. She was available as a conversation partner during the students' midmorning break.

We were interested in analyzing the possible effects on classroom interaction of bringing in someone who was not a teacher, and, in particular, in exploring the assumption in the earlier students' feedback suggestion that a nonteaching NS would offer not only more practice but also a different type of communicative experience than would be available with a teacher. To assess the impact of the CA's contribution to the speaking strand, we decided to concentrate on the scenario classes because these would allow us to make the most direct comparison of interaction with teacher and nonteacher on the same topic and task.

Scenarios

A *scenario* (Di Pietro, 1987) involves a situation in which, through discussion, the participants attempt to resolve a conflict of interest. The scenarios in our program are based on firsthand reports by Edinburgh University international students of difficult situations they have encountered in their studies or daily life. Pedagogically, the advantage of simulating this sort of confrontation is that it exposes students to the natural unpredictability of such conversations. The classroom procedure is in five stages:

Stage 1: The teacher divides the class in half and gives the groups the role information for one of the two participants in the scenario. The students form a close circle, read their role cards, and discuss how they want to approach the problem and what they are going to say. Sample role cards are shown in Appendix B.

Stage 2: One player is chosen from each group to play the scenario in front of the class.

Stage 3: The players return to their groups for a debriefing in which all the students discuss the content and language and highlight any points that could be handled better or differently in the second round.

Stage 4: A second pair of players is chosen; they play the scenario again.

Stage 5: The teacher leads a whole-class review, discussing points noted during the performances. The teaching notes suggest four areas for feedback (see Figure 2).

One way in which we expected the student/CA talk and student/teacher talk in scenario classes to differ was that we thought students working with the teacher would focus more on form because they would regard the CA as having less authority in that area. We also assumed that there would be more negotiation of meaning—especially more requests for clarification—in interaction with the CA, for two reasons:

1. She would have less experience of NS/NNS interaction than the teachers and would therefore understand her interlocutors less well.

2. The students were likely to be less accustomed to the CA's Scottish speech patterns than to those of the teachers, both of whom were English.

Strategy	*Did they manage to get what they wanted?*
	Did one player come away the loser?
Information	*Did they use relevant role information provided?*
	Did they forget or change any details?
Communication	*Were there any breakdowns in communication?*
	How (and how well) did they resolve them?
Language	*Did they appear to manage to express their intended meaning?*
	Did their performance reveal any significant gaps in grammar, vocabulary, or pronunciation?

FIGURE 2. Structuring Scenario Feedback

◈ DISTINGUISHING FEATURES

Our classroom study to explore these assumptions involved recording student/ teacher and student/CA interactions at Stage 1 of the scenario (when the two halves of the class prepare for the first public performance). The recordings were made in nine lessons over Weeks 1–6 of the 1996 program: Five featured a lower level class (approximately 450–500 TOEFL) taught by Teacher B, and four a higher level class (500–550 TOEFL) taught by Teacher C. The 18 students in the two classes came from Bahrain (2); Germany (2); Iran (2); Japan (2); Korea (3); Nepal, Peru, Saudi Arabia, Spain (2 each); Thailand; and Turkey. Teachers B and C were similar in age (in their 50s), classroom experience (25–30 years, including extended periods in Africa), academic background (PhDs in applied linguistics) and origin/accent (southern English). Teacher B was female, and Teacher C was male.

Classroom Recordings

The audiorecordings were transcribed and analysed into *episodes*, defined as a series of speaking turns on the same topic. These episodes were further categorized according to who had initiated them: the students or the NS (CA, Teacher B, or Teacher C). Following Hancock's (1997) study of adult EFL learner interaction in role-play classes, we decided to adopt the categories of *literal* and *nonliteral frame,* derived from Goffman (1974). In our case, students were considered to be speaking in a nonliteral frame when either discussing or rehearsing the performance for Stage 2, and to be speaking in a literal frame when referring to or focusing on their lives beyond the classroom task. Talk in a nonliteral frame included three main categories: episodes dealing with *general procedure/task management*; *input* (on the content or language of the role card); and *output* (on possible strategies or language to be used at Stage 2, or in rehearsal). Talk in a literal frame was subdivided into *on-task* and *off-task*. Two examples of each category (from the Bank scenario) are included in Figure 3.

In some cases it was difficult to categorize literal frame episodes as exclusively off-task or on-task. For example, a Saudi student who said "I hate the banks' treatment here in this country" was raising an issue that was related in his mind to the current scenario but was not intended to influence his group's decisions about strategy or language for Stage 2. This suggests a need for a midway category between off and on, such as "Prompted by the task," to distinguish talk directly related to the task from episodes that are quite unconnected with it. However, for the purposes of our study, the important division was between literal and nonliteral frames, rather than between the subcategories within those frames.

Our analysis of Stage 1 episodes shows that in overall quantitative terms, the students' interaction with the CA was more like that with Teacher B than that with Teacher C. In Table 1, the *total* is the total number of episodes, *mean* refers to the mean number of episodes per scenario, and *share* is the proportion of episodes initiated by students or NS.

The topical episodes involving the CA tended to be more staccato (205 episodes in the nine CA recordings, compared with 160 in the nine teacher recordings). The CA was also more like Teacher B in terms of her share in initiating episodes— approximately 4 out of every 10 episodes; Teacher C initiated only 1 in 4 episodes.

We had expected language-focused talk to be more frequent in interaction with

Nonliteral Frame*

General Procedure

1. Is this one going to be filmed?
2. One out the group has to go up to practise

Task Management

1. Could you join this group?
2. Do you think you're now ready?

Input

Content

1. This student has cashpoint card?
2. OK the spelling + the spelling is different

Language

1. "Distrust" is opposite of "trust"?
2. (*pointing to the word "withdrawal" in the text*) This one?

Output

Strategy

1. So maybe we could try to think of a reason
2. Maybe they will ask + + + to have identification

Language

1. Yes this now situation is bad + I mean first how can I say? + + + 'I have some problem'
2. Yeah but we don't normally say "What is your identity?"

Literal Frame

On-Task

1. Yeah + some days ago + I went to my bank
2. How about your country... this situation ?

Off-Task

1. What means "cabaret"?
2. Oh I'm sleepy (*laughs*)

*Note: See Appendix A for key to transcript.

FIGURE 3. Nonliteral and Literal Frame Examples

the teachers than the CA, but that turned out not to be the case (see Table 2). *Input* episodes were those in which the discussion focused on the role-card texts, while *output* episodes were about the language to be used by the players in Stage 2. The less frequent form-focused episodes with Teacher C could reflect the higher proficiency level of his class, although the difference between the two classes was relatively small. The overall totals for this type of talk with the CA and the teachers are very similar: 30 language-focused episodes with the CA and 28 with the two teachers. However,

TABLE 1. INITIATION OF TOPICAL EPISODES (STAGE 1)

	Total	Mean	Share
Ss	115	12.8	56.2%
CA	90	10.0	43.8%
Ss	48	9.6	59.3%
Teacher B	33	6.6	40.7%
Ss	58	14.5	73.5%
Teacher C	21	5.25	26.5%
	365		

a difference emerges when we consider who was the source of those episodes. The CA initiated relatively more talk about language (36.6%) than Teacher C (33.3%) and, particularly, Teacher B (26.3%). The CA's initiations were primarily comprehension checks about the role card, as in Example 1.

1. CA: **is there anything you don't understand?*

   R: I couldn't understand + find exactly + "beginning to lose patience"
   CA: it means that they're + beginning to get + angry with you
   R: oh
   CA: you're beginning to annoy them + because you keep going back to see them + you know
   R: (laughs)
   CA: every time you come back they get + angrier + + that's that's what you think anyway
   M: (laughs)
   CA: but it might not be true
   M: no it's true (laughs)

TABLE 2. INITIATION OF FORM-FOCUSED EPISODES

	Input (text)	Output (task)	Totals	NS share
Ss	11	8	19	
CA	8	3	11	36.6%
Totals	19	11	30	
Ss	3	11	14	
Teacher B	—	5	5	26.3%
Totals	3	16	19	
Ss	3	3	6	
Teacher C	3	—	3	33.3%
Totals	6	3	9	

*Note: See Appendix A for key to transcripts.

However, language-oriented episodes were initiated by students more often than by any of the NSs, either as clarification requests (see Example 2) or as suggestions for expressions that could be used at Stage 2 (see Example 3).

2. **P:** **"tactfully" + can you explain me?**

    M: (??) it's carefully
    CA: yeah tact is + + (??)
    P: skilfully?
    CA: no + yeah you're probably being very polite with them +

3. **M:** **so we say "if you want to read it here you can + if not + I suggest" +**

    CA: "you go away" *(laughs)*
    M: *(laughs)*

A substantial amount of the time in Phase 1—137 out of 365 episodes—was spent discussing how to approach the task: what we have called *output: strategy,* to distinguish it from talk about the appropriate linguistic forms to use (*output: language*). We found that the CA was more proactive than the two teachers in initiating output-focused episodes, as indicated in Table 3.

In Table 3, we can see that the CA took the lead more often in encouraging the students to discuss what strategy to adopt at Stage 2, as illustrated in Examples 4–6, which show three consecutive episodes of talk between the CA and her group.

4. **CA:** **so we could maybe try to think of a reason +**

    F: (??)
    CA: sorry?
    F: (??)
    CA: so we could maybe try to think of a reason +
    F: official reasons
    CA: yeah + official reasons to check their ID
    F: account number + "you have been given an account number?" + so we should ask for this

TABLE 3. INITIATION OF STRATEGY-FOCUSED EPISODES

	Total	*Share*
Ss	47	63.6%
CA	27	36.4%
Total	74	
Ss	23	82.1%
Teacher B	5	17.8%
Total	28	
Ss	28	80.0%
Teacher C	7	20.0%
Total	35	

CA: hmhm + and it says you can't authorize withdrawal without proper identification anyway + so we could say + um "we need your identification before we give you money" + anyway + +

5. **CA:** **is there anything else? + + oh we need to decide as well**

F: decide what?
CA: whether we're gonna let them have the money or not + + I suppose it depends if they have any ID + + + I mean if they don't have any identification what can we do? + + + we'll give the money or not?
F: + + + but if he has the account number? + + + are we going to give it to him?
CA: so + if he has the account number? + + + are we going to give it to him?
F: we should give him the money
CA: (laughs) but what if he doesn't have any identification? + apart from the account number?
F: look at his eyes (laughs)
CA: yeah (laughs) + + +

6. **CA:** **is there anything else we can ask him? + + + are we gonna check the name as well** when he's written it down? + do we tell him that the spelling's different?

F: (??) the spelling's different
CA: should we tell him this or not? + do you think we need to tell him that we do have an account but it's + the name's + slightly different? + I don't know whether we should tell him that
F: it's difficult the identification

This tendency for the CA to be more proactive in strategic talk is borne out by the figures in Table 1, which show that interaction with the CA featured more and shorter episodes. It may be that she saw it as her responsibility to ensure that her groups completed the Stage 1 planning satisfactorily, and therefore coaxed them through their discussion, as in the three-episode example we have just shown. It could also be that she was less tolerant of, or less used to, the thinking time that some L2 learners need in this sort of activity. The teachers seemed more prepared to wait for the students to come up with suggestions for Stage 2.

Of the areas we have studied so far, the one in which Stage 1 interaction with the CA differed most from interaction with the teachers was in terms of the opportunities the students took to talk in a literal frame: that is, about their real lives.

There were twice as many literal frame episodes with the CA as with the teachers combined (see Table 4). In addition, whereas we found no instances of either teacher initiating off-task episodes, there were two occasions when the CA did. In one case, Example 7, a Korean student (P) has been talking about the problems of adjusting to British accents. When that topic comes to a natural end, marked by laughter and then a long pause, the CA switches to a new topic (Example 8).

7. P: I familiar with uh south + south southern southern English

CA: yes
P: pronunciation + I moved uh two weeks ago it's very confusing *(laughs)*

TABLE 4. INITIATION OF EPISODES IN LITERAL FRAME

	On-task	Off-task	Total
Ss	17	10	27
CA	4	2	6
Total	21	12	33
Ss	4	—	4
Teacher B	4	—	4
Total	8	—	8
Ss	8	—	8
Teacher C	—	—	—
Total	8	—	8

CA: and you're still + it's difficult to understand
P: I'm feeling familiar with + Scottish pronunciation
CA: yes + + there might be quite a few slang + words
P: but [Teacher C] and [Teacher D]
CA: they're all English yes (*laughs*) exactly
P: (*laughs*) + + +

8. **CA: where are you staying? +** do you have a flat or a...?

P: yeah flat
CA: are you just on your own?
P: yeah
CA: is it a private + flat?
P: private flat yeah

Strikingly, there was not a single case of a student initiating off-task episodes with a teacher, perhaps because students regarded such talk as off-limits, whereas they were willing to engage in such talk in interaction with the CA. In Example 9, a group working with the CA has been preparing a scenario about university accommodation and are now talking on task, in literal frame, when an Iranian student (R) raises a different and unrelated topic:

9. M: oh maybe yeah + four years ago I had university flat my rent was £227

CA: and how many bedrooms?
M: two bedrooms
CA: oh two bedrooms + + and did you have a dining room?
M: a dining room something like a + small kitchen
CA: and whereabouts?
M: Buccleuch Street + just very close to the main library
CA: oh Buccleuch Street + yeah
R: I would like to ask you some information + I have two children + a daughter and a son + my daughter is twelve and my son is nine

CA: hmhm

R: and I don't know which schools are good

CA: oh you'll need to find out about schools + um + you could try at the Institute + at 21 Hill Place + if you go into + I'm not sure but if you go into Reception + at Hill Place + we possibly have some + information sheets which would maybe have addresses + where you could contact different schools and ask them

R: I don't know how it is here + but in Iran there are a great number of schools

M: so you mean private or...?

R: yeah some different kind of private schools and also state schools + + + at the first stage I have to find a flat and after that I decide to find some schools

Z: you should make phone call + or write a letter + (??) in your flat area maybe + + easier

Why did the students talk more about themselves with the CA? One reason could be affective or interpersonal: They may have felt more able to do so as she was a younger person and a less authoritative figure, in the classroom at least. There may also have been a practical reason: They had more time to do so because, as we have seen, the CA tended to push them on to complete the planning stage adequately.

Questionnaire Responses

The qualitative aspect of our case study draws on the students' responses to a questionnaire (Appendix C) that provides glimpses of the motives behind patterns of interaction in class. Unfortunately, half the students (9 of 18) did not complete the questionnaire in full, but we believe the comments we did receive are enlightening, particularly in revealing students' perceptions of the relative merits of interaction with the two types of NS in their scenario lessons. In brief, analysis of the returns shows the following:

- Most found their teacher easier to understand than the CA (Item 1).

- Most found it easier, or as easy, to speak with the CA (Item 2).

- Most said that the differences they noticed between the teacher and the CA were in terms of accent and speed of speaking. Two thought the CA spoke less accurately. On the other hand, a further two described the CA's accent as "ordinary" and "natural" (Item 3).

In four of the five areas of linguistic improvement (vocabulary, pronunciation, listening, and fluency) mentioned in Item 4, the students reported that interaction with the CA benefited them as much as (or more than) that with the teacher. Only in relation to grammar did they feel that interaction with the teacher was more helpful. This could in part reflect occasional comments from the CA herself, in response to questions about grammar, such as in Example 10, in which a Japanese student (Y) has noticed that the instructions on his role card include what he thinks is a grammatical error. He queries the (gender-neutral) pronoun *they* in the text: "A foreign student comes into your branch, saying that they opened an account some days ago. They have not received their cashpoint card. . . ."

10. Y: but second "they"

 CA: that's talking about students
 Y: but
 CA: I know + it says + uh + that's singular
 Y: hm
 CA: sorry I have to read it + "they have not received" + + it is + referring to this student that's going to visit us
 N: "they" + I think "they" + speak about more than one
 CA: no they're just talking about one student + don't ask me to explain some grammar to you (*laughs*) + I don't think I'm qualified
 Ss: (*laugh*)

The final questionnaire item, on the general value of the CA to the EAP program, elicited predominantly positive replies. All but one of the students regarded the innovation as useful, listing the following among their reasons:

- It helps us to get used to native speakers. (three similar replies)

- It practices listening to normal speed English.

- You don't know exactly what kind of sentence will come next.

- We gain confidence with someone not so formal as a teacher.

One student felt that having the chance to talk to the CA was useful "under organisation, programming and controlling of an experienced teacher"; it was not clear whether he felt that had not been the case in his scenario lessons.

The only clearly dissenting comment—"What is really the role of the non-teacher?"—came from a Spanish student who had taken the EAP program although she did not intend to go on to university. It could be that, partly for that reason, she saw less point than other students in getting used to the speech of a (pedagogically) unqualified assistant, particularly one with a Scottish accent that she might well not encounter again in her future use of English. It may also be relevant that both this student and the one who commented on the need for control were among the linguistically weakest members of the lower level class—indeed, the Spanish student was the only respondent who opted to answer the questionnaire in her first language. It would be understandable if greater difficulty with the CA's speech reduced the value these two students saw in interacting with her.

◈ PRACTICAL IDEAS

Since the introduction of the CA into the summer program in 1996, we have explored other ways of involving CAs as additional NSs in the scenario lessons.

Ask the CA to Play the Scenario With the Class Teacher

Videotaping the two NSs doing a scenario in class allows you to replay extracts later so that the students can compare their performances with a sample performance by NSs. This enables you to draw attention to patterns of spoken language, which are normally less accessible than those in the written language (Carter & McCarthy, 1995). Examples we have found and pointed out to students in our recordings include the CA's use of local expressions such as *a wee bit, Where do you stay?* for *Where do you live?*, and *Will I . . . ?* for *Shall I . . . ?* The recordings also highlight some sociocultural assumptions underlying NS discourse, such as the stereotypical tendency of British people to play down problematicity (*I've got a bit of a problem, That would be quite difficult*), and their common softening of a refusal or retort with *actually*. Video replay makes such characteristics of communication more tangible (cf. Jones, 1999; Scarcella, 1990).

Ask the CA to Transcribe NS Videorecordings

Transcripts are undoubtedly a useful device for helping L2 learners focus on form (e.g., Johnson, 1996), but producing the transcript is time-consuming. The CA can provide invaluable help by doing a preliminary rough transcript and word processing it for the teacher to check and reformat as a student handout. This assistance allows the teacher to focus on form in the posttask phase, without needing to spend out-of-class time on the transcribing.

Use the CA as a Partner in Pair Work

In summer 1998, we changed Stage 2 of the scenario procedure: Instead of beginning with a public performance by two students, we had all the students play the scenario privately, in parallel pairs. With an odd number of students present, the CA worked with the unpartnered student; when numbers were even, she helped the teacher monitor the students' talk, deal with requests for language help, and listen in and comment on the pairs' recordings once they had finished.

Ask the CA to Help Students Self-Transcribe

The most recent development of the CA's role in scenario classes has been to help students transcribe their own Stage 2 scenario recordings. Clennell (1999b) has demonstrated the value of having EAP students record and transcribe interviews with NSs; this process helps focus their attention on features of input. We have extended that to getting the students to record and transcribe (parts of) their Stage 2 performances; they then edit and correct their original transcript, and pass it to the teachers for reformulation (Lynch, 2001). This has created a new role for the CA as consultant to students as they discuss corrections and improvements to their transcript.

A study of the 1999 classroom version of the extended procedure is now under way. The preliminary evidence is that the students found it useful, that it was manageable, and that it created natural conditions for what Swain (e.g., 2000) calls *collaborative dialogue* about spoken English.

◈ CONCLUSION

This case study has assessed the effects on classroom interaction of having a NS course assistant in scenarios classes in a presessional program. It suggests that the CA made an appreciable difference to the amount and the nature of NS/NNS interaction in class. The study has included quantitative analysis of classroom recordings of student/teacher and student/CA talk during the scenario, and qualitative analysis of students' perceptions, expressed in a questionnaire, of their opportunities to interact with the CA. The findings in both cases point to the value of the additional NS.

From the students' point of view, it may be that the most important difference the CA made to classroom interaction was that they were able to find—or take—more opportunities to talk about themselves (in a literal frame) when working with her than with the teachers. Although we have categorized some instances of literal frame talk as off-task, that label should not be interpreted in a negative sense. On the contrary, we agree with Hancock (1997) that certain types of off-task talk are beneficial and necessary for the interpersonal cohesion of the group and for the lesson as a social event, as well as reflecting what van Lier (1996) calls the *contingency* of real-world conversation. The evidence of our study is that the introduction of the CA has extended the social dynamics of NS/NNS interaction inside the EAP classroom—something that has been appreciated by both learners and teachers.

◈ ACKNOWLEDGMENTS

We would like to acknowledge the contributions of the CA, Teacher B, and Teacher C to this case study, and thank Cathy Benson and the editors for their comments on earlier versions of the chapter.

◈ CONTRIBUTORS

Tony Lynch is senior lecturer at the Institute for Applied Language Studies, University of Edinburgh, Scotland, where he works in EAP and teacher education. He has published books and articles on listening skills and classroom interaction, and, most recently, on learner autonomy in a university setting. He is now researching ways of helping students notice features of their spoken English.

Kenneth Anderson has been involved in EAP at the Institute for Applied Language Studies in Edinburgh since 1986. His interests include teaching academic writing, especially to students in humanities disciplines, and he is coauthor with Tony Lynch of *Study Speaking* (Cambridge University Press, 1992). He is currently engaged in research on learners' preferences for, and uptake of, different forms of feedback on their writing.

◈ APPENDIX A: KEY TO TRANSCRIPT

+	=	short pause (0.5–1.0 second)
++	=	medium-length pause (1–2 seconds)
+++	=	long pause (more than 2 seconds)
italics	=	a description of nonverbal actions or events, or a metacommunicative commentary
(??)	=	words that are not clear from the tape

◈ APPENDIX B: SAMPLE ROLE CARDS, FROM THE BANK SCENARIO

Student

It is the week before your course starts. A few days ago, you opened an account at a bank near the university and were given a piece of paper with the account number. Access to your account is by means of a cashpoint card, which you were told would be sent to your address. It has still not arrived. The money that you brought with you is nearly finished. You call in at the bank to see if you can take any money out. You have left the account number at home. The person you speak to is not the one you saw when you opened the account. How will you explain the position?

Bank teller

A foreign student comes into your branch, saying that they opened an account some days ago. They have not received their cashpoint card, and want to make a cash withdrawal. You ask for the person's name. Your records show that an account has been opened in a similar name but the spelling is slightly different. This makes you suspicious. You cannot authorise a withdrawal without proper identification. The customer would have been given an account number when they opened the account, so you ask for this. As the senior staff are out at lunch, you have to decide whether or not to let the customer have any money. How can you check the student's identity without appearing to distrust them?

Lynch & Anderson (1992). Reprinted with permission.

◈ APPENDIX C: RESEARCH QUESTIONNAIRE: COMPARING CONVERSATION WITH A TEACHER AND A NONTEACHER

Scenarios

Please think about your experience of talking to (CA's name) and (T's name) when your group was planning your role in the scenario. Then circle the answers that match your opinion:

1 a I found it easier to understand (CA).
1 b I found it easier to understand (T).
1 c I found no difference in understanding them.

If you have circled **1a** or **1b**, please say why it was easier to understand her:

2 a I found it easier to speak English to (T).
2 b I found it easier to speak English to (CA).
2 c It was equally easy (or difficult) to speak English to either of them.

Again, if you circled **2a** or **2b**, say why you found it easier to speak to her:

3   The main difference(s) in the way (CA) and (T) spoke was/were that...

4   Did you improve the following in the Scenario? If so, with which speaker? Put
     a cross to show your opinion:

	More with CA	More with T	Equally from both	Neither
vocabulary				
grammar				
pronunciation				
listening				
general fluency				

Outside the Speaking Class

5   Did you speak to (CA) in the Study Room?   YES   NO
6   Did you speak to her in coffee breaks?   YES   NO
7   If you have answered YES... what sort of things did you talk about?

8   Did you find it more useful to talk to her
     (a) in class, or
     (b) outside?
     Why?

General

9   Having a nonteacher (as well as a teacher) to talk to on the EAP Course is
     (a) useful
     (b) not useful because . . .

CHAPTER 3

Interlanguage Analysis as a Tool for Teachers

Victoria MacLeod

❖ INTRODUCTION

A large part of English language teachers' work involves the analysis and guidance of student output and, in particular, the identification and treatment of developmental errors. Examining what students can and cannot do linguistically gives teachers important information about their students' stages of language development (Tsui, 1995) and, therefore, directly affects teachers' daily practice, enabling them to provide learners with the most effective help. This case study provides a snapshot view of one student's current state of interlanguage development, revealed through an analysis of samples of the spoken and written language she produced in the classroom. The classroom in question consisted of a group of nine adult learners enrolled in a full-time academic English course at a private English Language Intensive Courses for Overseas Students (ELICOS) institution in Adelaide, South Australia.

This chapter aims to show how classroom research can be useful in suggesting likely pathways for future instruction focused on guiding students' transitional competence (Corder, 1974) toward more nativelike proficiency.

❖ CONTEXT

The Learner

Tina was a 22-year-old Thai student who had been studying intensive English in Adelaide for 3 months. Previous to this, she had studied English during the course of her primary, secondary, and tertiary education in Thailand, a period of about 15 years. Tina reported that her awareness of the importance of English first came about with her interest in science, which she had always wanted to pursue. She therefore started learning English in a tutorial school (in the afternoons after primary school), and this helped her gain entry to an elite government high school, where she studied science. Following this, she undertook a bachelor of engineering (in telecommunications) and then a master of business administration, but it was only during her postgraduate studies that she had recognized the need to resume her English studies and immediately made plans to study in Australia as a means of improving her job prospects. Following her arrival in Australia, Tina worked hard on her language skills and showed considerable progress. Like many of her peers, she appeared to attach a lot of importance to making her parents feel proud of her.

The Institution

The South Australian Adelaide Language Centre (SAALC) is a member of English Australia, formerly known as ELICOS, whose member schools provide a range of accredited English language programs for visiting students Australia-wide. Students can enroll in long- or short-term courses and for varying reasons—business, academic, vocational, or recreational. Many students go on to study at tertiary level or participate in work placement programs. The SAALC caters to young learners preparing for secondary school, as well as offering general English for adults. Having small classes means being able to offer the adult clientele flexible courses that can be tailored to meet the needs of individual students as necessary. Twice a year, a 12-week specialist academic course is offered under the title of Preparation for Cambridge First Certificate in English. Two teachers share the class, and the main focus is on the development of the knowledge and skills required to complete the five examination papers (reading, writing, use of English, listening, and speaking). Study skills and authentic examination practice are important components, and continuity is maintained through the use of a course book—currently *New First Certificate Masterclass* (Haines & Stewart, 1996).

◈ DESCRIPTION

Perhaps the most important feature of interlanguage theory, a term first coined by Selinker (1974), is its characterization of language as being constantly in the process of change and growth—a quasi-permanent state of change (Rutherford, 1987). A significant part of language teachers' daily work involves successfully ascertaining the states of interlanguage development of their students and designing appropriate learning activities—clearly, a very challenging task.

As Tina's teacher, I had noticed in her language evidence of some fascinating learning strategies. I was also intrigued by the discrepancies between her spoken and written language and her ability to communicate enthusiastically and successfully despite some fairly serious grammatical, lexical, and pronunciation problems. She was also very conscientious and interested in her own language learning and very willing to discuss it. Therefore, Tina was an ideal subject for this study, and I anticipated that engaging her in the verbalization of and reflection on her linguistic difficulties would afford her extra opportunities to address them (Swain, 1998).

Task 1

The first task was designed to gather a sample of Tina's speech and evidence of her conversational skills, which appeared to be compensating for her lack of accuracy. I set up an informal discussion on a familiar topic (learning English), having previously formulated questions that not only were of interest to me as a teacher and researcher but also appeared to evoke strong reactions from the students. Issues discussed included the effect of first language (L1) on second language (L2) learning, the learning of vocabulary, and the role of language in the development of thought and speech—important areas of study for myself as a master of TESOL student and also the site of daily struggles and triumphs for language students. Text 1 (the spoken text) is a transcript of excerpts from the discussion. As can be seen, the talk was lively and interesting, and involved students—even though turns were often teacher allocated (see Lines 1–2, 4–5, 18) because students appeared reluctant to speak while being recorded.

Text 1. (Spoken)*

Line	Speaker	Speech
1	<T>	So, like the differences between YOUR language and ENGLISH, how
2		do they…how do they affect your English when you're SPEAKING?
3		* * * * * * *
4		Um and Tina, what about in THAI (<Ta> uh) how does that affect
5		YOUR English?
6	<Ta>	Uh my language is not have uh grammar or TENSE so for me when I
7		translate at first I just translate to uh present SIMPLE because we
8		use just present simple and we use TIME to tell WHEN (<T> uh) but
9		we don't have ah TENSE so is very difficult to me, (<T> mm) for
10		me…to speak English.
11	<T>	So do you find that ah, your VERB tenses are a problem…for you?
12	<Ta>	Yes and uh we don't have ah, adverb, adjective so for ME [laughs]
13		when I SPEAK I don't know which one is adjective, which one is
14		adverb (<T> mm) I just remember MEANING and I use THIS meaning
15		(<T> yeah) when, because when I speak I translate from Thai to
16		English so I, I don't know WHICH word is adjective, which word is
17		adverb so quite difficult
18	<T>	Mm and ah, how about Korean language?
19	<H>	We, we, we make sentence just like words and verb like that so we
20		don't have tense
21	<T>	Ah is that the same as Thai then, you don't have tenses?
22	<Ta>	But Thai
23	<H>	We can make past or something
24	<N>	But Thai language and English I think quite similar word order (<T>
25		yeah) so is quite easy for me to make a mistake but I just translate
26		word by word so is ah very, ah confuse some time because some
27		word I don't know ah? This one is adjective? No, no, no is o.k. is
28		the same MEANING is o.k. (<T> yeah) I think just is same MEANING
29		so I translate word by word
30		* * * * * * *
31	<T>	What happens if you're thinking in your OWN language and trying to
32		speak ENGLISH?
33	<Ta>	Longer…my, my, my sentence is longer, longer than if I think in
34		English because I have to think I translate so I have to think is more
35		long I can't say EXACTLY this way (<T> mm) so I have to MAKE a
36		long way to go to my POINT (<T> yeah) so is longer
37	<T>	Which is QUICKER?
38	<Ta>	If I think in ENGLISH…quick

*Note: See Appendix for key to transcript.

39   It's quicker…thinking…speaking (gestures with parallel hands) it's

40   <Ta>   speaking yes

41   <T>   quicker isn't it?

42   <Ta>   But I don't know, when I SPEAK because I speak too much so

43   [laughs] I don't know, NOW I don't know my thinking is a English or

44   Thai I'm not sure but for me maybe is a Thai, WHY I can't think in

45   English? So I'm not sure… I can, sometimes I speak English with my

46   friend but SOME word that I speak is a THAI because we have a

47   word order same (<T> mm) so some word (<T> mm) between we

48   have THAI so I know ah, THIS word is Thai (<T> mm, interesting) so

49   I'm not sure

50   * * * * * * *

51   <T>   O.k. when you're trying to learn new WORDS, what's a good way to

52   REMEMBER them?

53   <Ta>   I can learn word for ME if ah, some people especially FRIEND told

54   me this WORD we are speaking and they use this WORD and I don't

55   know this WORD and they told me the meaning this one is make me

56   more remember than I READ I don't know WHY (<T> mm) but for

57   me very easy (<G> yeah, make more impression) Yeah!

Task 2

For the second task, Tina wrote a homework assignment in preparation for the International English Language Testing System (IELTS) speaking subtest (see Text 2). She was instructed not to use a dictionary and not to erase anything. The aim was for her to give detailed personal information of the sort she was likely to be asked about in the test. Tina's written text was produced several days after her speaking was recorded, so there is evidence of ideas overflowing from the class discussion into the second text.

Text 2. (Written)

Family name: —	First language:	Thai	1
Given name: Tina	Other language:	English	2
Nationality: Thai	Years of English study:	about 15 years	3

English language courses: Intensive English, GMAT, General English   4

Educational background and qualifications: 5

    1)   Bachelor of Engineering (Telecommunication)   6

    2)   Master of Business Administration (General Management   7

Reasons for taking the IELTS: 8

    1)   To use for making resident visa (Australia)   9

    2)   To use for finding a good job   10

Other Future Plans: 11

  After finishing this course, I'm going back to Thailand to work. Now I don't   12

know yet about my job, but I hope I can work in a communicative company. I think   13

I want to work in a big company about 10 years and then I want to work in a small   14

company and at the same time I want to open my shop. I think experience that I   15

small
learn from a ~~big~~ company will help my shop and ~~xxx~~ connection from a big company   16
will help me to import or export my products.   17
     18

My English Study Experience: 19
    I started study English when I was 5 years old in kindergarten, but I didn't learn   20
anything about English because I think it isn't necessary for me. After primary school,   21
I would quit from school and worked with my parents. They had a restaurant, a coffee   22
shop and a grocery. But my life changed after I studied science and I knew I loved it   23
and wanted to study it in high school. And this time I became aware about my English   24
because I wanted to study in a government high school. So I began to study English in   25
a tutorial school but I learnt just how to make a good score in exam. However, after   26
I could study in a government high school. I didn't mine or want to study English any   27

                                                                                    e
more until I finished bachelor degree and worked in a big company. I kn~~o~~w I had   28
                            was   e
to study master degree and English ~~is~~ very importance for me. But in this time, I kn~~o~~w   29
it's quite late to study English, especially pronunciation.   30
     31

My English problems Which Are Effected By My First Language.   32
Speaking & Pronunciation   33
    Because Thai language doesn't have accent at the end of the word, so when we are speaking 34
it's difficult for everybody to understand. And I think our dictionary doesn't use phonetic, we use 35
Thai to tell how to pronunciation.   36
Grammar   37
    Because Thai language doesn't have tense same as English, thus at first I used present simple 38
while I spoke about past events. Sometimes I don't understand why I have to use tense to tell 39
the time because in that sentence or you already know about time that I refer to in my speaking. 40
So when I speak I always make a mistake about tense because I have to think about   41
vocab and grammar at the same time. And usually I translate Thai to English word   42
by word because our language has word order similar with English. But after studying   43
English in Australia I get used to some sentence, for example "How long have you been here?" 44
"I have been here for 6 months.", so when Thai people asked me this question I had to   45
translate from English to Thai. It's sound stupid for some people but I ~~ho~~ don't know why 46
it happen. After I studied here for 3 months I began dream in English and thought in English 47
sometimes. So now I don't know I translate from Thai to English or not.   48
Reading   49
    If I can use dictionary, reading is a part of English which is easiest, because I can translate 50
word by word. Sometimes I have a problem about meaning of word. I don't know which   51
meaning can I use. Because one word in English can have more than 10 meaning in   52
Thai.   53
Listening   54
    For me I never mind about grammar so when I listen I listen just main verbs   55
                        o
or main work because tense d~~i~~sn't have meaning in my language, for example, "have ever 56
been, are going to, will…".   57

My Opinion about Learning English in Thailand: 58
   Now in Thailand, we have a lot of international schools which teach every subjects   59
in English and there don't teach Thai language, so students who finish from these school   60
can't speak Thai. However fee of these school are quite expensive but we have other school ~~that~~   61
which teach English more than 70% and fee are cheaper. And most Thai parents want to   62
send their children to these school. Even though all of these school are in Bangkok, thus most   63
Thai people can't speak English, especially the poor ~~parents~~ or quite poor student don't have a   64
chance to study in school. which are most status in Thai.   65
   I live in Bangkok so I want to give information only about learning English in   66
                            mix
Bangkok. Most teenagers in Bangkok like to speak ^ Thai and English ~~mixor~~ together. Because it   67
make them look like have a high education, or they think it's cool to speak like these. When I   68
                                  d
studied in University and I had to present a report if I spoke more English wor~~ks~~ than Thai words   69
it looked professional and I could get a good score.   70
   Another thing that I think it effect to Thai is most superstars in Thai finished from ~~intr~~   71
International schools or went to study in USA or England so they can't speak Thai very well or they   72
speak Thai accent English. And these effect to young people who want to copy or to imitate them   73
Another reason that make English important in Thailand is most of the companies were   74
tookover by European companies, so if you can't speak English or understand English, they don't   75
want to receive you or they will sack you. In my opinion, we will speak English more than Thai   76
in Bangkok or we won't use Thai in Business in the future.   77

◈ DISTINGUISHING FEATURES

On analysis, Tina's language use in its spoken and written forms varied though it was still apparently systematic, its variability appearing to depend on the linguistic, situational, and psycholinguistic contexts in which it was produced (Ellis, 1997). By examining Tina's use of language and the appearance of nonstandard forms, I gained valuable insights into how her output was affected by her developing interlanguage parameters, the linguistic choices she made, the situations in which she was performing (informal vs. formal, spoken vs. written), and the time she had available for planning and reflection.

Errors

Like native speakers (NSs), Tina produced some nonstandard forms that would be considered "mistakes" caused by distraction or inattention, rather than "gaps in her knowledge" or errors (Ellis, 1997, p. 17). For example, in her speech and writing, Tina repeatedly used the lexical item *word* accurately, though it suddenly appears as "work" in her writing (Text 2, Line 56). Judging by her general use of this item and also the context of the sentence, this was just a mistake. This conclusion is confirmed by Tina's later amendment of "works" to "words" in Line 69 (Text 2). Similarly, the word *mind* appears as "mine" (Text 2, Line 27) and then correctly as "mind" (Line 55)—with the same contextual meaning. Other mistakes of a similar nature included the use of "effect/effected" instead of *affect/affected* (Text 2, Lines 32, 71, 73) and on several occasions some confusion of *this* with *these* (Lines 60, 61, 68, 73). In spoken and written forms, phonological factors rather than a lack of knowledge are a more likely explanation for these discrepancies, including pronunciation transfer from her L1, Thai, which does not, for example, stress syllable-final segments or differentiate length in the vowels /i:/ and /ɪ/. Clearly, careful error analysis can help teachers identify the source of deviant forms and determine priorities in terms of their correction and treatment.

Spoken Versus Written Language

Some interesting observations can be made from a comparison of modes in Tina's speech and her writing . First, her speech in Text 1 shows a considerable amount of repetition and a lack of variation in grammatical structures and lexical items. A common occurrence is the use of fixed expressions and formulaic phrases such as "I don't know" (Text 1, Lines 13, 16, 42, 43, 54–5, 56) and "I'm not sure" (Lines 44, 45, 49), which may be due to these types of informal and often colloquial expressions being a more common feature of conversational style. Although some of the same collocations appeared in both her writing and her speaking, they are not used as frequently in the more formal mode of her writing; for example, "word by word" and "make a mistake" each appear only once (Text 2, Lines 42–3, and 51, respectively). It is also interesting to note the accuracy in the use of these fixed expressions in both modes, thereby possibly supporting the theory that language is more readily internalized in chunks. For example, of the 28 correct uses of articles in Tina's writing (see Table 1), almost half of these involved collocations and fixed expressions such as *at the same time, a lot of, a part of, get a good score, tell the time, have a chance, at the end,* and *find a job.*

Tina's speech (Text 1) also showed a tendency for overelaboration, a communication strategy commonly associated with nonnative speakers (NNSs) who lack confidence and therefore overelaborate to ensure that their message is transmitted (Tarone & Yule, 1989). Nevertheless, her discourse strategies appeared to be systematic, her utterances tending to be organized into short speeches with a beginning, middle, and end. Moreover, they were well constructed, exhibiting competent use of cohesive devices such as *so, but, and,* and *because.* See, for example, Lines 33–36 from Text 1:

> Longer…my, my, my sentence is longer, longer than if I think in English **because** I have to think I translate **so** I have to think is more long I can't say exactly this way **so** I have to make a long way to go to my point **so** is longer.

TABLE 1. ANALYSIS OF TINA'S CORRECT USE OF ARTICLES

	Omission of a/the	Correct use of a/the	Incorrect use of a/the	Omission of it	Correct use of it	Incorrect use of it
Text 1 (spoken— 400 words)	9	2	4	8	—	—
Text 2 (written— 960 words)	13	28	1	—	9	1

Interestingly, there is also what appears to be a kind of topic + comment structure ("longer…my sentence is longer," Line 33). Whether this is evidence of L1 transfer (structural or discoursal) is unclear, but its use certainly serves to emphasize the topic, making it more salient and easier to process (Clennell, 1995). Whereas Tina's writing is also cohesive, she shows no tendency to conclude each paragraph with a repetition of the opening point, unlike her speaking (see again Lines 33–36 above).

Tina's use of the pronoun *it* and the definite and indefinite articles also varied. In her speaking, she largely omitted or used these items inappropriately, but they appeared with more frequency and varying degrees of accuracy in her writing. Table 1 shows that her usage of these items in her writing was much more accurate. In fact, in her speech, the ratio of omissions/incorrect usage to correct usage for articles was 13:2, and in her writing, 14:28 (i.e., 1:2). For the pronoun *it,* the ratios for omission/incorrect usage to correct usage show opposite trends, at 8:0 for speaking and 1:9 for writing. These figures are interesting in that they demonstrate the influence of the psycholinguistic context on the variability of learner errors (Ellis, 1997): That is, extra time, conscious attention, and the opportunity to plan output can affect learners' language and ultimately be more indicative of their true linguistic abilities. These psycholinguistic variables have implications for how teachers organize classroom activities and anticipate students' potential output. Furthermore, this kind of research can highlight differences between spoken and written modes of language and remind teachers of the importance of bringing such distinctions to students' attention, especially if learners are to master nativelike stylistic features.

Evidence of Grammaticization

The process of grammaticization (Rutherford, 1987) was also evident in Tina's spoken and written language. First, Tina showed conscious attempts to apply her linguistic knowledge about the rules and structure of English through what appeared to be her confusion with the adjective *communicative* (Text 2, Line 13) with *communications,* the use of *confuse* (Text 1, Line 26) and *importance* (Text 2, Line 29) as adjectives, and *pronunciation* as a verb (Text 2, Line 36). According to interactionist theory, the feedback, and particularly negative evidence (Ellis, 1997) she received in response to these approximated forms would have encouraged Tina to modify her language and ideally produce more accurate target language forms. Thus, her use of grammatical and lexical approximation was an important communication strategy.

Second, Tina displayed erratic use of final *s*. In her writing, her addition of *s* to plural countable nouns was fairly logical. In her spoken text, however, she used no plural nouns at all. Interestingly, in both texts, she omitted plural *s* whenever she used *some* before the noun; though *sometimes* she used both with and without a final *s*. The appearance of other errors, such as the substitution of *isn't* for *doesn't* and incorrect subject-verb agreement with *it* as subject, also showed similar variation. Thus, Tina displayed systematic variability in her linguistic choices; her behavior is supported by studies showing that the use of one linguistic form can trigger the use of another form, regardless of its grammatical accuracy (Ellis, 1997). Further, her vacillation between accurate and inaccurate use of these forms could be evidence of a firming-up process taking place in the learner's mind (Prabhu, 1987). Such variations could be expected eventually to disappear from Tina's language as they are replaced by forms closer to those of the target language (Allwright & Bailey, 1991).

It is also likely that negative transfer was responsible for some of these variants (particularly in Tina's use of final s, verb tenses, and word order), as Tina herself suspected. The teaching implications here would be to consider students' "built-in" syllabuses (Corder, 1974, p. 24) as determiners of error production and language acquisition in addition to learners' L1 because it is often the unlearning of aspects of these features that can cause the most difficulties for L2 learners (Rutherford, 1987).

◈ PRACTICAL IDEAS

For teachers, the analysis of learner language and interlanguage development naturally leads to the question of how to act on the findings: How can we use what we observe in the classroom to obtain positive outcomes for our students? Outlined below are examples of how the data gained in this classroom research could be utilized in planning teaching.

Encourage Self-Assessment and Reflection

Use questionnaires, surveys, and discussions to direct learners' attention to their language learning—in particular, to their short-term achievements. For example, a simple technique involves having students rate their own abilities in different areas (e.g., speaking to other students, reading a magazine, understanding NSs, knowing vocabulary), and remembering what they could do when they first arrived in the country or started their course and then several weeks or months later. By casting their minds back to their early days, even the most skeptical of learners have to acknowledge some degree of progress and usually find this exercise interesting, as well as motivating and rewarding.

Such self-review also offers excellent opportunity for spoken practice, especially if it includes a one-to-one discussion with the teacher. Reflection on her learning not only helped Tina (and me as her teacher) identify her linguistic strengths and weaknesses, it also encouraged her to take responsibility for her learning. By knowing where she was, she was able to constructively adapt her learning strategies to all kinds of situations independent of the classroom. For example, despite receiving plenty of praise and encouragement from her peers and me regarding her oral skills, she remained unconvinced and set out to find Australians to practice with and correct her pronunciation, eventually moving in with a local homestay family in order to achieve this objective. Naturally, her skills improved with the increase in practice and exposure to authentic language.

Offer Controlled Pronunciation Practice

Identify one or two problems and focus on correcting them. For example, with Tina, difficulties with final consonants such as the plural s and past tense marker ed were letting her down by giving her spoken English an elementary sound it did not deserve. Games are an enjoyable and nonthreatening way for language learners to practice the pronunciation of final sounds. Bingo involving the use of minimal pairs would be one way. With a learner like Tina as the caller and the rest of the class relying on her accurate pronunciation of words such as *socks* versus *sock* or *six* versus *sick* to win the game, there would be plenty of incentive for such a learner to succeed in an amusing, nonthreatening atmosphere.

Tina also worked independently on identified problems, such as her difficulty in pronouncing the lateral *l,* explaining to the class how she had learned to imitate Britney Spears's tongue positions (with relative success) from watching music videos at the weekend. This was another example of a positive outcome from Tina's taking responsibility for her own learning, and it underlines the fact that ultimately the learner—not the teacher—determines whether the correct form is acquired or not (Tsui, 1995).

Dictation and information gap tasks would also be useful for all language learners, particularly if successful completion of the task necessitated correct pronunciation. For example, one partner could describe a set of pictures to the other so that both finish with the same pictures arranged in the same order. The pictures themselves would incorporate important differences such as *red flower* versus *red flowers* or *sheep* versus *ship*, and other minimal pairs.

All these kinds of activities can be adapted for a variety of pronunciation problems.

Use Relevant Models

Present students with authentic written materials that show varied and appropriate use of the features on which you would like them to focus.

In Tina's case, models displaying appropriate use of connective devices and punctuation would have been very suitable at her stage of learning. Although her use of connectives, referencing, and punctuation was reasonably accurate, in her speech she had a tendency to overuse *so* as a connector, particularly with adjectives: "so is very difficult" (Line 9), "so quite difficult" (Line 17), "so is quite easy" (Line 25), "so is very confuse" (Line 26), "so is longer" (Line 36). In her writing (Text 2), her use of *thus* was inappropriate, although not wildly off the mark:

> Because Thai language doesn't have tense same as English, thus at first I used present simple while I spoke about past events. (Lines 38–39)

> Even though all of these school are in Bangkok, thus most Thai people can't speak English…. (Lines 63–64)

Furthermore, Tina often used conjunctions correctly in her writing, but her sentence structure and punctuation were incorrect. For example,

> I don't know which meaning I can use. Because one word in English can have more than 10 meaning in Thai. (Lines 51–53)

> After I studied here for three months I began dream in English and thought in English sometimes. So now I don't know I translate from Thai to English or not. (Lines 47–48)

A range of authentic or semiauthentic texts is available from course books as well as in newspapers, letters, magazines, and brochures. These texts can be adapted for classroom use by, for example, having students compare them with less or more effective examples, turning them into cloze exercises by deleting certain features, or using them as writing frames or skeletons for students to incorporate their own material. A useful resource here would be *Writing Matters* (Brown & Hood, 1989). By comparing their own work with successful, authentic samples, language learners such as Tina could easily improve their writing.

Build Vocabulary

Encourage the use of monolingual dictionaries—to build up students' repertoires of lexical items and discourage their use of literal translation, which is often not particularly helpful. You could discuss with them ways of recording new vocabulary and encourage effective learning strategies, such as organizing frequently used items into logical categories. By the same token, encourage students not to make endless lists of unrelated, obscure words to be memorized.

Tina's tendency to repeat herself may have been due to a lack of vocabulary because NNSs often resort to repetition rather than use more effective strategies such as circumlocution and approximation (Tarone & Yule, 1989). Therefore, activities that incorporate these circumlocutions and approximations would be appropriate for learners like Tina. These activities could include orally describing pictures of selected objects to a partner (or team), who tries to guess what the object is. Describe-and-draw information gap activities are also useful because they require learners to describe a situation in detail and cope with any consequent communication problems. A relevant resource would be *Intermediate Communication Games* (Hadfield, 1990). Tina's self-initiated interaction with NSs was very helpful to her in learning new words and expressions in a meaningful and communicative context, and this strategy is worth encouraging in other students.

◈ CONCLUSION

This case study has demonstrated some advantages of analyzing learner language as a means of providing pedagogical clues to interlanguage development. An investigation of Tina's spoken and written language enabled both Tina and me, as her teacher, to identify some of her learning strategies and provided valuable insight into her language acquisition processes. At the same time, the analysis revealed the important influence of context (linguistic, situational, and psycholinguistic) on her language production. Knowing this enabled me to provide a more detailed assessment of her stage of linguistic development and subsequently to plan appropriate action to cater for this. I believe that research of this kind encourages teachers to work with rather than against natural processes and in partnership with their students. It can also assist teachers in creating optimal conditions for language development rather than merely trying to fill empty vessels.

◈ CONTRIBUTOR

Victoria MacLeod is a recent master's graduate in TESOL education from the University of South Australia, in Adelaide. She is currently working in the South Australian branch of the Commonwealth Department of Immigration and Multicultural Affairs.

◈ APPENDIX: KEY TO TRANSCRIPT

<T>	Teacher
,	1-second pause
<Ta>	Tina
…	Pause of more than 1 second
<G>	Another student
<H>	Another student
[laughs]	Paralinguistic behaviour
WHY	Stress marked word
* * * * * * *	Abridged text
(<G> yeah)	Backchannel response

CHAPTER 4

Characteristics and Effect: A Teacher's Interactional Adjustments

Hao Sun

◈ INTRODUCTION

This chapter examines characteristics of a prospective ESL teacher's interactional adjustments as well as their effect on learners' comprehension and participation in group discussion. I use the term *interactional adjustments* here, also known as *conversational adjustments* (Long, 1983a), to refer to conversational modifications used by native speakers (NSs) at a discourse level to facilitate communication with nonnative speakers (NNSs) or to assist their language learning. Interactional adjustments differ from linguistic adjustments (Long, 1983a) in that the latter are realized in the form of discrete lexical items or syntactic structures, whereas the former are made at the suprasentential level.

Issues regarding the relationships between input, interaction, and language development have gained significant attention in the field of second language acquisition (see Ellis, 1994, for a detailed discussion). Long (1983b, 1985) and Long & Robinson (1998) stress the importance of modified interaction, involved in negotiation of comprehensibility and meaning, for acquisition. Long (1983b, 1996) proposes an interaction hypothesis, which holds that interaction between learners and other speakers is crucial for language development and addresses the inadequacy of comprehensible input alone, particularly with adults, a position advocated by Swain (1985, 1995) and Swain and Lapkin (1995). Swain emphasizes the significance of output, stating that output, among other functions, is one of the triggers for noticing linguistic gaps, a process that leads to modified output.

Related to language development are the concepts of *scaffolding* and *zone of proximal development* (ZPD). The notion of scaffolding, which can be traced back to Wood, Bruner, and Ross (1976), stresses the positive role and supportive conditions a knowledgeable participant can create for a novice in social interactions. It is closely related to Vygotsky's (1978, 1986) concept of the ZPD, which highlights language development through learners' interaction with more competent interlocutors in meaningful activities and the role of teachers' support and intervention in learning (Mercer, 1994). Central to this concept are the ideas that learning with assistance is an important feature of human development and the idea that the right kind of cognitive support can expand a person's problem-solving ability (Mercer, 1994).

In second language (L2) development, interactions with NSs constitute opportunities for learning as well as negotiation of meaning. Furthermore, comprehensible input has been recognized as influential in language development. Adjustments in teacher speech have been the focus of many studies, and such modification seems to serve the purpose of clarifying information and eliciting learners' responses (Chaudron, 1988).

◈ CONTEXT

This case study grew out of my observations of teacher/student interactions in an ESL class taught by preservice teachers[1] enrolled in a practicum class. During my observations, I noticed that teachers demonstrated different styles of interaction with students, and the outcome, as manifested in student response and participation, was different, particularly in teachers' interactions with lower level students. The lack of necessary interactional adjustments for the students seemed to constitute one of the problems. Videotaped interactions enabled me to compare teachers' interactional styles, and one of the teacher learners, Trish, stood out as an instructor who was able to follow learners' responses closely and adjust her interactions accordingly. Such observations motivated and prompted me to further examine characteristics of Trish's interactional style and its effect on learners.

The ESL class under discussion was offered for an MA TESL practicum. The class was not listed in the university course catalogue, nor was it part of the English language program provided by the language center affiliated with the university. There were five students enrolled in the practicum. As the faculty member teaching the practicum, I was also responsible for the ESL class offered to the community. Because the teacher learners taught the ESL class, I was able to observe their teaching as well as participate in some of the small-group discussions.

Our ESL class was open to any NNSs in the local community interested in improving their English language skills. Twice a week, the class met for 75 minutes over a 12-week period. Most of the learners were spouses of international students enrolled at the university in town, and a few were immigrants who had arrived in the United States not long ago. In our first ESL class meeting, we asked all learners to fill out a questionnaire on their language needs and goals for improving English. The questionnaire provided us with essential information regarding learners' goals as well as perceptions of the strength of their language skills. We also informally assessed the students' listening and writing skills through the use of a video excerpt. In addition, the use of a self-introduction activity on the first day gave us a general idea of the learners' language skills in speaking.

It became obvious to us after the first class that the learners' ESL proficiency varied tremendously, ranging from beginning to high intermediate level. In addition, although some learners intended to pursue academic study at universities in the United States, others were anxious to improve their general ability to communicate verbally. It seemed essential to divide the learners into two classes, so this is what we did. One class was to focus on conversation skills (hereafter the C class); whereas the

---

[1] The term *preservice teachers* refers to the TESL students enrolled in the practicum; *teacher learners* or *teachers* alternatively refer to the same group. The term does not mean that these teachers are necessarily inexperienced; *preservice* is only used in the sense that they are currently engaged in professional training.

other class was geared toward academic preparation (hereafter the A class), with an emphasis on the integration of the different, relevant skills. Teachers were then selected accordingly. For each class, one teacher would be in charge of teaching assignments for a given week while other teacher(s) of the same class would observe and help out with group or pair work.

My discussion here focuses on interactions in the C class. There were 13 learners in the C class, and their countries of origin included Bulgaria, China, Egypt, Korea, India, Thailand, Turkey, and Vietnam. The greatest challenge for the instructors of this class was the wide range in learners' language skills. At the higher end, two learners were able to converse fairly well with NSs. At the lower end, the learners who were true beginners had great difficulties even following classroom instructions delivered at a normal rate. In general, most of the learners were able to engage in basic communication.

◈ DESCRIPTION

One of the most effective ways of learning and teaching for the C class was teacher-fronted small-group interaction. This interactional structure turned out to be crucial for the success of the C class due to the specific characteristics of the class: First, it was extremely difficult to provide instructional content and input at the level and speed appropriate for everyone in the class, given the considerable disparity in the learners' language proficiency. Second, most students were reticent, especially for the first few weeks, with only the two relatively fluent students participating most of the time. Third, because this was a class emphasizing spoken language, it was critical to ensure that the learners were able to comprehend class interactions and that everyone gradually became comfortable participating. Last, the fact that there was more than one instructor for the class was both a disadvantage and an advantage.

Multiple teachers called for learners' frequent adjustment to different instructional styles, but this need for adjustment meant that learners required additional time to feel comfortable in class. However, it is precisely because more than one instructor was available in this class that more individualized interaction with different learners was possible. In brief, teacher-fronted small-group interaction was an effective pedagogical option in our multilevel class.

The small-group format with a teacher in each group offered more individualized and appropriate input. It also made learner participation less overwhelming. However, the group interaction format described here is not typical of group work discussed elsewhere. In our C class, the group format was not always designed for learner interaction. Instead, it was often intended as a miniclass where a teacher was present to guide interactions and provide any necessary directions at a rate and level appropriate for the students involved. Such an interactional format seemed to be a necessary and useful initial step for the learners to adjust to participation. From a teaching perspective, the teacher-fronted group interaction was fairly effective considering the learners' lack of prior experience and skill at participation.

The research question for this study emerged after I had observed several classes and viewed videotaped lessons taught by different instructors. Videotaping was an arrangement I discussed with the teacher learners prior to the beginning of the course. The purpose of the videotaping was to promote and facilitate professional growth. All the teachers were informed that one of their classes would be videotaped, and the schedule was set up after both classes began. The first taping was conducted approximately the 5th week of the 12-week session, and the last one was completed in the 11th week.

During my observations, I noted that teachers' explanations or questions were not always understood in class. Group discussions also manifested teachers' different interactional patterns. Because of the general complexity of classroom interaction, it is impossible as well as inappropriate to attribute any interactional outcome to one particular aspect of the interaction. What prompted my interest in conducting this case study, however, was the interaction of one group with the teacher Trish, who consequently became the focus of this case study. Trish's interactional style demonstrated salient adjustment features that seem to have facilitated learners' comprehension and participation in the group discussions.

In the videotaped group interaction discussed below, what initially drew my attention was the high level of student participation. All four learners, who were usually reticent, seemed to be actively involved as demonstrated in the amount of information they shared and the questions they initiated. If the learners in this group were more active participants than other learners, what might have contributed to their participation? It is at this point that my research questions began to emerge. Due to pedagogical considerations, I did not conduct any interviews while the class was in session, even though the learners in the class were acquainted with me and were aware of my role given that I was often in class (alternating between the A and the C classes) observing, videotaping, or participating in small-group discussions.

After I reviewed the videotaped classroom interactions involving Trish and four learners who were at the low intermediate level, I formulated the following research questions:

- What factors might have contributed to the effectiveness of communication and high learner participation in this group[2]?

- What are the characteristics of the teacher's interactional style?

- How did the teacher's interactional style affect students' comprehension and participation?

- How did the learners perceive the teacher's interactional style in relation to their L2 development?

Although the distinctive language functions of lectures and conversations have been discussed (e.g., Chaudron, 1988), the type of teacher talk exemplified in the group interactions described here is difficult to categorize as either lecture or conversation because it combines features of both instructional explanations (teacher-to-student discourse) and genuine exchange of information (between conversational partners). As a teacher, Trish strove to provide comprehensible input while maximizing learners' participation—a difficult balance well maintained.

I videotaped Trish's teaching in the fifth week of the course, after eight sessions. By then, Trish had taught three class periods, and she was fairly well acquainted with every learner in the C group. The topic on the day of the recording was health, a

---

[2] Possible answers to this question are not included in this chapter because they do not all pertain to its focus.

continuation from her class a week before. In that class, Trish had introduced the class to some general vocabulary related to health. With the use of key words such as *sickness, symptom,* and *remedy* in context, Trish had shared with the class her home remedy for a cold, effectively demonstrating the appropriate use and meaning of the new words as well as providing an interaction model for the sharing of home remedies to follow.

The class period began with a brief review of the key words. Then Trish introduced the task: Each group was to work on two questions with the use of a handout, which included illustrations of various symptoms of different health problems and some vocabulary items. The two specific questions to discuss were

1.   What health problems do these people seem to have?

2.   What remedies can you use to treat these ailments?

The discussion specified in her lesson plan aimed to introduce new vocabulary and stimulate the meaningful exchange of information. The questions encouraged interaction by incorporating learning of the new vocabulary in the genuine sharing (i.e., Gass & Veronis's, 1985, two-way communication) of home remedies for the sicknesses listed on the students' handouts.

The videotaped session demonstrated several features of Trish's interactional style. Modified teacher talk in L2 classrooms typically involves phonological, syntactic, and lexical concessions and other features, such as slower rates of speech, pausing, and feedback (see Chaudron, 1988, for a detailed review). The discussion here focuses on its more global aspects, specifically, Trish's rephrasing and elaboration, repetition of student output, and discourse scaffolding. I chose to focus on these features because they seem salient and bear on the group interactions.

◈ DISTINGUISHING FEATURES

Rephrasing and Elaboration

Repetition is a common feature of modified teacher talk (e.g., Chaudron, 1988; Pica & Doughty, 1985), but with Trish, rephrasing or elaboration was more than simple repetition. Trish rephrased her questions or elaborated her explanations in a number of ways. However, all her rephrasings were alternative linguistic forms that any NSs might use with each other. By reformulating the same idea in different ways, Trish's main ideas were not only conveyed through different linguistic means, they were also reinforced. Thus, the processing time was increased, and comprehension was accordingly made more manageable. Furthermore, learners were exposed to enriched input that might aid their language acquisition and expand their linguistic repertoire in general.

Example 1 illustrates these features.

1.*

```
1    T:      ok - excellent-
2→           so:: if you get one of these ailments -
3→           what do you do -
```

---

*Note: See Appendix for key to transcript.

```
4→         what is your home remedy -
5          what do you do for a headache -
6    S1:   Aspirin
7    T:    Aspirin ^ =
8    S1:   Tylenol =
9    T:    or Tylenol ^ - anything else you can do -
10   T:    does that help you to - to sleep - to get some sleep -
11   S1:   {nodding}
12   S2:   {nodding}
13   T:    sometimes we call that bed rest - you need bed rest -
14         right - bed rest - meaning - sleep in bed - sleep - relax
15         - right
16         any other remedies you have -
17→        what if you have a stomachache -
18→        what do you do when you get a stomachache –
           [5.11 seconds]
19   S2:   I heard - my parents - (xx ) ago - in Korea -
```

In Lines 3 and 4, Trish asked the same question in two different ways, "What do you do?" and "What is your home remedy?", thus simultaneously reinforcing the message and facilitating learning. Similarly, in Lines 17 and 18, Trish first asked "What if you have a stomachache?", then "What do you do when you get a stomachache?" Although the *what if* structure is more succinct, being a reduced form, it is more complex syntactically. Consequently, it can be more difficult for learners to understand. On the other hand, the *what do you do* structure is more regular (Long, 1983a). Thus, the rephrasing of the *what if* question with *what do you do* probably provided a form that was more comprehensible for the learners. In addition, the change from *have* to *get* in Line 18 introduced another lexical option for the learners. In these ways, Trish skillfully reformulated her questions so that if the learners were not able to understand one version, they might understand an alternative form.

In her explanations in response to students' questions, Trish demonstrated a similar pattern. In Example 2, Student 4 (S4) raised a question about *ailment* in Line 2. This word had actually been discussed in the previous class period, but S4 did not seem to remember its meaning. Trish first asked other students if they remembered the word. Two students did and offered their opinions (Lines 5 and 7). Trish confirmed their answers first and then added her explanations. Again, her reply is characterized by more than one way of explaining the word. The expressions she used include "not too bad," "small symptoms," and "minor sicknesses." She further commented on the characteristics of ailments, including their possible effects on one's health and treatment options (Lines 12 and 14). One of the strengths of Trish's explanations is the meaningful and rich contexts she provided with definitions. These details enhanced students' comprehension.

```
2.

1    T:    ok - anything else - any other questions -
2    S4:   (number xx)
3    T:    ailment - does anyone remember -
4          we talked about it on Thursday
5→   S1:   unhealthy
6    T:    unhealthy ^
```

```
 7→  S3    illness
 8   T:    illness ^
 9   S3:   {nodding}
10   T:    yeah - all of these -
11→        ailment is usually minor - meaning - it's not too bad -
12→        it's ok for you - usually to cure yourself at home - right ^
13→        ailments mean small symptoms - minor sicknesses -
14→        they usually don't last very long - usually not too painful
```

In such ways, Trish not only assisted learners who might have had difficulty in understanding the original form of the question or statement, she also introduced learners to alternative forms for the same meaning. Remarkably, she was able to strike a balance between which information would be comprehensible and which would be beneficial to learn. When I asked Trish what she observed on the video, she mentioned that she was pleased to see herself offering some explanations that were appropriate for the students she was working with. In Example 3, her three versions for *recuperate* in Lines 4, 8, and 10 respectively provide an example.

3.

```
 1   S1:   what does re:cuperate -
 2   T:    recuperate =
 3   S1:   = recuperate
 4→  T:    yeah - that means the process of getting better
 5   S1:   ok
 6→  T:    so if you're recuperating
 7   S1:   uh hum
 8→  T:    it means you're getting better
 9   S1:   getting better
10→  T:    uh hum - very similar to recovery - right ^
11   S1:   recovery
12   T:    recovery - good question -
13         any words new to you -
```

In this case, Student 1 (S1), in Line 1, asked Trish about the meaning of *recuperate*. First, Trish defined it as "the process of getting better." Then, she elaborated: "so if you're recuperating, it means you're getting better." Her second explanation in Lines 6 and 8 removed *process,* a word that might have increased the difficulty for the learner if she did not know what it meant. *Getting better* is easier to understand than *recovery* and *recuperate*—as evidenced by the learner's repetition of this phrase (a strategy she frequently used on other occasions, too) in Line 9. Trish's third explanation introduced the word *recovery* to the learner. *Recovery* occurs more frequently and in a wider range of contexts, so it is more useful than *recuperate*. The introduction of *recovery* reflects Trish's awareness of students' need to learn and her judicious, balanced provision of comprehensible input, and opportunities and content for learning. Elaboration is generally recognized as beneficial (e.g., Nunan, 1995) because it can "compensate for linguistic complexity" by "adding redundancy to discourse through the use of repetition, paraphrases and appositionals" (Long, 1996, p. 422). Trish's interactional style is an effective example of elaborative strategies rather than simplified modification.

Repetition of Student Output

One of Trish's adjustments in response to students' output was her repetition of their utterances. Most of the literature on modified teacher talk discusses teachers' corrective feedback on student output (e.g., Brown, 1994; Long, 1983b, but aspects of other possible functions have not been fully addressed. Trish's repetition of student output seemed to serve multiple functions—confirmation checks, facilitation of noticing, reinforcement strategies, acknowledgment of student contributions, assistance with learning, and corrective feedback.

In Example 1 (Lines 5–9), after S1 said "Aspirin" and "Tylenol" (Lines 6 and 8), Trish repeated these two words (in Lines 7 and 9). First, with rising intonation, Trish's repetition may serve as a confirmation check for herself of what S1 had just said. Second, it might facilitate noticing, alerting the speaker to the gap, if there is one, between what she had intended to convey and what she had actually communicated. Specifically, if Trish's repetition were different from what S1 had planned to say, it would indicate to the student that she had not communicated successfully or been understood accurately. Thus, S1 would have been given an opportunity to repair. Third, repetition is also a reinforcement strategy for S1 to learn both the meaning and form of what she had said. In addition, the teacher's repetition acknowledged and reaffirmed the speaker's (learner's) contribution to the discussion. Although it is difficult to assess the immediate effect of such acknowledgment on learners, I believe such acknowledgment promotes and encourages learner participation in the long run, especially for learners who are new to classroom participation.

Fifth, Trish's repetition was a means of giving other students more time to comprehend S1's message without having to ask S1 to repeat what she had said. This assistance was probably necessary because students' utterances were not always clearly audible even though the teacher and the four learners were sitting together in a circle. Indeed, most of S4's utterances were inaudible on the tape due to her low voice. More advanced learners would have been capable of negotiating meanings on their own without the teacher, and taking the initiative in asking for and providing clarifications for themselves would have benefited such learners' language development. However, because these learners were beginners and inexperienced in this kind of interactional format, some assistance, assurance, and guidance from the teacher were conducive to learning—an observation that was confirmed in my interviews with the learners themselves.

In addition to the five functions described above, the teacher's repetition sometimes served as implicit correction. In Line 13 of Example 4, Student 2 (S2) suggested "rubbing hot towel" as a home remedy for backache. Due to his pronunciation, S1 did not at first understand S2's utterance, as indicated by her "uhm" in Line 14 and her immediate turning to Trish. In response, in Line 15, Trish confirmed S2's utterance as meaningful with her "OK," then immediately repeated "hot towel," thereby providing corrective feedback (Long, 1983a) to S2. Trish's repetition of students' utterances was judiciously selective, triggered possibly by factors such as that the repeated word or phrase was important for comprehension (e.g., S2's mispronunciation of "towel" in Example 4); or that the speaker's voice was too low for others to follow (as was the case with S4 in Example 2).

4.

1	T:	how about if your back (xx)
2		do you have a remedy for that - [4.42 seconds]
3	S1:	(xx)
4	T:	ok -
5	S1:	(xx)
6	T:	ok
7	S1:	an::d hot =
8	T:	oh::::=
9	S1:	(it's going to be) hot
10	T:	uh hum
11	S1:	really hot (xx)
12	T:	uh hum - uh hum and what would it do to your backache
13➔	S2:	rubbing hot towel - hot towel
14➔	S1:	uhm - {looking puzzled, turning to T}
15➔	T:	ok - hot towel
16	S1:	hot - yeah
17	T:	uh hum - uh hum -

In these ways, repeating learners' output assisted communication, learning, and classroom interaction, and generally served pedagogical purposes. Trish's use of repetition seemed to reflect her sensitivity to her different roles: as a teacher, a facilitator of interaction, and as a participant in communication. Such sensitivity is especially important in two-way interaction in which new, rather than familiar, information is being exchanged.

Discourse Scaffolding

Scaffolding refers to linguistic expressions or conversational devices used to respond to perceived learner difficulties or need for clarification. The two discourse scaffolding strategies relevant to this discussion are assistance with a missing word and an or-choice option.

Assistance With a Missing Word

Even in communication in one's native language, it is possible sometimes to find oneself searching for the precise word to convey an idea during a conversation. At such moments, we often seek our conversation partner's assistance by asking, for example, "What do you call that…?" Lower level ESL learners, however, may not have acquired such linguistic means or discourse skills, as Example 5 reveals.

5.

1	T:	anything else that's new -
2		do you ever use rubbing alcohol for anything -
3		rubbing alcohol ^ -
4	S2:	{giving an injection}
5	T:	uh hum
6➔	S2:	before we - we have -
7➔	T:	shots ^ - a shot ^ -
8	S2:	(xx) nurse - rubbing alcohol {rubbing}

```
9       T:    yes yes right - to disinfect to make sure that it doesn't get infected
10            - right ^ - sometimes - people use it to soothe muscles -
11            right ^ - sore muscles
```

S2 in Example 5 was trying to respond to Trish's question about *rubbing alcohol*. Other students did not seem to understand what the term meant. Yet, though S2 did, he did not know how to explain it. As can be seen on the video, he made the gesture of getting a shot and said, "Before we- we have-," and then turned to Trish for help. Trish noticed S2's difficulty in finding the right word to describe an injection, and provided the missing words: "shots - a shot." After S2's further attempts, including his specification of the "nurse" as the person who performs injections, Trish explained the use and functions of rubbing alcohol. Such assistance facilitated students' communication and learning.

The Or-Choice Option

The or-choice option (Long, 1983a) functions as a guide to narrow and clarify the speaker's meaning. In Lines 14 and 20 in Example 6, Trish utilized or-choice questions to help the learner clarify the meaning.

```
6.
1       T:    any other remedies you have -
2             what if you have a stomachache -
3             what do you do when you get a stomachache –
4             [5.11 seconds]
5       S2:   I heard - my parents
6       T:    uh hum
7       S2:   (xx ) ago - in Korea -
8       T:    uh huh -
9       S2:   person (vomit) for stomachache
10      T:    uh hum
11      S2:   they eat - salt
12      T:    salt -
13      S2:   yeah -
14→     T:    a lot of salt or just (some)
15      S2:   a lot of salt
16      T:    really
17      S2:   and - water {stirring gesture}
18      T:    o:::h and this should cure -
19      S2:   {nodding}
20→     T:    but do people do that now - or not any more -
21      S2:   uh: when I was a child -
```

Sensitivity

In my research, I was also interested in the development of Trish's interactional adjustments. I wondered how she developed her sensitivity to and awareness of her students' interactional needs, given that she had only limited experience working with ESL learners in a formal context. During the interview, I found out that Trish had actually worked with ESL learners as a volunteer conversation partner and a tutor for a few years before pursuing her graduate degree. What seemed to be important was her unusual sensitivity to learners' conversational responses. In response to my question about the development of her sensitivity and awareness, Trish commented that she had always paid attention to students' responses, whether these were verbal or nonverbal cues, but that she was not aware of any particular experiences that had had much impact on her interactional style; she thought her adjustments had probably just evolved over time.

Classroom Characteristics

Our ESL conversation class featured some special characteristics. First, students' language proficiency levels varied tremendously, and that was our major challenge. The wide range of learner language skills necessitated the format of teacher-fronted small-group interaction. This format was conducive to needs-based teaching in a nonthreatening environment.

Another factor was the number of teachers. In regular ESL classes, there is only one teacher per class. In our case, we had three student teachers. The availability of more than one instructor made small-group interaction with one teacher feasible and effective, and small-group interaction was a crucial contribution to the success of the class.

Furthermore, this study confirmed the positive role of teacher-modified talk that incorporated learners' perspectives. Research on modified teacher talk abounds, but learners' perspectives have not been well documented. This study has provided some valuable insights on this issue. The learner interviews confirm their appreciation of teachers' interactional adjustments and their belief in such modification as beneficial for learning and participation. The positive effect of such adjustments for this group of learners is demonstrated in their increased comprehension, their more active participation in group interaction, and their recognition and evaluation of the teacher's modified interactional style as facilitative.

❖ PRACTICAL IDEAS

In this section, based on observations and insights obtained in this study, I make specific recommendations on classroom interaction, student participation, and teacher discourse.

Use Teacher-Fronted Groups When Necessary

Group interaction with well-designed tasks in language classrooms can provide optimal interactional opportunities for meaningful communication in the target language and promote negotiation of meaning among learners. Furthermore, group interaction can foster learner independence. The promotion of student-group interaction, however, does not and should not rule out teacher-fronted group interaction completely. This study suggests that such an interactional format can be useful in some cases (particularly when a class consists of learners of different proficiency levels) and might especially benefit those students who need to make major adjustments to be able to participate in classroom activities or who need individualized instructional assistance.

Teacher-fronted group interaction provides a transition and a less intimidating environment for lower level students or learners who are not yet ready to participate in class discussions. In addition, some learners can benefit tremendously from a teacher's individualized encouragement, explanations, and instructions. A teacher's feedback, discourse scaffolding, and requests for clarification, among other means of assistance, may also contribute to learners' positive experience in expressing themselves. Granted, it is difficult to put such a plan into action when there are more than 20 students in the class with only one instructor. Therefore, teacher-fronted groups seem to be most appropriate when there is more than one instructor in the class. Nevertheless, it is still possible for an instructor to focus on one particular group, provided that other groups in the class are able to work on their own.

Call on Learners If They Find It Helpful

Many ESL instructors refrain from calling upon classroom learners to participate because they realize that learners might feel uncomfortable. A lack of volunteers generally indicates that learners are not ready to participate. To call on learners, therefore, can be perceived as forcing participation; this is not appropriate pedagogically from the perspective of many teachers who are NSs. It is true that it takes time for learners to become comfortable participating in group or class discussions if such practice is not what they are used to. However, calling on particular learners to engage them in a discussion is not necessarily always detrimental. In fact, it might be beneficial for some learners because eliciting individual students' responses or contribution might actually help them overcome the initial challenge of expressing themselves in front of their peers.

Hesitation or nervousness in volunteering a reply may derive from at least two different sources for learners who are not used to participating in classroom interaction. One, which is linguistic in nature, relates to speakers' sense of uncertainty about the correctness or appropriateness of their linguistic choice. The other concern is a cultural challenge: Learners from cultures that revere teachers will find it fairly difficult to ask a question in class, which, in their view, may constitute a challenge to the teacher; similarly, they may find it difficult to volunteer a response, which could be perceived as showing off by their peers (Flowerdew & Miller, 1996). In fact, students from these cultures will deem volunteering in class a violation of the principle that values humbleness in the individual. Given such possible disparities in perspectives regarding norms of behavior, teacher-elicited responses from nominated learners may, in students' eyes, legitimize their responses, and this may gradually facilitate their participation.

In fact, some students might be looking forward to such teacher elicitation. For example, one of the learners in the ESL class in this study told me during the postsession interview that he had even counted the number of times he could have been called upon (based on his calculation of the number of class sessions and the number of students in the class) to answer questions in class had the instructors actually called upon him and other learners—a perspective conveying a strong desire to participate that would be hard even to imagine if it had not been directly communicated. Although to nominate students has, therefore, some benefits, instructors certainly need to be sensitive to differences in learners, and, therefore, to exercise caution and discretion as to whom, when, and how often to nominate in the classroom.

Sensitize Yourself to Students' Readiness to Respond

My observations and interviews with some ESL learners suggest that when learners are ready to respond, they tend to look at the instructor, whereas if they are not ready, they avoid eye contact with the teacher. Schiffrin (1996) discusses some of the differences in display of involvement in U.S. classrooms. Certainly my observation is preliminary and does not hold true for every learner, but it is nevertheless essential for teachers to sensitize themselves to learners' different ways of displaying their readiness for participation. Teachers might also find it beneficial to ask individual students outside class if they feel comfortable about being nominated to answer questions.

Become Aware of Learners' Interactional Needs

Interactional adjustments—such as, requests for clarification, rephrasing of questions or explanations, and repetition of student output—can be particularly useful for lower level ESL learners in assisting them to communicate more effectively, to build up confidence, and to maximize learning based upon their own ideas and output. Such features of interaction are not part of every instructor's conversational style, however, and I do not suggest that all teachers should change how they converse. Nevertheless, it would be useful to help instructors and preservice teachers become aware of the assistance such adjustments might provide for learners in a pedagogical setting. It would also be beneficial if teachers became more sensitive to learners' interactional needs.

❖ CONCLUSION

Trish's interactional adjustments to ESL learners were effective in facilitating comprehension and participation. The ESL learners involved all expressed appreciation of her teaching and interactional style. The effectiveness of Trish's style cannot be judged on students' expressed preferences alone; the learners' active participation in the group discussion provides part of the evidence of their comprehension of the interactional input. Meanwhile, in our teacher education program, I will continue to encourage in-service teachers to utilize videotaped classes to examine, reflect on, and improve interactions with learners in an effort to maximize opportunities for learners' language development.

❖ ACKNOWLEDGMENTS

I thank the editors for their help with earlier versions of the manuscript and am grateful to Trvyan Ann Thomson for her support and participation. I also thank the student participants, who provided valuable input in this study.

❖ CONTRIBUTOR

Hao Sun is an assistant professor at Indiana University-Purdue University, in the United States. Her research interests include discourse analysis, intercultural communication, L2 teaching methodology, and L2 writing.

❖ APPENDIX: KEY TO TRANSCRIPT

T	teacher
S	student
(xx)	words not decipherable
( )	uncertain transcription
-	brief untimed pause
(5.0)	timed pause
underline	speaker's emphasis
=	latching (no obvious interval between turns)
/	beginning of overlap between two utterances
::::	stretched sound
^	rising (instead of falling) intonation; only indicated when the same utterances might have been produced with falling intonation
{laugh}	nonverbal gesture
→	feature referred to in discussion

CHAPTER 5

Teaching Spoken Language Skills Through a Reading Comprehension Text

Maya Khemlani David and Kow Yip C. Cheng

⬦ INTRODUCTION

Current teaching methodology, that is, communicative language teaching (CLT), stresses the contribution of learner interaction in language learning. CLT emphasizes communication that focuses on meaning and intention, rather than form (Johnson, 1982; Johnson & Morrow, 1981; Taylor, 1987). Communicative classroom settings help language learners because they focus on communication tasks. In such settings, group work tends to reduce students' anxieties about speaking and facilitates the development of spoken discourse skills.

In the study we discuss in this chapter, we supplied students with a reading comprehension text followed by five multiple-choice questions (see Appendix). The students were asked to find the best possible answer to each of these questions. For each question, they had to negotiate an outcome (see, e.g., learner negotiation toward identified communicative goals as examined in Crookes, 1986; Rivers, 1978). This negotiation involved them in discussion and interaction. We hoped that focusing on completing the reading task would encourage each group of students to use English.

Second language (L2) learners tend to resort to communication strategies when their target language resources fail them. Communication strategies enable language learners to "overcome obstacles to communication by providing ... [them] with an alternative form of expression for the intended meaning" (Bialystok, 1990, p. 35). Among the communication strategies L2 learners often employ are avoidance, appeals, paraphrasing, and literal translation. (For an overview of communication strategies, see Faerch & Kasper, 1983; Kellerman, 1991; Tarone, 1980.) In this study, students tended to resort to appeals and avoidance strategies: They appealed by asking a question or enlisting the help of a teacher or peer; they avoided a problem either by not speaking or by abruptly stopping soon after they had started.

Selinker (1988) proposed that someone learning an L2 goes through many interlanguage stages. These are psycholinguistic stages of language development during which learners who do not have target language competence produce forms that are deviant from the norm. In the task used during this study, the learners demonstrated different stages of interlanguage development. For example, those learners who could initiate repair were able to move from interlanguage to English forms.

Thus, our research was motivated by the current interest in communicative activities in the English language classroom and pair or group interactions. We set out to analyze task output generated by a set reading task in a classroom. We hoped that the set task and the resulting group interaction would generate an anxiety-free environment and make L2 learners' target language use less inhibited. We were especially interested to examine the kinds of communicative competence the set task generated.

◈ CONTEXT

The research was carried out with 15 first-year undergraduate students from the Faculty of Economics in the University of Malaya. These students were registered for an English language proficiency course. All undergraduates in the University of Malaya are required to register for an English language course (unless exempted because of a good grade in the School Certificate English paper, which follows the equivalent of 5 years of secondary schooling). Although this specific course emphasizes reading for academic purposes, it also encompasses other language skills.

◈ DESCRIPTION

The 15 students had varying ranges of proficiency in English and, at the time of research, had studied English in primary and secondary school 9–11 years. They were studying accountancy in the Faculty of Economics and Public Administration and were expected to have fair to average competence in English. As many of their lecturers worked part-time in the private sector and were more comfortable using English than Malay, they were taught in English even though their peers, who pursued business studies or rural development in the same faculty, had lectures in Malay, the national language, which is the medium of instruction in most Malaysian universities.

Although the students were Malaysian Chinese, the majority were most comfortable in Mandarin; two were most comfortable using English. The latter lived in the city of Kuala Lumpur, where the University of Malaya is, and where English is used extensively. For these two students, English was an L2. The majority of the students, however, had first attended Chinese vernacular schools for their primary education and then Malay national schools, where Malay is the medium of instruction. Most students also came from the nonurban areas of Peninsular Malaya, where English has the status of being a third or foreign language (David, 2000). Consequently, these students were not very fluent in spoken English.

We made use of this variety of abilities by grouping the students so that every group had one proficient speaker who was to act as the facilitator or group leader and who was given the task of ensuring that all members of the group participated in the discussion.

Although students' spoken proficiency in English varied, they had been taught reading skills and appeared to have mastered various subskills of reading, such as skimming, scanning, looking for main points, and inference. However, most of them still appeared diffident about using English and reverted to Mandarin as soon as the class was over. In order to encourage talk, they were set a reading task, which was in line with one of the major aims of the language course, namely, reading for academic purposes. The reading text selected was on the cockle industry in Malaysia. Because the course was an English for specific purposes (ESP) course, all texts were related to economics. The reading passage was followed by five multiple-choice questions, as this was the format used in the final examination. (For details of the written and oral examination structure of the ESP paper for economics undergraduates in the University of Malaya, see Yong & David, 1996.)

Furthermore, we hoped that the multiple-choice format would facilitate discussion because students had to choose an answer from four options for each question. Students were instructed to discuss the arguments in favor of or against each option and provide reasons substantiated from the text for their choice. We hoped that, in arriving at a group consensus on the answers, they would indirectly produce speech acts of soliciting opinion, agreeing, disagreeing, and resolving conflicts or disagreement.

We videoptaped four groups of students (Groups 1–3, consisting of four members, and Group 4, consisting of three) during the discussion, which lasted 3 hours. To minimize teacher interference, one of us (Maya) left the classroom during the discussion. The only instructions Maya gave were that the groups had to come to an agreement regarding the answers for each of the five questions and provide reasons for so doing. Additionally, so as to initiate and ensure discussion, Maya carefully selected the group facilitators to start the discussion for the first question. These student facilitators were to ensure that all members of their group participated in the discussion. The recorded interaction was transcribed. Analysis of the transcript revealed some characteristic features of classroom discourse.

❖ DISTINGUISHING FEATURES

Use of Speech Acts

It is common classroom practice for teachers to elicit information. However, all questions in the recording for this study were initiated by the students as they set out to determine the answers to the preset task questions. The student-initiated questions, therefore, were task authentic in that the questioners really needed the opinions of the other students in their groups. This factor stimulated student talk. In the resulting group discussions, initiation, response, and feedback (IRF) structures, which were entirely student initated, emerged (see Coulthard, 1979, 1981). Students responded to student questions such as, "What is your opinion?" and "What is your answer?" (see Student 2 [S2] in Example 1). At times, the original feedback of the initiating student was another question (see Student 1's [S1] response to S2 in Example 1), resulting in continued communication among the participants.

1. IRF Pattern

S1: What is your answer? *(eliciting)*
S2: B *(response)*
S1: Why? *(feedback)*

When a reason was provided, the listener would either agree, disagree, request clarification or elaboration, or assert an opinion and provide information or reasons for doing so. Negotiation would continue until a consensus was reached. The students used a wide range of speech acts (see Figure 1) and achieved communication despite their structural deficiencies in English. The figure shows their many ways of soliciting opinions, seeking agreement, agreeing, and disagreeing, both directly and indirectly. We want to emphasize that although the participants were not grammatically competent, they were able to come to a consensus based on logical reasoning.

Because the students were entirely responsible for the discourse, they found themselves having to use a diverse combination of speech acts in order to complete

Soliciting Opinions or Reasons

1   What are your opinions?
2   So would you give your view?
3   So what's your answer?
4   How about you?
5   What is the reason why you say B is correct?
6   Can you give more explanation?
7   Why you choose B?
8   Why do you prefer B?
9   Where can you find the paragraph/sentence which tells you this?
10   Where you found? (*on being told what the answer is*)
11   Why do you say that A is the answer?

Seeking Agreement

1   Are you agree with me?
2   Are you the same?
3   So are you agree with the answer B?
4   Do you agree?
5   You agree indirectly my answer eh?
6   I think the answer is C, you think so?
7   So can we select answer as C? Can we?
8   How about B? Can we select that? No?
9   So the answer is B? Do you agree or not?
10   This is my view. Are you the same?
11   So are you all agree?
12   So are you agree with my reason or what?
13   What do you think (*after providing explanation and examples*)?
14   Are you all agree with me? OK (*reinforcing*).
15   Cannot say 1043, isn't it (*after providing explanation and example*)?
16   The option B is really wrong, right?
17   This one is correct, right? I agree.

Continued on p. 53

Agreeing/Conceding

1   I agree same answer.

2   I agree with you and totally agree.

3   Since you note the point so I agree with you.

4   My answer same.

5   Yeh.yeh. I agree with you (*nodding head*).

6   You accept B as the answer, isn't it (*verifying*)? OK, lah. I also accept.

7   I agree with you wholeheartedly.

8   Alright.

Conditional Agreement

1   Actually A and B answer is very close.

2   I agree but…

Disagreeing (Direct)

1   No. I disagree with you.

2   I am not agree with your answer.

3   I think your answer is not suitable.

4   I still insist on answer B.

Disagreeing (Indirect)

1   Why is it A is not the answer?

2   Why are you so concerned about C (*and refers to text, implying C is not right*)?

3   If the price is not lower, how can demand increase, isn't it?

4   Why can't we accept A (*when told another option has been selected as the key*)

FIGURE 1. Speech Acts of Soliciting Opinion, Seeking Agreement, Agreeing, and Disagreeing

the communicative task successfully. This required them to focus on finding the solutions to multiple-choice questions, and to do so, they had to communicate through English.

Use of Openings and Closings

The study data showed that the students knew how to follow the basic rules of interaction. They were aware, for example, of the need to open and close interactions and, notwithstanding their limited competence in English—evidenced in their interlanguages (Selinker, 1988)—they were able to do so. For instance, as openings, they used varied ways of soliciting opinions. In Example 2, S1 asked "What about you all?" meaning "What is your opinion?", yet his peer understood him and in turn brought Student 3 (S3) into the conversation by asking, "What about your opinion?" S3 has evidently accepted S1's informal usage. Nevertheless, S3 went on to repeat the same question using formal English.

2. Openings: Ways of Soliciting Opinions

S1:   So my answer is C. What about you all?
S2:   My answer is A. What about your opinion?

The speech acts of agreeing and coming to a close after seeking consensus are vital components of spoken discourse. Example 3 shows the interlanguage used by a participant to indicate a close. The use of the particle *ah* in Example 3 is a Malaysian linguistic habit (see Kow, 1995). The particle used in conjunction with a falling intonation pattern functioned as a tag question as the speaker was seeking agreement to the point made. Another Malaysian variety of closing that was used was the particle *lah,* as seen in Example 4. The use of *lah* is functional. The particle acted not only as a form of closing but also, through a soft tonal ending, as an appeal to the listener (see Kow, 2000). Although these forms may be viewed as ungrammatical, they are nevertheless a creative way of communicating meaning and can be used as a launching pad to teaching English forms.

3. Bringing It to a Close: Use of Abbreviated and Condensed Speech

S1:   So are you all agree?
S2:   Agree
S1:   So?
S2:   So agreed
S1:   Clear, ah?

4. Bringing It to a Close: Using the *Lah* Particle

S1:   So are you agree with my answer or what?
S2:   OK, lah

Some groups were more sophisticated and even used preclosing utterances, as seen in Example 5.

5. Bringing It to a Close: Preclose Frame

S1:   Have you any questions or if not I will go to question 4?
S2:   So the answer is B *(forcing the issue to an agreement)*

Use of Turn Taking

The learners used a number of turn-taking strategies, both verbal and nonverbal, to select the next speaker: for example, nomination in conjunction with prosody, as in the use of the next speaker's name with a rising intonation suggesting a question (see Example 6, S1). They also used condensed structures such as "What about you?" (see Example 6, S2) to pass the turn, and body language such as eye contact with an intended respondent and hand gestures (i.e., whole palm upwards beckoning to the next speaker).

6. Nomination

S1: Mary? *(rising intonation)*
S2: What about you?

The success of the reading comprehension task in this study can be attributed to the persistence of speakers in getting the students they nominated to take the turns offered. Such persistence is shown in Example 7, in which S1 persisted three times before S4 responded. In his attempt to get S4 to respond, S1 transformed his question from a general "What is your opinion?" to a more specific "Do you agree with my answer or not?"

Is this persistence particular to a classroom situation? The student speaker must have been sure that it was only a matter of time before someone replied and that nonresponse was not meant to conceal knowledge. The listeners may have been inhibited or lacked confidence in front of other students in the group. Such persistence in pushing the nominated person to respond to a question is less common in social interaction in Malaysia. The speakers in the classroom setting must have concluded that interactants needed time to reply or may have assumed that they had not understood the question. The persistence on the part of S1 in Example 7 resulted in three reformulations of the same message, showing creativity on his part as the initiating speaker.

For instance, the general open-ended question in the first turn was transformed to a more specific *yes/no* question in the final attempt. Such instances could be used perhaps to show low-proficiency language learners that if they are not understood, they should try again, and then again if need be. It is clear from this study that in a classroom task requiring authentic, goal-directed interactions, speakers are stimulated to persist by repeating or reframing the statement until the listeners comprehend and respond.

7. Persistence Resulting in Reformulations

1   S1: My answer is X. What about you all? *(Looking at nobody specifically)*
2   S1: *(Realizing there were no takers, repeats question)* What is your opinion?
(Silence, yet S1 persists)
3   S1: Do you all agree with my answer or not?
(Finally, S4 responds)
4   S4: I agree with your answer.

It should be remembered that the group members who had been selected in this study to initiate the discussion on the first question generally felt responsible for the entire interaction. These students tended to be the more proficient L2 speakers and tended to take longer turns. In fact, in all four groups, there was a tendency for one or two participants to take longer turns.

Even among the less proficient learners, the discourse was coherent and cohesive. These learners used a range of communication strategies to overcome linguistic deficiency and complete the task set, among them minimal response either to confirm or agree with a response, or express interest. A brief *OK, yes, same answer,* and *same reason* indicated that they had nothing further to add. In Example 8, the rather long turn by S1, the more proficient speaker of English, is followed by a minimal response from S2, who brings the topic to a close. This tendency among the low-proficiency speakers in this study is corroborated in David (1992).

8. Variation in Length of Turns

S1: I think the answer is apparent from paragraph 4. You can see from the first line or last line. They say.... So it is very clear there is a decrease in the production of cockles. So do you all agree?
S2: Yes, agree.

Use of Adjacency Pairs

Adjacency pairs are utterances produced by two successive speakers in which the second utterance is a response to the first. The most common form of adjacency pair found in the data was question-answer (see Example 9).

At times, the more proficient speakers, appearing to realize the limited language proficiency of their peers, asked closed questions requiring only *yes/no* answers (e.g., "So do you all agree?"), thus showing their ability to adapt to different proficiencies among their interactants. However, not all questions warranted short replies, as speakers did, at times, ask open questions (see Example 10). Learners who were not proficient in English, faced with open questions requiring fairly lengthy explanations, still tended to use minimal responses such as those of the second speakers in Examples 8 and 11. In such cases, these speakers could see that even when they were not very proficient in English, they could still convey meaning by employing a communication strategy. Language teachers can highlight such communication strategies with learners who are shy and inhibited.

9. Question-Answer Adjacency Pair

S1: What is your answer?
S2: My answer is C.
S1: Do you all agree with the answer?
S2: Yes, we agree.

10. Open-Ended Questions

S3: So what are your reasons giving C?

11. Minimal Responses of the Less Proficient Speaker

S4: Same as Vincent.

The data indicated also that less proficient learners used short replies as evasive strategies to bring the discourse to a rapid close (see Example 12).

12. Evasive Strategies to Bring Discourse to a Close

S5: How about you, Chu Chu?"
S6: My answer also same with Sock Kiang and the reason also same.

A minimal or short response often used in the recorded discourse was *OK*. By using different intonation/stress patterns, students were able to change its function from questioning to responding or clarifying. For instance, in Example 13, the first *OK* had a rising intonation and performed the function of a question, whereas the responding *OK* had a different intonation and was a statement. The questioning *OK* normally brought a fairly long turn to a close and the acknowledging *OK* would function as feedback (Example 13).

13. Single-Word Items With Varying Intonation Patterns Performing Different Functions

S1:   OK?
S2:   OK.
S1:   Clear?
S2:   Clear.
S1:   Agree?
S2:   Agree.

In these ways, even those speakers who were not linguistically competent in the English were able to negotiate meaning; learners resorted to prosody, communication strategies such as minimal responses, Malaysian English, and nonverbal language to get the message across. These strategies were more in evidence possibly because the speaking took place in an anxiety-free environment.

Use of Repair Structures

Eriksen points out that "lessons are speech events characterized by the presence of frequent cognitive and interactional troubles and repair work" (cited in van Lier, 1988, p. 212). The data from this study show that repair was a strategy the students employed. Hence, the repair strategy is not just used in teacher-fronted discourse but can also appear in students' group interaction.

Repairs can be speaker initiated or set in motion by a listener. In this study, student speakers, when they were not initially understood—evident from the incorrect or inappropriate response of the next speaker, or at times, from nonresponse—persisted in repeating or reframing what they had said until the message was communicated.

Examples 14 and 15 show speakers' persistence in self-repair. In Example 14, S1 reframed his question three times, and it was only at his third attempt, when he used the communication strategy of circumlocution, that his question was understood and he was given the answer he sought. S1 thus resolved the misunderstanding by clarifying and elaborating his original request. In Example 15, a failure by the listener to comprehend the reason for a request resulted in S1 repeating his request and adding a reason for it. At other times, speakers self-corrected by replacing an inappropriate word with a correct one (see Example 16). To ensure that the meaning was understood in another instance, the speaker asked directly, albeit not in grammatically correct language, "Are you understanding what I mean?"

14. Self-Repair: Persistence

S1:   Where do you find the answer? (*He wanted to know why a specific answer was chosen*)
S2:   (*Reads relevant sentence in text*)
S1:   How do you know?
S2:   (*Starts giving reasons why the other options were not suitable, i.e., establishes how through a process of elimination, he had determined the key*)

S1: No, I just want to know how you all chose this answer. For me after I know A, C and D is not the answer, I know B is the answer. I just want to find out. One way elimination. Another way?

15. Self-Repair: Elaboration, When a Request Is Misunderstood

Restatement
S1: Will you read (*Meaning "Where is the answer; read the relevant paragraph/ sentence"*)?

Miscomprehension
S2: No (*Looking only at the surface form of the question and obviously not realizing the reason for the request*).
S1: Where is the answer? Will you read the statement (*Reframes request and elaborates*)?

Termination
S2: (*Reads*)

16. Self-Repair: Changing Lexical Item

S1: So Malaysia can *hike increase* the production of cockles.

Listeners who seek repair can either initiate it themselves or stimulate the speaker to do it. In Example 17, S2's "Yes" was not a really informative response; S1 did not hesitate to seek verification, which S2 provided. However, in Example 18, the listener interrupted to help a speaker who had a problem—manifested in two fillers ("uh"), followed by hesitation. He then, in quick succession (as S2), initiated several increasingly focused questions so as to facilitate the specific response he required from S1. In Example 19, repair was again carried out by the listener (S2), who corrected the speaker (S1); the latter apologized and then made the necessary repair.

17. Getting the Speaker to Initiate the Repair by Questioning

S1: My answer is D. How about you all?
S2: Yes
S1: Same?
S2: Same

18. Getting the Speaker to Repair by Asking Him Specific Questions

S1: Because of cleaner uh uh
S2: Why? Why you think so? What paragraph?
S1: Paragraph 2

19. Getting the Speaker to Respond to the Repair Made by the Listener

S1: Throughout the world
S2: Throughout the country
S1: Sorry. Throughout the country

A listener can also get a speaker to repair talk by appealing through, for example, a direct question, "What do you mean?", or through a question primed by a reason, "I am not very clear about your explanation. Can you explain?" Listeners in this study openly expressed the problems they faced in understanding other classroom speakers. Example 20 demonstrates one such open appeal. The learners, though grammatically not proficient, were communicatively competent appealers. They often echoed with rising intonation what they had not understood. This strategy encouraged a speaker to replace the repeated word or phrase with an easier item or explanation. Example 21 contains an instance of this. More strategically competent interactants were even able to anticipate the conceptual problems a speaker might have and complete an utterance for the speaker, as shown in Example 22, in which S1 helped S2 by anticipating the latter's reservations.

20. Informing the Speaker Directly That He Is Not Being Understood

S1:   It is not very economist
S2:   I'm not very clear about your answer
S3:   Let's leave the option first (*S1 didn't respond, so S3 intervened and resolved a potential conflict*)

21. Signalling to the Speaker That He Is Not Being Understood

S1:   My answer is D
S2:   D?
S1:   Yes, because…

22. Helping the Speaker by Repairing the Damage

S1:   (*Long explanation*) What do you think?
S2:   But the (*Hesitates, incomplete utterance*)
S1:   More than you suspect, more than half. Not exactly (*Anticipating the problem*). More than half means more than, not exactly (*A logic that was not apparent to S2*)

Incomprehension and repair sequences (statement-miscomprehension-clarification-termination) were, therefore, present in the data, with both self- and other-initiated repairs being quite frequent. The learners in this study had no inhibitions stating that they had not understood a speaker, something they indicated by asking questions when they had not understood an utterance, or even interrupting and helping the speaker repair the damage. Perhaps the small-group interaction and the goal of coming to a consensus encouraged such plain speaking and cooperation because the focus was not on the spoken discourse itself but on reading comprehension. Such directness does not always appear in interactions among non-English-speaking groups (Omar, 1995), but perhaps it could be more widely encouraged to alert students to the relationship between culture and communication (see Jariah Mohd & David, 1996). Certainly, in this study, adult learners, although not grammatically proficient, were communicatively competent and had acquired some of the skills of conversational cooperation and repair, such as requesting clarification, prompting, and helping out.

◈ PRACTICAL IDEAS

Structure Group Tasks to Encourage Conversational Skills

We have shown that a reading comprehension task can be used as a stimulus to talk among students. In this study, the reading comprehension text "Cockles" (see the Appendix) encouraged group discussion through the use of multiple-choice questions. With multilevel classes, this format caters to less proficient students by providing a structure for group discussion. Students have to assess the four choices for each question and come to an agreement on the best solution. Such interaction is meaningful and allows for learner negotiation toward a goal.

To further stimulate talk in such tasks, you can select a first speaker or coordinator whose role is to ensure that all members in the group participate and who can step into the breach should communication flag. Data in this study show that students who were focused on a reading comprehension task were able to practice English in a nonthreatening environment.

Make Students Aware of the Communication Strategies They Can Use

The students in this study used the following strategies to communicate meaning:

- intonation
- avoidance
- appeals
- minimal responses

It was then the teacher's role to point out to them that they had used these strategies. Although the students' attempts may be viewed as interlanguage, they were communicatively effective and good starting points toward higher levels of interlanguage and, ultimately, toward achieving proficiency in English.

You can utilize video- or audiotaped excerpts with less proficient students to show them how they can use strategies such as avoidance, appeal, and circumlocution to communicate despite limited vocabulary. As beginners, they can gain confidence through using the avoidance strategy (see Example 12). Later they can be encouraged to use the appeal strategy to seek peer assistance (see Example 19). Next they can graduate to the use of minimal responses (see Example 11) and the persistence strategy (see Example 14).

You can also discuss when and why to use different question forms with learners, making use of a database created from students' own language use. For instance, showing them their own creative use of question forms can give students a psychological boost (see Examples 8 and 9).

You can also use student data to increase learners' awareness of the cultural implications of language use. In our study, students were alerted to the use of the particles *lah* and *ah* (see Examples 3 and 4) as acceptable forms of closing in certain contexts but not in those where standard English was expected. You can combine this kind of teaching with raising students' awareness of how intonation can be used to convey meaning in different contexts. In our context, with some interlocutors, the teacher could point out that instead of using *Clear ah?*, students would be expected to use "That's clear, isn't it?" Thus, students can learn about language accommodation to interlocutors in specific contexts (see Giles, 1979).

Make Students Aware of the Different National Englishes

English being a lingua franca, it may be said that each country creates its own version, hence the presence of varieties such as Singlish, Manglish, and Spanglish. It is important that teachers be aware of these varieties and their functions. For example, Malaysian English is used to foster solidarity among Malaysians; it identifies Malaysians and their culture. In your own teaching context, you can point out to learners that although varieties of English exist and fulfill certain functions, for the sake of international intelligibility a certain amount of accuracy is required.

Use Videotapes as a Means of Feedback

Videotape can be used as in this study as an important means of student feedback. The students in this study were tertiary students, and at this level of study, you need to be sensitive about overtly correcting language errors (see David, 1994). Hence, the teacher in this study (Maya) took the role of a facilitator who introduced the study concept and range of communication strategies that could be used. After task completion, the students were asked to view their performance on tape and to identify the communication strategies they had used. This kind of activity provides feedback to the students on their range of strategies (for an earlier description of this technique, see David, 1992).

Another teaching strategy we have used is to videotape this reading comprehension exercise with a more proficient group of students and then show the recording to a less proficient group, whom we ask to comment on the pronunciation of certain lexical items. This can be a means of providing corrective feedback without being overtly corrective and could be an effective way to begin with sensitive or anxious students.

❖ CONCLUSION

A reading text and reading comprehension task together can form a powerful tool for encouraging talk. Students who are not linguistically competent in a target language are able to negotiate meanings, repair damage, and manage oral interaction. In this study, turn-taking and repair techniques were sophisticated, notwithstanding the relative structural poverty: Students had well-developed discourse systems and were communicatively competent at advanced levels. As adult learners, they were able to transfer discourse skills from their known languages to English. Hence, the reading comprehension task may be seen as a pedagogical tool that builds confidence by drawing upon students' communicative competence. The task in this study was a stress-free occasion in which students collaborated to find the solutions to a set of given questions. Although the students were focused on the reading comprehension task, unconsciously they were practicing and using English.

❖ CONTRIBUTORS

Maya Khemlani David is an associate professor in the Faculty of Languages and Linguistics, University of Malaya. She was the chief editor of *The English Teacher* (1994–1998) and is currently on the editorial committee of *Reading Online*. She has published articles in a number of journals, including *The Hong Kong Linguist*, *Language and Literacy*, *English Australia*, *South Pacific Journal of Psychology*, and *IJSL*. Her latest publication is *The Sindhis of Malaysia: A Sociolinguistic Account*.

Kow Yip C. Cheng is a lecturer in the Faculty of Languages and Linguistics, University of Malaya. Her first degree is in English literature, and she holds a master's degree in linguistics. Her PhD is in the area of child language. Her other areas of research include applied linguistics, Malaysian English, intercultural communication, and language testing.

◈ APPENDIX: READING TEXT FOR "COCKLES"

NAME _____

GROUP NUMBER _____

EZ204: BAHASA ENGGERIS II

TEXT 3
(1¼ hours)

ANSWER ALL THE QUESTIONS.

Section 1
The text below is followed by 5 questions each with 4 alternatives, A,B,C and D. First read through the passage. Then for each question, select the most appropriate alternative by circling the answer in ink.

1. The Malaysian cockle industry—the world's largest in terms of production—may soon gain acceptance in a big way into the foreign markets if the National Fisheries Development Board's (LKIM) plan to introduce a purification system materialises.

2. The board has engaged a foreign consultant to study the possibility of devising new technology to depurate cockles. The Kuala Lumpur-based Asean Food Handling Bureau, which is funded by the Australian Government, has also made a study aimed at coming up with a system to purify cockles and other shellfish. "The cockle industry has the potential of becoming a big revenue spinner for the country if the shellfish can be made cleaner," one source in the industry said in Kuala Lumpur. At present, some countries particularly Singapore, are reluctant to import Malaysian cockles because they are full of impurities. He said Malaysian cockles were found to contain a high percentage of bacteria because of pollution, caused mainly by sewage waste.

3. Industry sources said Singapore was keen to import cockles from Malaysia if they could be purified prior to export. They added that in Malaysia the problem of impurities did not arise because cockles were usually eaten only after they were boiled. However. in other countries people preferred to eat them raw or blanched as they feel boiling affects the taste and texture. The sources are confident that the introduction of a purification system will boost exports to countries like the United States, Hong Kong, Taiwan, Japan, Thailand and Singapore. A kg. of cockles, which costs about 50 cent locally, can fetch as much as $8 in some of these countries.

4. Malaysia produced 69,000 tonnes, or $66.2 million worth of cockles in 1981. The following year, production totalled 42,000 tonnes, about 30,000 tonnes of

which were exported to Thailand and 8,000 tonnes to Singapore. The production is mainly in Peninsular Malaysia, that is, about 2,085 hectares, with more then half of this in Perak. Other major cockles-producing states are Penang and Selangor. The cockle industry accounts for 11 percent of total fishery production in Malaysia. However, the cockle industry has in recent times been hit by a shortage due to premature harvesting. This caused production to drop from 111,000 tonnes in 1980 to 69,000 tonnes the following year and 42,000 tonnes in 1982.

1. The cockles in Malaysia could be highly export-oriented if attempts were made to:
   a. increase their production throughout the country.
   b. employ a consultant to look into the cockle industry.
   c. have them cleaner for export to foreign countries.
   d. control pollution caused by sewage waste.

2. Why are some people so particular about the impurities in the cockles? This is because those people
   a. would prefer to eat the cockles raw.
   b. are really fussy about their food.
   c. would want to make sure that the cockles are free from contamination.
   d. are strictly on a sea-food diet.

3. Why has the writer of the text reported that "the introduction of a purification system will boost exports" to some countries? This is because
   a. there will be a world-wide demand for cockles.
   b. the price of cockles in some countries is as high as 16 times its price in Malaysia.
   c. some countries have agreed to import large quantities of cockles from Malaysia.
   d. the cockles in Malaysia are contaminated with unhealthy matter.

4. From 1981 to 1982, there was
   a. an increase in the production of cockles.
   b. a demand for cockles by Thailand and Singapore.
   c. an over-supply of cockles.
   d. a decrease in the production of cockles.

5. From the text, the writer was trying to highlight the
   a. danger of impurities in cockles in Malaysia.
   b. potential of the cockle industry in Malaysia.
   c. effects of pollution on the cockle industry.
   d. demand for cockles throughout the world.

David, M. K., Tan, S. Y., Lim, S. L., Cheah, S. W. (1990). Reprinted with permission.

CHAPTER 6

Collaboration, Accommodation, and Co-Construction: Toward a Model for TESOL Research and Pedagogy

Charles Clennell and Sue Nichols

◈ INTRODUCTION

This chapter is about a learning process. It is a discussion and, at the same time, a demonstration of collaboration. We are inviting you to enter our collaborative process as we research the cooperative strategies employed by our students as they negotiate a task. Through our analysis of their interaction, we show them accommodating one another's input and co-constructing meaning. At the same time, by writing in our individual voices and also as a collaborative *we,* we hope to acquaint you with our differences and show how we have accommodated each other in both the writing of this chapter and the development of a specific classroom research program.

We discuss three learning processes in TESOL education and research practice called *collaboration, accommodation,* and *co-construction.* We recognize that they may not always be sequential, though we deal with them in that order. We describe our own teacher education context and outline a research project that demonstrates these practices in its planning, implementation, and evaluation. In the analysis of the data, we highlight cooperative features in the interlanguage talk of our learners and conclude by suggesting practical ways this process model could work within a TESOL research and practice setting.

Collaboration is now generally accepted as a prerequisite for successful learning and teaching outcomes in Western educational settings (e.g., see Stierer & Maybin, 1994, for a discussion of Vygotsky's influence on educational thinking). The term *accommodation,* however, is less well known. We are using it here in two ways: first, in its sociolinguistic sense (Giles & St. Clair, 1979), to explain how people change their style of speaking—for example, adjusting their accent to fit more closely with that of their interlocutor—"in order to show that they are aligned socially" (Hatch, 1992, p. 56), or, as is the case with nonnative speakers[1] (NNSs) in our study, aligning their pronunciation to that of their partner in order to be more easily understood (see Jenkins, this volume). But we also think that, at a deeper level, this process of adaptation may reflect a willingness by NNSs, when talking together in a second language (L2), to accommodate (or reject) different belief systems and cultural

---

[1] See Jenkins (2000) for detailed discussion on use of the term *nonnative speaker.*

perspectives. Considering the range of cultural and linguistic resources our learners have to deal with when communicating in English, this adaptation process is clearly as important as it may be uncomfortable; these sites of cross-cultural interchange can often be "places of struggle and contestation" (Pennycook, 1996, p. 218).

We have chosen the term *co-construction* because it highlights the sharing and cooperative aspect of what intercultural studies call "joint text construction" (Neil, 1996, p. 19) or "joint-construals" (Clark, 1996, p. 212). We could have used the term *cobuilding* because we want to emphasize the hard work involved in negotiating and reconstructing these shared meanings at a textual level (see Burton & Daroon, this volume). Moreover, as with accommodation, this cobuilding work may operate both at the sociocultural level as the creative interplay between different "Discourses" (Gee, 1990, p. 143) in a Bakhtinian dialogic sense, but also at the linguistic level as the realizations of this interaction through cocreated text.

◈ CONTEXT

We began coresearching the cooperative process described in this chapter in 2001, with a research project that continues as of this writing. Our writing format is designed to foreground the issues of collaboration, accommodation, and co-construction. We have produced two kinds of accounts:

1. a consensus account written in first-person plural and representing the outcome of our co-construction

2. individual accounts written by each of us in the first-person singular

These enable us to show the value of maintaining our separate, different voices while demonstrating how we have accommodated each other's different interests and perspectives. Thus, in the following sections, we separately and together describe the research process:

- how we chose a topic

- how we arrived at agreement on a particular research methodology

- how we established a workable analytical framework

We go on to describe a sample analysis of the same data from two different perspectives and conclude with practical ideas for how this cooperative model might work in similar TESOL settings.

Before we start, some background on our TESOL context: We both work as teacher educators within the Division of Education, Arts and Social Sciences, at the University of South Australia in Adelaide; part of our shared work in 2001 was to deliver a master's program in TESOL. Our internal students come mainly from non-anglophone, specifically southeast Asian/Pacific Rim, countries, though, in 2001, the class also had single representatives from Kenya, Norway, and Russia.

Choosing the Research Topic

Selecting a topic was the first challenge in collaboration. As our individual accounts show, we came from different knowledge bases and professional backgrounds. However, we shared some common ground. Both of us had worked with international postgraduate students from diverse cultural and linguistic backgrounds. We both valued students' cultural knowledge and saw this as an invaluable learning resource. So we both wanted a research project that would treat difference as productive. Additionally, we were both interested in spoken discourse although we had different approaches to its theorization and analysis. One of our first decisions was that the project should focus on this aspect of communication. In a real sense, the construction of a research topic was ongoing as we spoke about how to define the field in which we worked. The agreed title of the project was "Investigating Intelligibility Issues in the Interlanguage Talk of Nonnative ESOL Teachers Carrying Out Academic Pair Work Tasks." Each of us will now tell our own story about arriving at that topic.

Charles's Perspective

As a pronunciation teacher, I prefer to adopt a "variationist approach" when it comes to providing models of "good" English (see Pennington, 1996, p. 17), and so believe that teachers should give learners a range of L2 models and not become distracted by debates about standardized accents or correct forms. Hence, my main interest in this topic could be summed up as a practical question: What phonological model (or multiple models) of English should we be offering our teacher learners to take back with them to their home countries, given that their use of English in 80% of cases will be with other NNSs?

However, it became clear that Sue and I would be approaching the topic of intelligibility between NNSs of English from somewhat different perspectives, both in terms of our research approach and the focus of our interest. In one sense, I was aware that Sue's approach could be seen to have a positive construction (What is it possible for my NNSs to achieve, and how can I help them toward this goal?), whereas mine tended toward deficit (What problems do typical NNSs encounter, and how can I help them overcome them?). In the past, I think I had felt safe keeping myself occupied with so-called linguistic-only matters, but at this point, I was able to risk looking further afield and consider that "questions of difference, identity, and culture are not merely issues to discuss, but pertain to how people have come to be as they are, how discourses have structured people's lives" (Pennycook, 1999, p. 340).

Constructing the Research Question

Sue's Perspective

When we embarked on this project, I did not know too much about Charles's area of expertise. But I did believe we could have a constructive research relationship. This was largely because whenever Charles and I started talking, I never knew just where these conversations would take us. Gender relations, the nature of knowledge, popular culture, literary theory, aesthetics, religion—our conversations, however brief, were always argumentative, unpredictable, and broadening. It was this experience of exploration that I believe set the climate for our research collaboration.

It was Charles who came up with *point of potential breakdown* as a research focus. This term immediately became a point of difference between us. It indicated our different research histories and conceptual maps. I had spent a lot time working with so-called at-risk students and had become sensitive to the role of language in defining these students and setting limitations on their achievement. *Breakdown* seemed in the same family as *failure* and *underachievement*. Nevertheless, any conversation that could be analyzed for points of potential breakdown could also be analyzed from a different viewpoint. Charles encouraged me to formulate an alternative perspective that could complement the points of potential breakdown emphasis.

I am interested in how conversation partners co-construct knowledge in an exchange; how they negotiate using the resources of topic knowledge, group membership, and discursive repertoires. In previous research, I had discussed how educational settings make particular kinds of literate and communicative competence salient, advantaging some learners and disadvantaging others (Nichols, 1998; Nichols & Najar, 2000). My interest in sociocultural knowledge leads me to see all communication participants as experienced discourse practitioners and all conversations as involving the negotiation of difference. This kind of negotiation was evident between Charles and myself as we jointly constructed the research question. It was not immediately evident how point of potential breakdown and co-construction could gel into a single research focus, but we decided to go ahead with the project and keep talking.

❖ DESCRIPTION

We chose our own NNS English teacher learners as our research focus for three reasons:

1. We wanted to have contributors who had a high level of proficiency in English, who were studying in an academic setting, and who shared a vested interest in the outcome of the study.

2. We wanted to emphasize the potential pedagogic significance of global English both at a linguistic level (What degree of formal accuracy do NNSs need to be understood?) and a sociocultural level (What does it mean to be a speaker of an international language?).

3. We wanted contributors to participate in two ways: as co-observers in the recordings of a specific task and as participants in the task itself.

Out of the 20 volunteers, 6 were selected to act as observer/recorders, and the remaining 12 were split into pairs (of different first language [L1] background) to carry out the task in the study.

Designing the Study

Sue's Perspective

In our discussions about the study, it became evident that Charles and I had different experiences of research as well as different agendas. An example was our decision about the task on which we would ask the NNS pairs to collaborate. I was keen that this task be open-ended for the reason that this would prompt the pairs to negotiate their way through it. Charles, it seemed to me, felt that closed-type activities would create the kind of performance pressure that might reveal more about communication difficulties. I argued strongly that the task should facilitate co-construction of meaning: That is, participants should be encouraged to discuss openly the knowledge that was relevant to the completion of the task.

A concept map seemed to me ideal for the purpose. A concept map is a visual representation of a domain of knowledge on a specific topic. For two people to collaborate on producing a concept map, they need to negotiate which topic words will be included and how they will be placed. This activity inherently involves decisions about knowledge because each topic word represents part of a field of knowledge. It is unlikely indeed that any two collaborators would understand and articulate any topic exactly the same way. How much less likely when the collaborators are from different cultural and language backgrounds?

Another advantage of such a task was that the exchange would produce two textual records: the recorded conversation that took place during the completion of the task and the concept map itself. I was excited about the prospect of working with these two elements: the visual-symbolic and the oral transcript. It built on some work I had been doing on an expanded definition of literacy incorporating nonlinguistic modes of representation (Nichols, 2001).

Charles's Perspective

Looking back on this time, I can see that I was undergoing a considerable shift of attitude as far as the research design was concerned. For example, I was obliged to negotiate the actual tasks I would like our NNS subjects to perform. From Sue's perspective, the task needed to be as natural as possible. I agreed with this in principle, but from my perspective, the task also had to allow for points of potential language difficulty or points of potential breakdown in the exchange of specific information so that I would be able to observe the participants' different communication strategies (Clennell, 1995). I do believe, however, that context (which includes the underlying interpersonal relations) has an important influence on how NNSs choose to realize their meanings in a given text and therefore wanted us to find an activity that would allow the subjects to speak freely on a topic in a realistic academic setting as well as allow me to research how participants addressed points of potential breakdown linguistically.

We therefore selected an academic task that the participants practice regularly in their master's program and that also reflected the content of the participants' courses and would allow them to speak freely about concepts with which they are familiar. At the same time, it allowed us to observe as many as possible of "the events going on around when people speak and write" (Halliday, 1991, p. 5).

The Data Collection Process

The data were obtained from six pairs of participants performing a specific academic task, namely the completion of a concept map around the topic of TESOL. Prior to carrying out the task, the six dyads and the six trained observers were invited to listen to a set of instructions as to how this concept map task might be successfully completed. While carrying out this task, each pair was audiotaped and was observed by a volunteer NNS observer who had previously been instructed by the researchers on how to complete an observation sheet. This checksheet listed various verbal and nonverbal indicators of communication difficulty. On each occasion that the observers noticed such an occurrence, they were asked to note the counter number and assign a symbol as code for the event.

Transcription and Follow-Up Introspective Interviews

During the transcription stage, we noted occasional difficulties in identifying the actual wordings or understanding the particular speaker's pragmatic (intended) meaning. To correct these discrepancies, we invited the participants to return for a posttask interview, and each pair had the opportunity to listen to their recording and talk about the task as they followed the transcript. Additional notes were taken during these introspective interviews. A full transcript of the recordings of the six dyads was made and detailed analyses of the transcripts carried out from two perspectives: One of us (Charles) carried out a conversational analysis from a sociolinguistic perspective, which investigated points of potential breakdown indicated by such phonological or syntactic cues as hesitations and pauses, lexical repetitions, unfinished utterances, and other paralinguistic features identified in the observation schedule. The second analysis, performed by the other of us (Sue), looked at the development of the task itself as a realization of the participants' underlying knowledges and experience, and plotted the progress of co-construction reflected in the final map itself through the linking of its component topics. At the same time, the individual contributions toward the completion of the task were noted and quantified.

In the next section, we provide a sample analysis of the same point of interaction from these two distinct perspectives. The sample is taken from the interaction recorded between Miho (an experienced EFL teacher from Japan) and Hanna (a graduate of English language and literature from Norway, without EFL experience). The two are in the initial stages of making a concept map of TESOL, and we meet them at a point where they are discussing basic terminology. Though both are fluent speakers of English, Miho's knowledge of the topic is clearly greater than that of her partner.

◈ DISTINGUISHING FEATURES

Analyzing Collaborative Talk From Two Perspectives

Charles' Analysis: Points of Potential Breakdown in the Talk Between Miho and Hanna

In the following example, there are two examples of points of potential breakdown, which I had identified in the observation notes and confirmed during the posttask interview.

1.*

1 H: shall we just put this TESOL in the – in the middle/
2 M: yea +
3 H: in the circle/
4 M: yep +
5 H: ++ then we're supposed to take everything+ that's+that's connected to TESOL
6 M: yea
7 H: is that the point/

---

*Note: See Appendix for key to transcript.

 8 M: I think so + ah +
 9 H: is that correct+ though/
10 M: yea + but before that we've got + two ++ oh this is MY idea of it + (H laughs) + is this alright/
11 H: yea
12 M: that's er +++ er++
13 H: do you want to put it at too small a level/ + do you mean that that should be a level under + or is it just something you had + you want to take around
14 M: no this is + erm + TESOL has + erm + has two branches +
15 H: /uh
16 M: one is + erm + English + for speakers + of other languages +
17 H: uh + + yes
18 M: Do you think so
19 H: yea
20 M: and one's + E F L + that's + that's + erm + English. English as a foreign language
21 H: OK +
22 M: that's all [I'm about to?] + but yet+ erm + this is + English + to speakers of other languages + meaning + teaching + English to speakers + in an English speaking + environment
23 H: mm
24 M: like teaching + like Chinese people\
25 H: mm
26 M: English + in Australia + (uh uh) + English + + as a foreign language + meaning + like + + erm + what I'm doing in Japan\
27 H: OK + when you're teaching English in that country
28 M: as a foreign + yea/
29 H: OK + where they don't speak English + + yea
30 M: and TESOL is + is er + + kind of er + + mm + +
31 H: the main + main word for everything
32 M: yea + yea + it + erm + er + bridges + it + kinds of + er + bridge word (mm) + for these two + yea + + and + so + what's next/
33 H: maybe we should put everything that's + kind of + connected to + TESOL + erm +
34   and [[connecting]] what's similar + like the curriculum and (yea yea) + so on +
35 M: so how do we put that +
36 H: if you just put + it down here + and then we can try to make the connect + connection + (yea) after
37 M: yep + + + + is that alright/

Miho, in Turn 10, proposed that, according to her ("oh, this is MY idea": a metacomment), TESOL has two... and at this point she paused to search for a suitable word. This hesitation, combined with verbal fillers (Turn 12), clearly indicates a point of potential breakdown. While she was doing this, her partner, Hanna, in Turn 13, wanted to know if this division would mean shifting to a subcategory (different level) in the diagram they were drawing. But Miho did not understand what Hanna was referring to by "different levels" and her contradiction "no" in Turn 14 was intended to express her confusion and at the same time allow her to return to her original problem—the two subdivisions of TESOL.

At this point (Turns 14–17), it seems to me that they were really talking at cross-purposes, even though superficially at least they appeared to be in agreement. This momentary breakdown can be seen as a point where each speaker was grappling with a different communication difficulty. Hanna was generally unclear about the meaning of the acronym *TESOL,* and the subtle difference between *TEFL* and *TESL* was still confusing her. At the same time, Miho (Turns 14–18) was struggling to express what she meant by a *collective* (i.e., *umbrella*) term. She began with the offer of the synonym "branches" (which she admitted later to being a lucky guess) in Turn 14 and then proceeded to amplify each branch with a short explanation for both the acronyms *ESL* and *EFL.* Hanna was writing and drawing as Miho explained this distinction (Turns 19–24).

Another point of potential breakdown is evident in Turn 30, when Miho signaled her uncertainty with a typical circumlocution ("kind of er"), followed by a nonverbal filler and a pause. At this point, although Hanna was still unclear about these semantic complexities, she was quick to help in the clarification process, first by completing Miho's unfinished utterance with the offering "main word" (Turn 31), which Miho partially accepted, before trialing an alternative, "bridges," in Turn 32; this appeared first as a verb and then later in the same turn as a qualifier ("bridge word"). Hanna indicated mutual understanding by her request (Turn 33) to change topic. This short sequence illustrates characteristics of both accommodation and co-construction at work.

It is interesting that in the posttask interview, Hanna admitted to me that she was even then unclear about the distinction between ESL and EFL but, at the time, had copied it down nonetheless. Miho also confirmed that, suspecting her partner still had not understood her, she twice sought confirmation of understanding (Turn 28, the final rise on "yea"; and Turn 37, a further confirmation check with rising tone on "is that all right"). There seems to be a paradox here of a resolution of a specific communication difficulty set within a larger, remaining confusion. Whereas Miho and Hanna had resolved the immediate problem of the term *umbrella,* they had still not agreed on their understanding of the distinction between EFL and ESL.

Sue's Analysis: Co-Construction of Topic in Miho and Hanna's Interaction

I am always a little hesitant about admitting this, but often when I go to analyze data, I am not entirely sure what approach I am going to take. That was certainly the case with this study because I had never before analyzed a conversation that accompanied the activity of producing a concept map. A skim of the transcripts revealed the conversations had revolved around two task-related issues: (a) the selection of terms to appear on the concept map and (b) the placement of these terms in relation to each other. Conversations had also included non-task-related talk, but, at this stage, I decided to focus on the talk explicitly related to the task.

One of my starting assumptions was that effective task collaboration would involve substantial contributions by both partners. Further, I assumed that, for this to occur, both partners would need to actively offer terms for inclusion in the concept map. At the same time, effective co-construction would mean that participants would be willing to accommodate one another's knowledge and to modify their own contributions in the interests of producing a single map of their joint knowledge.

The analytical task I set myself was to map the co-construction of the topic

(TESOL) over the course of the whole conversation. I decided to focus on nominal words and clauses because a skim of the transcripts revealed that these were the dominant form in which participants offered terms for inclusion in the concept map. I mapped each nominal item every time it occurred, noting the speaker and the turn (these were numbered). Each new nominal item was plotted as a new column (see Figure 1). This means the map can be read horizontally as a complete set of nominal items in the order in which they entered the conversation. When nominal items were repeated later in the conversation, they are recorded in the same column as the initial appearance of the item. Therefore the map can be read vertically to indicate the persistence of particular items. Each participant is coded with a symbol so that individual contributions to the conversation can be compared. The balance of turns and items between speakers was strikingly evident in the completed analytical map.

	1.	2.	3.	4.	5.	6.	7.	8.	9.	10.
1.	TESOL H									
5.	TESOL H									
14.	TESOL M									
16.		English for speakers of other languages M								
20.			EFL M	English as a foreign language M						
22.					English to speakers of other languages M	Teaching English to speakers in an English speaking environment M				
24.							Teaching like Chinese people M			
26.				English as a foreign language M				English in Australia M	What I'm doing in japan M	
27–29				as a foreign M						When you're teaching English in that country where they don't speak English H
30.	TESOL M									
33.	TESOL H									

FIGURE 1. Concept Map of Conversation on TESOL Topic

Below I show my analysis of part of the conversation, which was transcribed and reproduced as Example 1. This analysis focused on two issues: the thematic development of the conversation, and the relative balance of the participants' contributions.

Because this conversation revolved around defining categories, an analysis of its thematic development can help us understand how the two participants jointly handled this task. The balance of contributions appears rather unequal and weighted in favor of Miho, who initiated eight terms other than the topic term *TESOL,* none of which Hanna iterates. In contrast, Hanna initiated one term, which Miho did not repeat. Miho, it seems, was taking the role of knowledge provider.

TESOL was the most mentioned item (five appearances, see Figure 1, Column 1). It was the only nominal item that both speakers used, and its semantic importance is indicated by their initial agreement that it should appear in the center of the concept map. The term *TESOL* can be considered the primary theme: Its iteration by both speakers in Turns 1–5 and then again in Turns 30–33 (see Example 1) signals the boundaries of this unit of discourse.

Following the agreement to place *TESOL* in the center of the concept map, the speakers turned to deciding the main branches or subcategories for this concept. Miho nominated two (see Example 1, Turns 14–20); these are shown on the concept map (Figure 1). The second of these items (*English as a foreign language*) became the subject of most of the thematic development in the remainder of the transcript (see Example 1).

After introducing this term (Turn 14), Miho repeated it in Turn 26 and followed up with a fragmented version in Turn 27. In Turn 26, she also attempted two restatements of the theme, as "English in Australia" and "What I'm doing in Japan." These restatements progressively shifted the emphasis toward a more contextualized representation of the concept, first through the inclusion of place ("in Australia") and then through the addition of action and person ("What I'm doing") to place ("in Japan"). The use of first person gave Hanna the option of drawing on her prior knowledge (as a fellow class member) of Miho's teaching practice. These contextualizations appeared to invite Hanna to indicate the extent of her understanding. Hanna had already signaled her agreement through brief affirmations, but this was not sufficient to prompt Miho to move on to another category. Miho appeared to be seeking a more definite indication of understanding.

In Turns 27–29, Hanna finally offered the following: "When you're teaching English in that country where they don't speak English." This could be read as providing her own restatement of the concept *English as a foreign language.* However, though this appears as two turns in the transcript, it was spoken as one unit that overlapped Miho's turn (Turn 28). Hanna's restatement contained three elements: person ("[When] you're"), subject ("teaching English"), context ("in that country where they don't speak English"). A further look at the thematic development of the conversation suggests the semantic steps Hanna followed to reach this restatement.

The subject part of Hanna's statement ("Teaching English") formed part of the central category *TESOL* and so could be considered part of the theme in development. Hanna's choice of person did not reflect Miho's use of first person ("What *I'm* doing in Japan") but instead took the second-person form ("When *you're* teaching English..."). This variation can be interpreted in two conflicting ways: Either Hanna was literally reflecting Miho and reinstating her specific context, or she was using the second person as a generalizing strategy (i.e., *you* implying *or anyone*). Hanna's treatment of context suggests the latter might have been the case. Miho had previously identified three specific contexts for teaching English: "like Chinese people" (Turn 24), and "in Australia" and "what I'm doing in Japan" (Turn 26). Hanna appeared to produce a generalization on the basis of two of these contexts to achieve "in that country where they don't speak English."

The analysis of thematic development shows that Hanna's participation was more active than it would appear if only number of turns and topic initiations had been taken into account: Following this thematic development, Hanna was able to approximate the problematic term. This analysis also shows Miho's participation to have been collaborative rather than dominant. Her many restatements of the term—and, in particular, her progressive contextualization—helped Hanna develop a version of it. Miho's collaborative intent is evident in her refusal to accept Hanna's simple affirmations as indication of comprehension. Miho was clearly seeking more complete, mutual comprehension.

This analysis has caused me to rethink my initial assumption that effective task collaboration would involve relatively equal contributions by both partners—that is, if I were to assess equality through number and length of turns. In this case, the contributions of the partners were by no means statistically equal; however, their persistence in achieving shared knowledge was not unequal for all that.

Combining Charles's and Sue's Perspectives: Co-Construction in Analysis

Any work of analysis is a work of meaning construction. By allowing ourselves as researchers to use different analytical strategies, we created the opportunity for different meanings to be produced. However, for this to be a genuinely collaborative exercise, we had to consider how our analyses could co-construct meaning about Miho's and Hanna's interaction. As we discussed this issue, we became aware of the metaphors we used to express our approaches to research. Through focusing on these metaphors, we were better able to understand how our separate approaches might combine. The metaphors we found useful were the *spotlight* and the *map*.

Charles's analysis was like a spotlight in that it focused on particular moments in the interaction between Miho and Hanna. The intensity of a spotlight allows details to be illuminated that might not be apparent to the naked eye. At the same time, a spotlight can be harsh and unflattering. Charles's focus on points of potential breakdown meant that the conversation was analyzed in terms of communication problems.

Sue's analysis was like a map in that it outlined the terrain covered in the interaction. The territory this map represents was the domain of topic knowledge that was brought into play during the interaction. Whereas the diagrammatic representation shows the pattern of topic construction at a glance, it does not portray the moment-to-moment conduct of the interaction. Together these two perspectives enabled a fuller construction of meanings for this piece of discourse than would have been possible for either alone.

A spotlight-wielding researcher and a mapmaking researcher do not always agree about what they see. For instance, we had many discussions about the use of terms such as *confusion, negotiation,* and *breakdown* to describe aspects of the interaction. One great advantage of our different perspectives was that it allowed each of us access to a friendly critique, a way of addressing the inevitable dark spots or off-the-map areas in our work.

◈ PRACTICAL IDEAS

This cooperative process can be applied to TESOL education programs. Our English language training (ELT) approach focuses on promoting English as an international language (EIL) and emphasizes phonology teaching and learning. We illustrate the three cooperative processes of collaboration, accommodation, and co-construction from two distinct viewpoints: (a) how we reflect cooperative practice in our teaching behavior and (b) how we as teacher educators encourage and support cooperation with and among our teacher learners. We finish this section with a few suggestions on the importance of reflection.

Collaboration
Work Openly and Constructively With Others

To reflect this participatory spirit in TESOL practice, as teachers, we need to

- encourage an atmosphere of open-endedness in our teacher education classrooms by not always insisting on clearly defined learning outcomes or products; this may be particularly important in the context of EIL and the international debate currently in progress

- demonstrate that unfinished business can not only be tolerated but welcomed and that learning is an ongoing and incomplete process; this incompleteness could be effectively verified through action research projects that emphasize the cyclical nature of learning

- encourage our teacher learners to be critically aware of the underlying sociocultural issues at curriculum and individual program content levels; to do this, we need to provide opportunities in our TESOL courses for them to critique curriculum and other educational documents (Phillipson, 1992), and compare and contrast the sociopolitical issues they identify across cultures

- invite NNSs from a range of cultures and professional backgrounds to speak to and with our teacher learners on a range of topics, including discussions on what constitutes good or acceptable varieties of English

- collaborate with colleagues across disciplines to discuss EIL issues and their impact on study programs in different content areas

Accommodation
Value Difference in Our Classrooms

This means we need to foster an atmosphere in our language classrooms such that diversity of opinions, cultural values, and beliefs are fully acknowledged and appreciated. Less well understood, perhaps, is that to encourage this valuing of difference, we first of all must

- recognize our own prejudices and be prepared to articulate them if necessary to ourselves as part of our own developing self-awareness

- maintain an openness to differences and reflect in our teaching the belief that to hold one's own views is not to deny the value of others', and that through this diversity of opinion, a new richness of resources and ideas can be explored

- develop dialogic relationships with our teacher learners so that TESOL classrooms become places where accepted norms and assumptions can be tested and challenged through discussion

- design tasks that seek out different TESOL contexts and compare these differences, striving to reach a consensus on, for example, what might constitute a common phonological core (see Jenkins, 2000): For example, pronunciation teaching could focus on EIL issues and identify specific differences between Norwegian and Mandarin Chinese philologies

- value the use of NNS models of English not only for pronunciation work but also for listening and speaking texts

- make use of NNS/NNS texts in the TESOL program for analysis at lexico-grammatical and phonological levels to demonstrate interlanguage developmental stages

- develop an awareness of strategic competence in NNS interlanguage by illustrating different kinds of communication strategies (see, e.g., Tarone & Yule, 1989). For example, have teacher learners identify and describe their own communication strategies in their L1 and consider how they can be applied to L2 learning

- be openminded about what constitutes good and or acceptable English, both in what we model in our own language usage as well as in what we expect from our teacher learners

Co-Construction

Jointly Negotiate New Meanings With Learners and Colleagues

To exemplify this process, we should

- demonstrate our own willingness to work together first with colleagues but also with our teacher learners to produce a lesson plan, an academic paper, a conference report, and so forth

- report on the process of collaborative academic writing from our own experiences and model this process in our teaching by analyzing the mode of the co-constructed texts from a textual perspective (see Halliday, 1985)

- provide opportunities in our classrooms for teacher learners to jointly produce a discussion paper, for example, on pronunciation teaching issues in two different Asian contexts and later write it up for a ELT conference presentation

- encourage the expression of individual voices within a group report summary written up by different members, to be published in a monthly ELT bulletin

- focus classroom group work on meaningful interactions that encourage negotiation and joint construction: for example, designing a pronunciation syllabus based on EIL common core features (Jenkins, 2000) in order to make the English phonology syllabus more effective in a specific TEFL context

- allow teacher learners to select their own activities and texts when working round specific ELT issues such as pronunciation teaching or curriculum design, and, as teacher educators, be ready to critique, improvise, and expand on what is produced when necessary

Reflection

Value the Process of Reflection as a Means to Learning

The process of reflection is important for us as practicing classroom teachers and as a means for encouraging our teacher learners to evaluate and absorb new experiences. This invitation to reflection, so to speak, recognizes that assimilating and processing input requires time and space (both mental and physical) for learning to take place. Our teaching sessions can better acknowledge this need for space and time so that we as teacher educators and our teacher learners can reflect on learning activities without the extraneous pressures so often exerted by willing (but anxious) teachers to extract a tangible product in more traditional classrooms. This reflection time can be accommodated well in such activities as journal writing or informal chat at coffee breaks.

◈ CONCLUSION

In this chapter, we have discussed a process model that has practical potential in TESOL contexts for research and classroom teaching. We have demonstrated our collaborative principle as coauthors in the creation, implementation, and writing up of a specific classroom research project with our teacher learners. This project has involved them as research assistants in its implementation, and as participants through carrying out an academic pair-work task.

Also in this chapter, we have compared a sample analysis of a specific interaction from one of the transcripts to illustrate how these different perspectives were able to enrich the overall understanding of the speech event as well as providing evidence of collaboration, accommodation, and co-construction in an EIL context. Finally, we extrapolated various practical ideas for reinvigorating our TESOL settings—ideas that express this cooperative process in achievable, realistic forms.

◈ CONTRIBUTORS

Charles Clennell is an adjunct senior lecturer in TESOL at the Underdale Campus of the University of South Australia, in Adelaide. He has contributed to the TESOL master's program over a number of years in the fields of phonology, discourse analysis, and interlanguage studies and has published many papers in TESOL journals on learner language, prosody, and the grammar of spoken discourse in English language teaching.

Sue Nichols is a key researcher at the Centre for Literacy Policy and Learning Cultures, University of South Australia. She conducts research in the areas of higher education, secondary curriculum, and gender and education. She teaches research methodology in several postgraduate programs and finds her teaching practice a productive area for action research.

◈ APPENDIX: KEY TO TRANSCRIPT

Feature	Symbol	Example in transcript
Sense (tone) group division	+	In Turn 20: and one's + EFL
Significant extra pause	++(+)	In Turn 26: English ++ as a foreign
Rising tone on preceding word	/	In Turn 32: what's next/
Falling tone on preceding word	\	In Turn 26: in Japan\
Backchannelling	( )	In Turn 26: (uh uh)
Unclear but likely interpretation	[ ]	In Turn 34: and [connecting]
Emphasis or contrastive stress	CAPitals	In Turn 10: MY idea

PART 2

International Contexts of Learner Interaction

CHAPTER 7

Intelligibility in Lingua Franca Discourse

Jennifer Jenkins

❧ INTRODUCTION

In recent years, interaction among nonnative speakers of English (NNSs) has increased to the extent that it is now the most frequent type of spoken English discourse (cf. Crystal, 1997; Graddol, 1997). Within the TESOL profession, this has led to a small but growing interest in the study of English as an international language (EIL). In essence, EIL refers to the use of English as a lingua franca among its NNSs rather than to interaction among its native speakers (NSs) or to NS/NNS interaction (respectively English as a native language and English as a second/foreign language). The profession is even beginning to witness the emergence of whole volumes dedicated to EIL issues (see, e.g., Gnutzmann, 1999).

Much of the discussion, however, has focused hitherto on political and ideological issues such as those raised by Pennycook (2000), while the practical implications for EIL pedagogy remain largely unexplored. As far as pronunciation is concerned, very little has been written about the means of safeguarding mutual intelligibility in communication in which all participants are, by definition, NNSs speaking English with a range of second language (L2) accents. The result is that teachers have been provided with scant, if any, guidance as to how to translate EIL ideology and theory into classroom practice and, in particular, into concrete pronunciation models and relevant pronunciation activities. TESOL pronunciation pedagogy thus remains firmly rooted in methodologies designed to improve learners' phonological intelligibility and acceptability when they interact with NSs rather than with each other.

This case study indicates possible directions for research into phonology for EIL and ways in which such research can feed directly into pronunciation teaching. The study formed part of a larger research project designed to investigate the (un)intelligibility of pronunciation and learners' use of phonological accommodation strategies in EIL interaction in order to redefine phonological error and, ultimately, to produce guidelines for the teaching of pronunciation for EIL use.

The original project (1995) involved exploratory and pilot studies to establish the existence of an EIL intelligibility problem grounded in pronunciation; several years of field data collection from pair-work and group-work interactions in multilingual EFL (i.e., in reality, EIL) classrooms; two sets of recorded pair-work tasks (of which one was a small-scale longitudinal study); and a controlled experiment into the ability to produce and interpret tonic stress (i.e., the most important word).In this chapter, I report on one section of the research: the longitudinal study of a group of students preparing for the advanced-level, paired speaking examination that forms one examination of the University of Cambridge Local Examination Syndicate (UCLES) Certificate of Advanced English (CAE). Although the study was devised as part of the larger project, there was a more immediate pedagogic aim: to increase the students' prospects of success in the speaking examination. I hoped, first, that placing the students in pairs with a partner who had a different first language (L1) would reduce the number of serious pronunciation errors because of the greater potential threat to their partner's understanding than would obtain for same-L1 pairs; and, second, that if students remained in the same pairs during the preparation period they would, over time, gain an increased understanding of one another's L1-influenced pronunciation as a result of such direct and lengthy exposure to it.

◈ CONTEXT

The study was conducted in a London language school. The six students in the CAE class were recorded at biweekly intervals over a period of 10 weeks between their arrival on the course and the CAE examination, the final recording being made 2 weeks before the examination. On four of these occasions, they were recorded interacting in the different-L1 pairs to which they had been assigned for the examination. On one occasion, at the end of the period, however, four of the students (two Swiss-German and two Japanese) were recorded interacting in same-L1 pairs. The purpose of the latter interaction was to determine whether, as predicted, the same-L1 paired students would increase their L1-influenced pronunciation as a result of accommodating one another. If so, this would also have the advantage of demonstrating to the students themselves—who had commented that they found the English of members of their own L1 easier to understand—that their pronunciation was less accurate in these pairings than in their different-L1 pairs.

Two of the students were Japanese females (J1 and J2); three were Swiss-German males (SG1, SG2, and SG3); and one was a Swiss-French female (SF). All six students were in their 20s, with the youngest (J1) being 21 and the oldest 27 (SG1). Five were graduates of universities in their own countries, whereas one, the youngest, was to return to Japan to complete her degree after taking the CAE examination. The three Swiss-German students were bankers; the Swiss-French student worked in an insurance company; and the older Japanese student in an information company. All six students had taken a placement test before entering the CAE class (2 weeks prior to the first recording), and all were found to have reached levels of proficiency in English ranging from high intermediate to low advanced.

In terms of their pronunciation needs, the students on arrival demonstrated the standard problems of speakers of English from their L1 backgrounds. For example, the Japanese students regularly confused the sounds /r/ and /l/ and tended to elide word-final nasals and nasalize the preceding vowel sound so that, for example, the word *animation* was pronounced [æniˈmeɪʃɔ̃]. The Swiss-German students frequently substituted /w/ with /v/ (and occasionally vice versa) and devoiced word-final consonants such that, for instance, the word *size* was pronounced [saws]. In addition, at a more holistic level, the Japanese students tended to be less vociferous, to pause longer before speaking, and to speak more slowly and carefully than the Swiss-German students.

◈ DESCRIPTION

The six students were all engaged on a 12-week program of 5 hours' study a day, 5 days a week, leading up to the CAE, which has five examinations: In addition to the speaking examination, there are also examinations in reading, writing, listening, and use of English (the latter focusing on grammar, syntax, and level of linguistic formality). The language school's CAE program prepared students for these papers by concentrating on matters relating to grammar for half the day and on the four skills (reading, writing, speaking, listening) for the other half. Preparation for the speaking examination involved a considerable number of classroom pair and whole-group discussions as well as negotiation, information-exchange, and problem-solving tasks; specific pronunciation work; and the five practice interviews that also provided the study data.

Because the recorded practice interviews were the main focus of the study (although they were supplemented by interviews with the students and by questionnaires), a brief account of the format of the interview is useful at this point. The CAE interview always involves two candidates (except where the examination centre is entering an odd number of candidates, in which case by default there will be one group of three). There are also two examiners, one acting as an interlocutor at points where the candidates need instructions, and the other as an assessor who only speaks, if at all, in the final stage of the examination. At the time of the study, candidates were assessed on five criteria, each on a 1- to 8-point scale: fluency, accuracy and range, pronunciation, task achievement, and interactive communication. However, minor adjustments were made by UCLES in 1999 to the assessment criteria and scales.

The interview itself consists of four phases. In the first phase, the candidates are asked to chat with one another in order to find out about one another's homes, countries, families, interests, future plans, and the like. The second phase consists of two information gap activities. In each case, one candidate speaks for approximately a minute while the other listens and performs a task such as drawing what is described, identifying which of several similar pictures has been described, or noting similarities and differences between the picture that has been described and their own picture. The listener is permitted to ask questions to clarify and confirm but is encouraged to wait until the speaker has had a long turn before doing so. Roles are then reversed and the procedure repeated.

The third phase of the speaking paper is a problem-solving task in which, with the help of picture prompts, the two candidates collaborate and negotiate to reach agreement (or agree to disagree). They might be asked, for example, to decide which of a pictured group of inventions has had the greatest impact on people's lives, which topics should and should not be taught to teenage schoolchildren, or which of a number of items best symbolizes the 1990s. The final phase, which—because it involves at least one of the examiners—was of no interest in this study of NNS/NNS interaction, entails developing the theme of the third phase into a broader-based discussion. The whole examination is expected to last about 15 minutes although the majority of examiners overrun by at least 5 minutes. The practice examinations for this study each lasted considerably longer (typically 30–40 minutes, although during the 2-week period after the final recording, the students were given timed practice conforming to the stipulated time limits of the examination proper).

The practice interviews were all recorded and replayed immediately to the students. This gave all of us an opportunity: I could elicit from them further information relating to the precise causes of the intelligibility problems that had arisen during the interactions, and they could identify moments of unintelligibility that had not been obvious at the time they occurred. The replays were also intended to offer the students themselves insights into their performance and their success (or otherwise) in communicating with one another. In particular, it was predicted that they would become increasingly aware of those pronunciation idiosyncrasies (largely L1 transfers) that rendered their speech unintelligible to one another. In this way, the recordings also had a sound pedagogic purpose and, in the light of the findings, would have been beneficial even had they not been part of a study.

A final, crucial feature of this study is that intelligibility was assessed in relation to ongoing interaction rather than in experimental situations. Thus, it was possible to identify which pronunciation features related to communicative success or failure in genuine NNS/NNS exchanges as opposed to merely testing the participants' nonparticipatory understanding or their understanding only of words (or even sounds) uttered in citation form (see Jenkins, 2000, for a more detailed discussion of the issues involved in assessing phonological intelligibility). Assessing ongoing interaction also enabled me to observe the participants' attempts to adjust or accommodate their pronunciation in order to anticipate and remedy unintelligibility for their interlocutors—an important phonological communication strategy for which experimental settings make no allowance (see Giles & Coupland, 1991, for a full account of accommodation processes).

The Data

What follows is a discussion of a selection of the study data focusing on two main areas:

1. This point focuses on the longitudinal aspect of the study and the effect on the participants' productive/receptive phonological and accommodation skills. In other words, to what extent did the participants improve (a) their productive pronunciation skills in relation to their listeners' needs, that is, in order to reduce phonological unintelligibility for their listeners; and (b) their receptive pronunciation skills as the result of prolonged exposure to their interlocutors' (L1-influenced) accents? In this regard, I examine data showing the effect of the interlocutor's L1 and the effect of task type on the participants' pronunciation.

2. By relating this study to my wider research, I highlight those features that seem to be crucial to learners' phonological repertoires if they are to be able to make effective use of their accommodation skills in EIL interaction contexts. These features can be considered as candidates for an EIL pronunciation core.

Although improvement is not guaranteed, teachers can usually expect their students to demonstrate improvements in the areas taught during a course. And given that pronunciation was one of the main classroom foci for these students and one of the variables on which they were ultimately to be assessed in the speaking examination, I predicted at least some replacement of L1-influenced pronunciation features with more targetlike pronunciation as the program progressed. This prediction was, indeed, borne out by the evidence, insofar as all six students, by the end of the 12 weeks, had demonstrated their ability to replace several of their L1-influenced pronunciation features, particularly sounds, in certain discourse situations.

However, it was not a question of overall improvement: Not all L1-influenced pronunciations improved. Rather, the students were selective in the items they improved and, in addition, the improvements were not monolithic but depended on the needs of the particular interlocutor and on the demands of the specific activity in which they were engaged. The students, in effect, developed their phonological accommodation skills during the program. But whereas traditionally, the accommodation strategy of convergence involves making one's speech more like that of an interlocutor, these students met their different interlocutors' needs not by converging on the latter's pronunciation, but by meeting them halfway on a pronunciation that was closer to the target item.

A case in point is the older Japanese participant's (J2) pronunciation of the sounds /r/ and /l/. Early in the study period, she regularly confused them, even when there was a serious risk of unintelligibility for her Swiss-German interlocutor (SG2). In the second recorded interview, J2 was describing a picture in which there were three red cars. What she actually said was "three led cars," which noticeably confused her interlocutor. In the follow-up discussion, SG2 asked what she had meant by this, saying that he had thought she had been referring to "three let cars," in other words, cars to hire. He had managed to identify which of six possible pictures she had been describing but had achieved this in spite of rather than because of her description.

Four weeks later, in the fourth set of recorded interviews, the same two students were engaged in a similar activity. This time, J2 referred to a *grey house* as a [gleɪ] house. SG2's response was to remain silent and frown. J2 noticed his difficulty and immediately repeated the word *grey* correctly as [gɹeɪ]. SG2 understood her meaning, and the interaction progressed. Afterwards, SG2 commented that he had initially understood J2 to have been referring to a "clay" house and had been confused because none of his pictures contained one.

Interestingly, SG2 added that he had grown used to J2's (by now more intermittent) confusion of /r/ and /l/ and had been listening for it. He had nevertheless trusted the phonetic information rather than his knowledge of his interlocutor's pronunciation problems and the visual contextual information on the page in his hand. In other words, over the period in question, SG2's exposure to this particular pronunciation idiosyncrasy of his interlocutor had not facilitated his ability to cope with this Japanese transfer.

On the other hand, J2's ability to identify the effect of the transfer on her intelligibility and to adjust her output (i.e., to accommodate) in relation to her interlocutor's need had improved. However, this improvement did not merely represent an overall improvement in phonological competence or the loss of the L1-influenced pronunciation of the sound /r/ but also, perhaps more importantly for

EIL, the development of the ability to replace it when communicatively necessary in order to be phonologically intelligible for a particular different-L1 interlocutor.

To demonstrate this factor, I will discuss an extract from the fifth interview, recorded at the end of the study period. This time, J2 was paired with J1, the other Japanese student. Two weeks previously, in the final interaction with her Swiss-German interlocutor, J2 had only confused /r/ and /l/ once. In addition, she had produced sounds influenced by transfer only 4 times out of 30 possible candidates for transfer (i.e., a rate of approximately 13%) in relation to three selected variables: (a) the mispronunciation of /r/, (b) the substitution of both /ɜː/ and word-final schwa with /ɑː/, and (c) the omission of word final /n/ with nasalization of the preceding vowel. When interacting with her Japanese interlocutor, however, J2 produced sounds influenced by transfer 10 times out of a possible 26 candidates (i.e., a rate of almost 40%) in relation to the same three variables. Example 1 comes from the information exchange task (Phase 2) of the final interview. J2 was describing a geometric pattern to J1, who was trying to draw the pattern as she spoke. Words affected by L1 transfer are transcribed in the line immediately below. In the example, J2 both substituted /l/ with /r/ ("line" in Line 9) and three times produced the flapped [ɾ] instead of the approximant [ɹ] ("cross" and "write" in Line 7, "line" in Line 8). In addition, there are several instances of the replacement of schwa (Lines 1, 3, 5) and /ɜː/ (Lines 1 and 2) with the sound /ɑː/, and two instances of the loss of word final /n/ and nasalization of the preceding vowel (Lines 7 and 9).

1.*

1 Mm inside the square there is ah circle which touches each line,
           skweɑː   ˈsɑːkl   ˈtʌtsɪz

2 um four (line)... in outside four line... and...in the middle of the

3 circle and square there is small square, but the corner, corners
   ˈsɑːkl   ˈkɔːnɑː ˈkɔːnɑːz

4 ah touches the cross xx square. And, how can I say that...just the
                                                              dæt

5 smaller square than the big one... (J1) The square which is
   ˈsmɔːlɑː   d̪ə

6 between the paper...xx and mm... in the big-biggest square there

7 is, you can see the cross, ah no no, not cross, mm...and uh   write
     kæ̃   kuɾɒs   ɾaɪt

8 the straight line in the middle (J1) The middle draw ah...ah, well
          ɾaɪn

9 you can see the cross in the line, and, okay, triangle, just triang-
     kæ̃   ɾaɪn

10 four triangles (big-big one), four triangles...and please divide the

11 triangle into two.

---

*Note: See Appendix for key to transcripts.

At first sight, this compares very negatively with J2's phonological performance in all four information exchanges with her Swiss-German interlocutor. Moreover, the same phenomenon was observed when the two Swiss-German participants were paired with one another. On the other hand, all four participants pointed out that they had found the interlocutor who shared their L1 easier to understand than their different-L1 interlocutor. All four, nevertheless, were astonished when they listened to their same-L1 interviews and heard for themselves the extent of their phonological transfer in these recordings.

If this outcome is considered within an accommodation framework, however, the picture becomes very different. Instead of interpreting the large number of L1 transfers in the same-L1 interaction as errors, we can, instead, consider both the increase in transfer in the same-L1 interaction and the replacement of transfer with more targetlike forms in the different-L1 interaction as attempts to accommodate toward an interlocutor in order to increase intelligibility. Over the study period, J2 (along with the other five participants) gradually worked out which of her pronunciations caused problems for her different-L1 interlocutor and attempted to remedy the situation by first acquiring the target replacements in her phonological repertoire, and then employing them when necessary (and, by the same token, not employing them when not necessary).

The same accommodation phenomenon was revealed in this study in relation to task type. Even within the different-L1 pairings, the attempt to replace L1 transfers that might have caused intelligibility problems for the interlocutor was not uniform. In particular, the data showed a marked increase in replacement of transfer during the second phase of the interview, the information exchange, as compared with the first phase, the chat. To demonstrate this, I will look at two further extracts (see Examples 2 and 3), both from the second practice interview with participants SG3 and SF: Example 2, a short extract from their Phase 1 chat and Example 3, from SG3's information exchange.

2.

SG3 and SF, Extract From Interview 2, Phase 1
SF: Erm, so where do you come from?

SG3:   I come from Switzerland.
                    ˈswɪtsəlænt

SF: Which part?

SG3:   Er central Switzerland.
                ˈzentrʊl ˈswɪtsəlænt

SF: Uh huh.

SG3:   I live in a quite a small village near Lucerne and er on the lake of
             lɪf   ˈwɪlɪtʃ   Lucerne.

SF: Uh huh.

SG3:   as well, a very nice area.
                        weri

SF: Yes, it is.

SG3:   Erm, I have a beautiful view to the Alps.
                                 fjuː

SF: Uh huh.

SG3:   And yeah, I like it there very much.

SF: That's lucky.

3.

SG3, Extract from Interview 2, Phase 2
  1   Okay, my picture shows a living room er... at the front wall there
                                                                 frɒnt

  2   hanging er three pictures and the picture er show plants or kind of
                                 ˈpɪktʃəs

  3   plants, I don't know (how) they're called exactly, and er, there is a a

  4   cupboard also at the wall
           ˈkɒbəd

In Example 2, L1 transfer affects 7 items out of 45, whereas in the second, it affects only 3 items out of 43. Of equal importance is the fact that most of the L1 transfers in the chat occur on important content words ("Switzerland," "village," "central," "view") and involve consonant sounds such as /w/, /v/ and /dʒ/, which, as will be discussed below, play a key role in maintaining phonological intelligibility in EIL interaction: In other words, they are core sounds. On the other hand, although there is potential for substitution of /w/ with /v/ in Example 3 ("wall" in Lines 1 and 4), in practice, it does not occur. In fact, only one transfer involves a consonant sound, and although this occurs on a key word, it is simply a case of terminal devoicing of the plural morpheme -*s*. The other two transfers relate to vowel quality, with /ɒ/ being substituted for the sound /ʌ/ in "front" (Line 1) and "cupboard" (Line 4). Vowel quality, it will be argued later, provided it is consistent, has a limited effect on phonological intelligibility in EIL interaction, much as it does in interaction between NSs of English with different regional accents.

Examples 2 and 3 provide evidence of a pattern that emerged in all the interviews for each of the three pairs of students, and again in a replication of the study with a larger number of participants from a wider range of L1 backgrounds. That is, the participants appeared to make fewer attempts to replace transfer with more targetlike production of sounds in the chat than they did in the information exchange. They confirmed that this was indeed so in their responses to a question in the follow-up questionnaire, in which they were asked if they had tried to alter the way they spoke at any particular points in the practice interviews. They also admitted, in response to another question, that they had not always expressed not understanding their interlocutor during the Phase 1 chat because of the risk of either their or their interlocutors' loss of face.

The evidence from both sets of comparisons (i.e., same vs. different L1 of interlocutor, and chat vs. information exchange) indicates, then, that the participants were attempting to engage in a form of accommodation by making the effort to be more targetlike in their production of sounds in those situations where it would enhance intelligibility for their interlocutor. As noted, this was the case for speakers with an interlocutor from a different L1 but not for speakers from the same L1. And even within the different-L1 interactions, the effect was far stronger when the outcome depended on the successful exchange of information than it was in chats, where nonunderstanding could more easily be disguised.

However, in order to accommodate in this way, speakers need not only to have acquired the skill of making spontaneous speech adjustments but also to have the critical target items within their phonological repertoires. This is all the more important because, despite regular exposure to another L2 English accent, EIL receptive phonological skills appear to be slower than productive skills to improve (see, e.g., the problem caused above by the substitution of the /r/ in the word *grey*, which occurred 6 weeks into the program).

The receptive problem appears to relate to an inability, even at relatively high levels of proficiency, to make use of context in interpreting nontargetlike pronunciation. On several other occasions in the practice examinations, a listener had clear contextual cues, often in the form of visual evidence, yet preferred to trust the acoustic information even where it did not make any sense whatsoever. If the acoustic information resulted in a nonword, listeners simply assumed it was a word that was unfamiliar to them; if it resulted in a word they knew, they tried to make it fit the visual information rather than vice versa. For example, the "led" cars became "cars for hire." Either way, the result was mis- or nonunderstanding. Given this difficulty in using contextual cues to compensate for inaccurate pronunciation, the accurate production of core items is critical. I now turn to the issue of what these items are.

The EIL Phonological Core

This study yielded 40 instances of communication breakdown. That is, there were 40 occasions when either the listener signaled nonunderstanding during the interaction itself, or admitted to it during the replay of the recording and discussion of the interaction. Of these 40 instances, 27 related to sounds, and a further 2 to other aspects of pronunciation. From the evidence provided by this study, along with that from the replication, my field data, and tonic stress experiment, I devised a core pronunciation for EIL, what I call the *lingua franca core*.

According to the lingua franca core, a phonological error in EIL involves an error in the following main areas:

1. the consonantal inventory, except for substitutions of /θ/ and /ð/
2. consonant clusters in word-initial and word-medial positions
3. vowel length contrasts
4. tonic stress production and placement

For the purposes of EIL, any variation from NS production outside these areas should be regarded as features of regional L2 accents of English. This includes vowel quality, weak forms, other so-called features of connected speech, word stress, and pitch movement (see Jenkins, 2000, for full details and explanation). The implications for teaching of this reduced pronunciation syllabus are discussed below in the section on practical ideas.

◈ DISTINGUISHING FEATURES

The overall distinctive nature of this study of NNS spoken discourse derives from the fact that it approached the topic from an EIL rather than an ESL/EFL perspective. Its overriding concern was to investigate productive and receptive obstacles to phonological intelligibility when NNSs communicate with each other rather than with NSs. Because the participants were in a multilingual learning environment (in the sense that they did not share the same L1), it was possible not only to investigate the role of phonology in NNS/NNS discourse more thoroughly than would otherwise have been possible, but also to carry through the underlying principle—that of working towards a goal of NNS/NNS mutual intelligibility—into daily teaching and regular preparation for the forthcoming speaking examination. So although this was intended as a study of lingua franca discourse, many of its procedures could be carried out as a part of pronunciation teaching for learners whose aim was international intelligibility.

Three main features, all originating from the focus on NNS/NNS interaction, distinguish this study and its implications for teaching from most other pronunciation studies and teaching programs.

Observing the Effects of Pronunciation on Interlocutors

Because the study involved the participants in communicating directly with one another in classroom tasks and examination practice, they were provided with authentic evidence of their EIL productive and receptive skills. Over a lengthy period, they had regular opportunities to observe at first hand the effect of their L1 pronunciation transfers on an interlocutor's understanding and to assess the relative risk to intelligibility of their individual transfer types. Although they had not, by the end of the study period, achieved targetlike production of all high-risk items all the time, they had improved their performance substantially in this regard. At the same time, they had not improved their performance of certain other phonological features such as weak forms, even though these were taught in class. This is not surprising, given that weak forms (the production of the vowel sound in words such as *to, from,* and *of* as schwa) do not increase intelligibility for a fellow NNS.

During the study period, the participants also, both by default in their multilingual classroom and by design in the examination practice, gained extensive exposure to other L2 English accents. This provided them with the opportunity to work out where the differences lay between their own accents and those of a different-L1 interlocutor. However, here the results, though promising, were not as strong. It seems that during an interaction, especially when a processing overload co-occurs with an interlocutor's L1 transfer, the tendency is to trust what has been heard. This, in turn, is compounded by the difficulty in interpreting contextual cues, as described above. It seems that there is a need for teachers to provide specific contrastive work in their classrooms, to promote and maximize the potential benefits of the available exposure to a range of L2 accents. This, however, is something that did not form part of the study/program under discussion.

The Role of Accommodation Skills in Effective Pronunciation

The second feature that distinguishes this study from others is that it took account of accommodation skills instead of regarding the participants' pronunciation as monolithic. It is well known in accommodation theory that we have a tendency to adjust our speech in the direction of that of our interlocutors (i.e., to converge), for either affective reasons (to be liked by our interlocutors), communicative efficiency reasons (to be more easily understood by them), or both. What has been little considered hitherto is that L2 speakers are likely to engage in the same strategies insofar as their repertoires enable them to do so.

It could be argued that as important as targetlike pronunciation of core sounds for successful EIL communication is the ability to adjust pronunciation according to the needs of the specific interlocutor in the specific speech situation, whether this involves more accurate pronunciation or not. This is a skill that remains to be taken into account in many oral examinations. Candidates are still regularly assessed according to their intelligibility for the (usually NS) assessor and in relation to their overall accuracy of pronunciation regardless of its appropriateness for their NNS interlocutor or in relation to the different tasks being carried out. This study and its replication point to the need for a serious conceptual shift as far as communicative speaking examinations are concerned.

In terms of the teaching program itself, the provision of activities, both in class and in examination practice, designed to foster the students' development of accommodation skills meant that they gradually discovered which of their pronunciation features caused serious problems for their interlocutors and therefore required adjustments toward the target, particularly in information exchange tasks.

Pronunciation Error Versus Intelligibility

The third distinguishing feature of this study was its relationship with and support for my larger program of work to design a core of phonological intelligibility for EIL. The main factor separating this from other research in the field is that so-called pronunciation error is not being defined as deviation from an NS norm. Instead, the claim is that in EIL, pronunciation error should be defined in relation to the communicative effect on intelligibility for an NNS interlocutor. Still more controversial is the claim that any items that do not figure in this core of intelligibility should be regarded as features of the L2 regional accent variety of the (NNS) speaker. Thus, for the first time, to my knowledge, NNSs who do not live in L2 countries where English has internal official functions are being permitted the sociolinguistic right to regional accent variation.

◈ PRACTICAL IDEAS

The study has generated a number of practical ideas for those teachers whose learners wish to be internationally intelligible in English. These follow.

Focus Learners' Attention on Phonological Core Features

To be able to adjust their pronunciation in the direction of more targetlike production as a means of accommodating EIL interlocutors, learners need to acquire the relevant features. As a basis for any practical EIL activity, they need to have mastered not the entire NS pronunciation inventory, but only those features designated as core. This implies a pedagogic emphasis on consonant sounds other than /θ/ and /ð/, vowel length contrasts, word-initial and -medial consonant clusters, and tonic stress. Learners who wish to be able to understand the pronunciation of NSs as well as NNSs—and this will be the vast majority in countries where English is the L1—will, of course, need receptive classroom focus on the noncore features, too.

Minimal pair activities, preferably of the semicommunicative type promoted by Brown (1997) for Singaporean learners of English, can be focused easily on specific L1 pronunciation problems. Learners work in pairs with one asking a question and the other replying. Each question and each answer is selected from a choice of two (see, e.g., Example 4).

4.

Question 1: Where did the driver leave his cap?

Question 2: Where did the driver leave his cab?

Answer 1: Outside, with the engine running

Answer 2: On the table

(from Brown, 1997, pp. 26, 69). Reprinted with permission.

Note: Answers are not necessarily in the correct order.

I have adapted Brown's idea for learners from other L1s. For example, for Korean learners, one of the problem areas on which I have focused is the conflation of /f/ with /p/ because of the difficulty in producing the former. Thus, a typical question is: "Can I make you a coffee?/copy?" with the answer being selected from "Yes, black with two sugars, please" and "Yes, please—I'll read it later."

The same principle can be used to work on tonic stress. Hancock (1995) provides a minimal pair activity in which one learner asks a question using one of two possible choices for tonic stress placement (the choices being indicated by the underlining of the two words). The other learner, instead of providing the appropriate response this time, has to identify the speaker's meaning from one of two possibilities (see, e.g., Example 5).

5.

What time does your plane leave?

I know what time the airport bus leaves, but when does your plane leave?

Or:

My plane leaves at midnight. What about yours?

(from Hancock, 1995, p. 105)

Minimal pair activities of this sort are as appropriate for monolingual as for multilingual groups of learners because the correct answer to each question depends entirely on accurate pronunciation and recognition of the target item.

Develop EIL Accommodation Skills

Here it is important to take into account both productive and receptive accommodation and the implications for both monolingual and multilingual classrooms.

In multilingual classrooms, it is relatively easy to set up activities in which learners from different L1 backgrounds communicate with one another. The main feature of such activities should be that they provide direct evidence to the interlocutors of which of their pronunciation items cause intelligibility problems for one another and therefore need adjusting. Any activity involving dictation is useful in this regard because, after the activity is completed, the speaker and listener can compare notes and discuss whether any anomalies are the result of a productive problem or receptive difficulty. A variant of this type of activity is describe-and-draw, in which one learner describes a scene, object, or the like while the other draws (and perhaps labels) it.

Communicative dictation-type activities of this kind are less effective in monolingual classrooms as learners will find it easy to interpret one another's L1-transferred pronunciation in longer utterances—as was demonstrated earlier in relation to the same-L1 pairs in the study. However, a technological solution to this problem should not be too difficult to organize. For example, videoconferencing activities could be set up between classrooms in different-L1 countries. Such activities could be arranged between learners who intend later to communicate in English with representatives of each other's L1s, where this is known.

Learners' focus during such dictation activities is usually on the production and reception of sounds, so there is a need also for activities that direct their attention specifically to the use of another crucial core pronunciation feature, tonic stress. However, there is as yet a dearth of published material focusing on the use of tonic stress in a more communicative manner and in which there is scope for genuine accommodation. One exception is Gilbert's (2001) pronunciation book for beginners. The general principle of her tonic stress activities is still similar to that of Brown's (1997) and Hancock's (1995) minimal pairs, but Gilbert's activities are more communicative to the extent that they allow learners to manipulate tonic stress within conversations rather than in a simpler two-line question/answer format. The conversations, admittedly, are short and simple, but, in this regard, it is important to bear in mind the beginners at whom they are targeted and for whom the exchanges are likely to prove challenging. The activity in Table 1 is preceded by a listening-and-repeating stage in which tonic stress has been introduced.

It should not prove difficult to create longer, more complex conversations of this sort, though preferably with a successful outcome depending on accurate tonic placement by one speaker in response to the other, as in Hancock's minimal pairs.

With regard to receptive accommodation, exposure to different L2 English accents tends to occur by default in multilingual classrooms. However, learners need to have specific training in the crucial differences in each another's accents because they cannot be expected always to produce the core items with total accuracy; nor

TABLE 1. FINDING THE MOST IMPORTANT WORD

1. Circle the most important word in each sentence.
2. Say these conversations two times with a partner.

1. The Shoes

Jean:	What's wrong?
Joan:	I lost my shoes.
Jean:	Which shoes?
Joan:	My tennis shoes.

2. The Dog

Jim:	What's the problem?
Mike:	I lost my dog.
Jim:	What kind of dog?
Mike:	A brown dog. A small brown dog.
Jim:	I saw a small brown dog. It was at the supermarket.

3. A Letter

Bob:	What are you doing?
Jenny:	I'm writing a letter.
Bob:	What kind of letter?
Jenny:	A business letter.
Bob:	What kind of business?
Jenny:	Personal business!

(from Gilbert, 2001, pp. 44–45). Reprinted with permission of Cambridge University Press.

can they be expected to interpret L1-influenced pronunciations when their concentration is fully engaged on a complex task. One solution is for accents to become a classroom topic alongside, or even replacing, some of the usual course book topics (e.g., food, health, sports). Learners could provide each other with translations from a NS accent such as general American or received pronunciation into their L2-influenced variety, and classroom discussion could then focus on the differences. In addition, NNS/NNS texts recorded from the learners themselves could be used as the basis for both listening activities and for a more specific pronunciation focus. Learners could be guided to analyze each other's accents and, in the process, to identify the core features or their absence and, in the case of the latter, to consider the effect on intelligibility.

In monolingual classrooms, any such exposure to a range of L2 English accents will have to be provided by means of technology. At the most basic, this could take the form of audio or video recordings, but it means that the teacher, rather than the different-L1 learners themselves, will have to be the expert in highlighting and contrasting the accent differences.

Web sites could also be involved. For example, the *BBC World Service* (n.d.) enables learners to access a wide range of varieties of British English and engage in tasks to familiarize themselves with these. The same concept could easily be extended to a wide range of NNS varieties of English, though this is an enterprise that remains for the future.

◈ CONCLUSION

The study described and discussed in this chapter is one of the first of its kind to consider the role of pronunciation in spoken discourse in an EIL context. It provides evidence, along with the larger project of which it formed a part, of a need to gather empirical data from NNS/NNS interaction in order to assess which items have the potential to cause phonological unintelligibility in EIL settings, and to discover the extent to which NNSs are able—or can be trained—to accommodate to one another by making pronunciation adjustments.

Clearly much more work is needed in these areas. Further testing of the lingua franca core has begun so that it can be refined and extended in relation to specific L1 learners if necessary (see, e.g., da Silva, 1999; Walker, 2001). Recently, complementary work has been taking place in the field of pragmatics (e.g., House, 1999; Kasper, 1998) and has just begun in the field of lexicogrammar (Seidlhofer, 2000, 2001). Apart from these studies, there has been little work on EIL varieties and even less on EIL accommodation strategies.

Any large-scale change in this direction, however, will first require a marked change of attitude among not only NSs but also NNSs themselves, who, as Lippi-Green (1997) points out, tend to be "complicit in the process" (p. 242) of their own linguistic subordination.

◈ CONTRIBUTOR

Jennifer Jenkins is senior lecturer in the Department of Education and Professional Studies, King's College, London, where she also directs the MA in English language teaching and applied linguistics and teaches sociolinguistics, phonology/phonetics, and World Englishes. Her main research interest for many years has been phonological intelligibility in EIL. She is the author of *The Phonology of English as an International Language* (2000, Oxford University Press) and *World Englishes* (2003, Routledge).

◈ APPENDIX: KEY TO TRANSCRIPTS

Unintelligible speech is indicated by xx
Parentheses indicate probable but uncertain transcription
Pauses of more than three seconds are indicated by ...
(J1) indicates that the listener spoke at this point

CHAPTER 8

The Rest of the Iceberg: Articulatory Setting and Intelligibility

Joan Kerr

❖ INTRODUCTION

A second language (L2) learner's accent may cause little or no interference with the communication of a message, even though the listener is aware of differences from a native speaker's (NS) speech patterns. It may, however, be a major hindrance to effective communication if the listener is frequently unable to recognize words or has to concentrate hard on decoding sounds rather than taking in the content of the message. Jenkins (2000) rightly points out that we can no longer assume that listeners will be NSs of English; we need, therefore, to give considerable thought to the features of spoken English that are most important for speakers to acquire in order to make themselves intelligible to the international English-speaking community.

The aim of pronunciation teaching should not be to bring about an accent as close as possible to some norm of NS English, but rather to give learners the understanding and skills to make themselves intelligible to the international community of English speakers. We need, therefore, to be very clear about what sort of modification of speaking style is necessary for general intelligibility.

In her discussion of English as a international language (EIL), Jenkins (2000) describes a lingua franca core phonology—comprising those aspects of pronunciation that are the most important for mutual intelligibility between speakers of English from a range of NS backgrounds. As well as certain consonants and consonant clusters, this phonological core includes certain manners of consonant production such as aspiration, maintenance of vowel length contrasts, and nuclear stress production within words and word groups. Most important for the purposes of this chapter, however, Jenkins goes on to remind us that there is an aspect of speech production fundamental to segmentals and suprasegmentals, the aspect known as *articulatory setting*. Articulatory setting (referred to by some authors as *voice quality setting*; Abercrombie, 1967; Esling, 1987, 1996; Esling & Wong, 1983) refers to the patterns of movement and tension in the articulators—vocal folds, lips, jaw, and tongue—that become habitual to NSs in producing the sounds and sound combinations of their own languages (Abercrombie, 1967; Esling, 1987, 1994; Esling & Wong, 1983; Honikman, 1964; Laver, 1980). Given that the motor processes used in speech are complex and require a high degree of skill, becoming automatic in the speaking of one's first language (L1), changing them is a difficult task, as anyone who has ever learned a L2 knows. Learners of an L2 may well be completely unaware of this aspect of speech, yet a different articulatory setting interferes with pronunciation of another language in ways that may seriously compromise the segmental and suprasegmental features nominated by Jenkins as central to EIL intelligibility. It may be, therefore, that modifying articulatory setting could have widespread effects on intelligibility as a whole.

For me, the real interest of articulatory setting is the effect it has on vocal resonance. It is not only the sound of individual phonemes, but the entire quality of the speaker's voice that is affected by the way he or she uses the vocal folds, lips, tongue, jaw, and soft palate. Listening to the English of a NS of German, a NS of French, and a NS of Cantonese, you will notice that not only are certain vowels and consonants pronounced differently, but the actual sound of their voices is different. It is this quality that we try to copy when we imitate a particular accent.

The issue of articulatory setting is of particular interest in Australia because there are many students of English from Asian language backgrounds—that is to say, speakers of tonal languages that have a very different syllabic structure and phoneme distribution from English. Speakers of Cantonese and Vietnamese in particular seem to have significant difficulty with the pronunciation of English (Macneil, 1987). In working with them, I became very aware of their different vocal resonances. I wondered what the relationship might be between the resonance differences and their overall level of intelligibility. The project described here is the outcome of that wondering.

The chapter describes a pronunciation program for a Cantonese speaker, based on the speech pathology technique known as *changing focus of resonance* (CFR). The details of the program are preceded by a discussion of how vocal resonance comes about and how the different phonologies of Cantonese and English might be conducive to different vocal resonances. The last section of the chapter makes some suggestions for classroom practice based on the findings of the study.

◈ CONTEXT

This single-case study was carried out as part of the master's degree in TESOL at Deakin University, in Australia, in 1998. The subject, CC, was a Cantonese-speaking male, 56 years old, born in Hong Kong but resident in Australia for 9 years. He was a qualified medical doctor but unable to practice in Australia because of his language difficulties. He worked part-time as an acupuncturist. CC had completed several years of full-time and part-time study in English language programs before enrolling in an undergraduate degree course in a health-related field. He completed this degree with maximum support from language and study skills advisers at his university. However, his study adviser felt that he had little chance of employment because of his poor intelligibility. So CC was highly motivated to improve his spoken English as he knew it was an obstacle to employment in his chosen field. At the time of the study, he was not receiving any other help with English.

An assessment of CC's production of English sounds in single words using the Weiss Comprehensive Articulation Test (Weiss, 1978) indicated numerous conso-nant and vowel errors, and substitutions (see Kerr, 1998, for full details). In addition to his difficulties with pronunciation, CC had marked difficulties with English vocabulary, syntax, and listening comprehension. Although he had studied in an English-speaking environment, his use of English outside his work and study was limited as his wife did not speak English, and his social life revolved around the Cantonese-speaking community. Example 1, from my conversation with CC, illustrates the nature of his difficulties in expression:

1.*

R: Did you live in a house or an apartment?

CC: Er, u,usually in Hong Kong is all, mm, the/ the, the apartment, the high building, the apartment, very [kraʊ]

R: Do you think that you made the right decision to come to Australia?

CC: Pardon?

R: Do you think that you did the right thing to come to Australia?

CC: Er/ this/ this is/ difficult to say this, because the everyone have the different situation. You must (xxx) go away/ go forward, you can't see back. You must always/ see the forward. You see the forward, you/ you come here not to/ wrong and right, because you, you choose this. You must/ (xx) keep going.

R: Yes. Is your daughter happy in Australia?

CC: She happy, because I think the young/ people more/ easy for/ cope with/ yeah, more easy for/

R: to adjust

CC: Yeah, adjust.

R: And what about your wife?

CC: Mmm, I think she (xxx). Maybe she might/ [maɪn], mind, yeah, she might be…

R: Mmm

CC: Yeah, because the language a problem, and find a job is a problem.

R: Uhuh. Yeah. Yeah. Would you go back to Hong Kong, do you think?

CC: Er, I got some/ er, relative/ and friend in Hong Kong, sometime go back and visit them, but the, I/ I like/ live/ the Australia.

R: Mmhm?

CC: I like the, the/ this environment. I enjoy this environment. The living is good.

R: Mm? What is good about it? What is it that you like about Australia?

CC: Yeah, in here you/ like the/ like the/ you very freedom. You can do your/ everything yourself/ if not di,disturb the other. You get the/ er, freedom.

R: And that's not like Hong Kong?

CC: Not like Hong Kong, no, because the Hong Kong you must the/ when you/ working you/ very competition, yeah, you must get very stress..

R: Mmm

CC: Every day you work the long time, and you must the/ a lot of time spent for the/ er/ the personality.

Vocal Resonance

Figure 1 shows the areas of the vocal tract referred to in this chapter. The shaded area represents the posterior resonating space that is postulated for NSs of Cantonese.

When we speak, the sound produced by the vocal folds resonates in the spaces of the pharynx, mouth, and nasal cavity. It is resonance that gives the voice its

---

*Note: See Appendix A for key to transcripts.

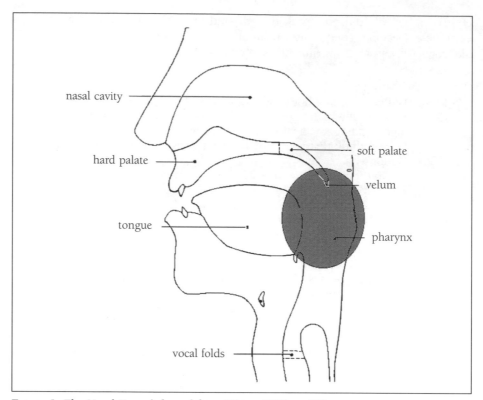

nasal cavity

hard palate

soft palate

velum

tongue

pharynx

vocal folds

FIGURE 1. The Vocal Tract (adapted from Weiss, 1978, p. 27)

carrying power. We all have an individual character to our voices because of individual variations in the size and shape of the resonating cavities. But the size and shape of the resonating cavities are also altered by the movements of the articulators. For example, a different oral cavity size and shape will be produced by rounding the lips or opening the jaw more widely.

A very important resonance difference is produced by the positioning of the velum. If the velum is raised to block off the nasal cavity, the voice resonates in the mouth but not in the nasal cavity, whereas a relaxed velum allows the sound to travel through the nasal cavity as well as the mouth.

I had noticed that the voices of my Cantonese-speaking students tended to have a posterior and nasal resonance. In other words, they tended to keep their jaws fairly closed and use a lot of tension in the back of the tongue so that constriction was created and, therefore, the voice could not travel freely forward to resonate in the front of the mouth. There also seemed to be more use of the nasal cavity as a resonator than is usual in English. Was there any evidence that these resonance features were related to the phonology of Cantonese?

Articulatory Settings in Cantonese and English

Cantonese is a largely monosyllabic language that has fewer consonants than English and does not use consonant blends. An analysis of Cantonese phonology based on the work of Kao (1971), Hashimoto (1972), Ramsey (1987), and So and Dodd (1995) showed that 86% of Cantonese syllables end in a consonant or a glide. Of this 86%, 42% end in a nasal, as opposed to 27% for glides and 17% for stops. The single most commonly occurring sound was the posterior nasal /ŋ/. Thus there appears to be a common syllabic pattern in which the movement of the tongue body as the syllable is produced is back toward the velum, which is relaxed to allow the sound to travel into the nasal cavity. This creates a large posterior resonating space as indicated in Figure 1. In addition, for nasal sounds, the mouth is kept relatively closed so that the major part of the sound travels through the nasal cavity rather than through the mouth.

Kao (1971) also analyzed vowel frequencies in Cantonese syllables and found that the back vowel /a/ was by far the most frequent, making up 41% of syllable nuclei, with the next most common vowel making up only 12%. (See Kerr, 1998, for a detailed analysis of these data.) The analysis of Cantonese phonology, therefore, suggests that it is conducive to a posterior resonance pattern.

By contrast, an examination of English phonology showed that the alveolar sounds—made with the tongue tip against the alveolar ridge—have the highest frequency of occurrence (Crystal, 1995; Knowles, 1987). These alveolar consonants in English can occur initially, medially, or finally. In addition, English contains many consonant clusters that contain an alveolar segment, such as blends with s, n, or t. Most English words are polysyllabic (Crystal, 1995), and there are relatively few restrictions on which consonants can occur in which positions in a word. These features of English suggest that an efficient tongue setting would be one that allows quick movement toward these anterior consonants and blends at any time. Analysis of the vowel system of English shows that front and center vowels and diphthongs ending in a fronted component are the most frequent (Crystal, 1995; Knowles, 1987). Therefore, it would seem that the articulatory activity in speaking English is located more in the front of the mouth, and that the resonances heard in the commonest vowel sounds are anterior ones.

The position in which the tongue body is held makes a significant difference to vocal resonance, as has been demonstrated by many researchers (Andrews, 1995; Honikman, 1964; Laver, 1980). Two other features that have been shown to be important are the relative roundness or spread of the lips and the degree of openness of the jaw (Abercrombie, 1967; Arslan & Hansen, 1997; Beddor, 1991; Fry, 1979; Kingston, 1991; Ladefoged & Maddieson, 1990; Nolan, 1983). If a Cantonese speaker speaks English with the tongue tensed back, the jaw relatively closed, and the velum relaxed, anterior consonants and vowels will not be clearly produced, syllables will be nasalized, and the voice will have a less carrying timbre than that of a speaker who maintains a more anterior setting.

Principles of the CFR Program

The program described here was based on four main principles:

1. anterior focus of resonance
2. vowels rather than consonants
3. awareness of the difference between heard and written English
4. a conscious technique

Anterior Focus of Resonance

The CFR technique is used by speech pathologists for professional voice-users, such as teachers who need to project the voice without creating undue strain on the vocal folds. The technique is also used with people who have too much or too little nasality in the voice. CFR involves teaching the person to remove the focus from the larynx itself and to attend to the kinesthetic feedback from the bones of the head and face as the voice resonates. A relaxed jaw, tongue, and pharynx are encouraged so that the sound can travel forward without constriction. When the sound resonates against the hard surfaces of the hard palate and teeth rather than being muffled by the softer tissues at the back of the mouth, the voice projects better.

In addition, CFR aims to sustain resonance over a full phrase by increased duration of vowels in stressed syllables and by linking between words. This sustained resonance counters the choppy speech pattern that often accompanies excessive laryngeal tension (Andrews, 1995; Fawcus, 1986; Moncur & Brackett, 1974).

Vowels Rather Than Consonants

The resonance of the voice is heard mainly on the vowels, which are the most prominent part of the English syllable (Fry, 1979; Pennington, 1996) and carry the pitch and stress information (Ladefoged & Maddieson, 1990; Pennington, 1996). Jenkins (2000) argued that the placement of nuclear stress—that is, the stress on the most prominent syllable in a word group—is one of the core elements in the EIL phonology. In general, Jenkins' core phonology places high importance on vowels. She points out that most of the world's languages have around twice as many consonants as vowels, whereas English has a potential 20 vowels to 24 consonants. For many students, therefore, the vowel system could be difficult to learn (Jenkins, 2000). Given the importance of nuclear stress, if the stressed syllable is produced with a vowel sound that is unclear or ambiguous, the potential for misunderstanding or a complete failure of communication is considerable.

Practically, a focus on vowels in the way described in this CFR program enables us to concentrate the learner's attention on features of articulation that are very visible and easy to sense, such as jaw opening and closing, and lip rounding or spreading. Such features may be easier to learn and habituate than more complex articulatory patterns in which tongue movements and postures are finely specified.

Raising Awareness of the Difference Between Heard and Written English

The peculiarities of English spelling should not be underestimated as a source of pronunciation error. I believe that learners should be taught to trust the ear rather than the eye when learning new words and to understand that there are many cases in English when the spelling may mislead them. In my view, this means that the phonetic alphabet, in particular the symbols for vowel sounds, should be available to them as a tool for indicating how words sound.

A Conscious Technique

Given the complexities involved in altering one's articulatory setting, learners cannot reasonably be expected to transfer a new setting consistently to all situations, particularly when they struggle with the grammar or vocabulary of the language. If, however, they can become confident enough with the basic technique, they may be able to call on it in situations of particular need. For this reason, the program put a strong emphasis on using field-specific vocabulary (Anderson-Hsieh, 1990) so that the participant could develop confidence in certain situations of high importance to him, such as job interviews.

◈ DESCRIPTION

At a preliminary discussion, in accordance with Deakin University ethical guidelines, I explained the program and gave CC a plain-English statement of the nature and purpose of the work. I had intended to have 12 seventy-five-minute individual sessions spread over 6 weeks, but this proved impossible for CC, and the 12 sessions were carried out once weekly, with occasional breaks of a week because of CC's other commitments. Therefore, the work was spread over 5 months in total. Before the teaching sessions, I took two sets of baseline measures 2 weeks apart. Each baseline consisted of the Weiss Comprehensive Articulation Test (Weiss, 1978) and a conversation sample.

Session 1

The main concepts of the program—using the front of the mouth and concentrating on clear vowel production—were introduced. I used a simple diagram of the mouth to show what I meant by the front of the tongue and the back of the tongue. CC repeated some English words after me—for example, *lip, meet, sip, ban*—all words using the tongue tip or lips and front vowels to demonstrate using the front of the mouth. Then I asked him to say some single words in Cantonese, and he was able to identify that he used the back of his tongue more.

Next, we reviewed the concept of vowels and consonants, with the vowels identified simply by the letters *a, e, i, o, u*. CC imitated my production of various long vowels (e.g., /ɑː/, /iː/, /ʊː/) followed by my production of various voiceless consonants in isolation (e.g., /p/, /t/, /k/). I chose long vowels and voiceless consonants to make the distinction between the length and loudness of vowel and consonant sounds as strong as possible. CC could hear that the vowel sounds were much louder and longer than the consonants. We then moved onto saying short words (e.g., *part, read, sound*) and discussed the fact that the part of the word listeners hear most clearly is the vowel component.

I then gave CC the vowel chart shown in Appendix B, and he practiced the vowels and diphthongs following my model. I instructed him to keep the tip of his tongue behind and touching the bottom teeth, and to concentrate on opening and closing his jaw and rounding his lips to change the sound. The vowels rely very much on how much speakers open their jaw and how much they round their lips, not nearly so much on precise positions of the tongue, as you will find if you experiment with saying vowel sounds with your tongue tip or blade in different positions. I described diphthongs as *moving sounds*; again we focused on feeling how the jaw and lips moved from the first part of the sound to the second.

I was not concerned that CC's vowel should sound exactly like my model, but only that the length or shortness and the degree of jaw opening and lip-rounding were observed so that the sound was approximated. At this stage, the vowels and diphthongs were not associated with any key words because I wanted CC to concentrate on the feeling of the lips and jaw moving to change the sound and did not want him to fall into any habitual patterns of producing the sound.

Sessions 2 and 3

The idea of bringing the voice forward was reinforced by demonstrating how sounds produced at the front of the mouth set up vibrations in the bones of the nose, cheeks, and upper jaw. Following the initial stages of the CFR technique outlined by Fawcus (1986), CC began by cupping his hands around his mouth and nose and intoning *bm-bm-bm-bm* on a continuous sung tone. The combination of the labial and the nasal gives strong vibratory feedback from the lips and the bones of the front part of the face, the hard palate, and the nasal cavity. Cupping the hands around the mouth and nose intensifies this kinesthetic and vibratory feedback. We moved onto intoning short syllables with front, central, or strongly lip-rounded vowels in combination with tongue tip or lip sounds (e.g., *bee, noo, tore*). In this way, the concept of keeping the voice forward was maintained by using combinations of sounds that produce strong vibratory feedback at the front of the mouth. We then practiced with the hands held away from the mouth and nose in a megaphone position, as a cue to keep the voice forward. From then on, I used this megaphone gesture to indicate to CC when he needed to bring his voice further forward.

Vowels and diphthongs were then practiced in chains of syllables requiring jaw opening and closing (e.g., *yahyahyah, armarmarm*), and lip rounding and spreading (e.g., *wahwahwah, moomoomoo*). At this stage, CC was trying to combine attending to the anterior resonance with moving his jaw and lips freely. We then moved from chains of syllables to single words and short phrases, first producing the word or phrase in a prolonged, singsong manner, then repeating it in a more conversational tone. Once we began using phrases, I started to tape CC's production and play it back to him to demonstrate the increased clarity of his voice when he was bringing the voice forward.

Sessions 4–6

These three sessions focused on relating the heard word to the written form of words that were particularly important to CC in everyday life or in the field of work he hoped to enter. I found that although he very often did not know how to pronounce words that he must have heard or seen many times in the course of his studies, he was capable of pronouncing them intelligibly following my model.

I prepared a summary sheet listing words containing the common spellings of each vowel or diphthong. For example, for the diphthong /ɪə/ the listed words were *ear, here,* and *beer.* We discussed the fact that English contains a number of different spellings for vowels and diphthongs and that it is important to be able to relate a spelling to a particular sound. I then said a word from the summary sheet, and CC referred to his vowel chart (Appendix B) to identify which vowel or diphthong he heard.

We continued working on CC's ability to identify the vowels and diphthongs in my production of spoken words and phrases. Increasingly, we used work-related vocabulary and common words I had noticed that CC mispronounced. I said the word or phrase, and CC identified and wrote in the vowels and diphthongs, referring to his vowel chart as much as he needed; he then practiced the phrase after my model. The only consonant corrections I made (at CC's particular request) were for the *ch* sound, which CC pronounced as /s/ or sometimes as /t/. I audiotaped him for the purpose of feedback, and I continued to cue him to keep his voice forward. I did not attempt to bring his vowel production closer to mine, but merely pointed out to him when one vowel could be confused with another. For example, if he produced *beat* as *bit,* I pointed to the short /ɪ/ on the chart and said, "That sounded more like this one to me," and allowed him to work out what he needed to modify.

Session 7

We began to carry the CFR technique over into conversation, using easy autobiographical information and exchanges typical of a job interview or a telephone conversation in which he had to request information about an advertised job. These conversations were unscripted, but I noted words and phrases that were not clearly produced so that CC could work out from my model what the vowel sounds should be. We used taping and playback extensively for feedback on the clarity of his voice.

Sessions 8–12

We continued conversational practice, first role-playing job interviews in which CC had to use work-related terminology and progressing to less predictable exchanges that made more demands on his language. For example, we talked about his attitude to gambling, smoking, and various superstitions. We also continued to work on stabilizing pronunciation of relevant terminology with practice reading from work-related materials. CC continued to write in the correct vowel or diphthong, from my model if necessary. Cueing was given where necessary by the megaphone gesture, and I played the tape back so that he could assess for himself whether he was maintaining anterior resonance and keeping his voice going. It was noticeable that the more linguistically demanding the topic, the more difficulty CC had in maintaining the anterior resonance.

CC commented throughout the program that this was an easy technique to learn and that he felt more confident of people understanding him when he paid attention to keeping his voice forward. He also mentioned that it was much more difficult for him to do this when he was trying to deal with an unfamiliar situation or a topic that stretched his command of English.

◈ DISTINGUISHING FEATURES

This program differs from many other approaches to pronunciation teaching in its focus on the gross determinants of voice quality—in particular the forward or backward positioning of the tongue body, jaw opening, and lip rounding—and its suggestion that paying attention to vowels and diphthongs can produce an improvement in intelligibility even in the presence of consonant errors. Further, it suggests that working with field-specific materials may be a more efficient method of bringing about a functional improvement in intelligibility than using drills or exercises to target specific phonemes. It is an approach that tries to focus on fundamental aspects underlying speech—the rest of the iceberg, so to speak—rather than on individual sound substitutions or distortions. The outcomes of the program are briefly presented below. More detailed information and discussion is available in Kerr (1998).

Pre- and Post-CFR Measures of Change

I administered the Weiss Comprehensive Articulation Test, and another speech pathologist who did not know the nature of the project, and did not know that the three tapes (two baselines and a posttreatment tape) were of the same subject, scored it. There was no significant reduction in CC's pronunciation errors on the articulation test.

In the original project, four NSs were asked to transcribe as much as they could of sentences randomly extracted from baseline and post-CFR conversational samples, and I found (Kerr, 1998, 2000) that the judges were able to transcribe more extended sections of most of the sentences in the post-CFR sentences. This improvement occurred in the absence of any significant change in intelligibility as measured by the articulation test, which tests individual phonemes in single words, suggesting that the improvement was not due to more accurate production of particular phonemes, but to some factor operating at phrase or sentence length.

In an extension of the original project carried out recently, I asked a nonnative English speaker to do the same transcription task. Details of this judge and her transcriptions are contained in Appendix C. Although the difference is not as marked as in the NS transcriptions, these data also show that the nonnative listener was able to transcribe more extended sections of most of CC's utterances on the post-CFR sample. It is clear in the transcriptions in Appendix C, however, that due to her limited knowledge of English, the judge was not able to fill in the gaps in what she understood, as NSs tend to do. This suggests that clarity of the key information words—usually nouns and verbs—is even more important for intelligibility in EIL than it is in conversation between NSs.

What are we to make of these data? Although there are methodological problems with my study (1998) that make it impossible to draw firm conclusions, the findings suggest that some change had occurred in CC's speech that made it more likely that listeners would understand phrases, or groups of words, where previously they had understood only isolated words. This may have been because his voice was better projected in general or better sustained over long phrases, or because the vowels in the stressed syllables (nuclear stress) were more salient. The CFR technique aims to bring about just these changes.

◈ PRACTICAL IDEAS

I am not suggesting that this approach in its entirety would be useful for improving pronunciation in all L2 speakers, but it could be particularly relevant to speakers of Asian languages, specifically, Chinese, Vietnamese, and Korean. In my experience, speakers of European languages generally have difficulties more related to particular consonant or vowel sounds and, perhaps, stress patterns than to their general voice quality. However, even for these students, it may be useful to focus on English vowel and diphthong qualities because of their central role in prosody—that is to say, in the appropriate placement of nuclear stress and, for more advanced students, the ability to use pitch and stress to convey nuances of meaning or feeling. Of course, there will always be a place for working on consonants and consonant blends that a speaker finds particularly difficult. Consonants were not addressed in the program described here because of the nature of the research question, not because they are unimportant to intelligibility.

Some suggestions for using aspects of this approach in the classroom follow.

Focus on English Vowels and Diphthongs and Teach Them Through Use of Some Basic Cues

As suggested above, it is possible to teach a fair approximation of the English vowels and diphthongs by using the relatively gross cues of jaw opening/closing and lip rounding/spreading. Diphthongs are particularly helpful in getting students to attend to the way their lips and jaw are moving because they are produced precisely by moving the jaw, lips, or both as the sound continues.

Encourage Students to Compare Differences in the Way They Use Their Voices When Speaking English and When Speaking Their Own Language

An excellent pronunciation text by Laroy (1996) encourages students to reflect on the way their "English voice" (pp. 34–35) differs from the way they use the articulators when speaking their own language. I have found the overhead transparency given in Appendix D useful as the basis for class discussion and comparison of languages. (As it was prepared for speakers of Asian languages, the description of English has been simplified to concentrate on the most important adjustments these learners need to make.)

Students enjoy speaking snatches of their own languages and trying to say whether they think they speak in the mouth, the nose, the throat, and so on, and it seems to help their awareness of these aspects of speaking English. Even when students have quite strong transfer of articulatory patterns from the L1 to English (as was the case with CC), they usually have some capacity to appreciate that attempting to produce English words after the teacher's model involves different patterns.

Teach Pronunciation as an Integral Part of General English Activities

The program described here was carried out with an individual learner, but I agree emphatically with Jenkins (2000) that pronunciation can and should be taught as an integral part of the general activities of an English class. My own practice in classroom teaching is to ally pronunciation work with general listening work, building in identification of the vowels and diphthongs in any new words or phrases and practicing them with attention to lip and jaw movement.

When learning new vocabulary, students learn first of all how to say the word, with the correct vowel qualities, rather than simply writing it down and looking up its meaning. Classroom posters or individual student dictionaries can be kept in which the new vocabulary is entered under the vowel or diphthong symbol of the stressed syllable. Doing this reminds students that a variety of spellings are possible for a given vowel or diphthong and that they need to rely on their ear rather than their eye when learning how to say the word.

Address Pronunciation as Part of Teaching
New Grammatical Structures

I have commented above that CC was better able to use the technique when he was speaking on topics that were relatively undemanding for him linguistically. Given the cognitive load involved in learning new grammar as well as in getting the articulators to move in different ways, it makes sense to give a lot of attention to pronunciation as part of the learning of new grammatical structures. There is a place here for drills that concentrate on the sound of the spoken structure in a way that starts to integrate the motor pattern with the meaning. This might be done in several ways.

- Focus on the vowel qualities of phrases spoken as a whole, for example, in the past continuous tense the schwa /ə/ in *was* or *were* and the full vowel sound in the first syllable of the verb, so that the sound pattern meshes with the rhythmic pattern. The phrase can be written on the board as *I wəs weɪting, they wə taːking, we waɪ̯ting* and practiced rhythmically, emphasizing the full vowel on the stressed syllable. It does not matter if students produce a fuller version of the vowel in *was,* but it is important that they lengthen and dwell on the vowel in the stressed syllable of *waiting* so that it becomes the salient word in the phrase. This approach integrates learning of syntax with attention to the placement of the main stress in a word group—one of Jenkins' core principles for EIL intelligibility.

- Have students mime the phrases slowly and silently, concentrating on the articulatory movements needed to produce a particular grammatical structure.

- Have the students practice a more complex structure very slowly, with the vowels drawn out, and only gradually increasing the speed of utterance.

❖ CONCLUSION

Every ESL teacher is a teacher of pronunciation. It is not necessary to know or use the technical terminology of phonetics textbooks. Do you use the tip or the back of your tongue? Is your jaw wide open, almost closed, or moving between open and closed? Are your lips round or spread? All of these features are easily visible or easily felt. When you listen to a spoken phrase, which words, which vowels are the most salient? Increasing awareness of these aspects of speech in yourself and your students is a simple but significant step in improving their intelligibility.

This case study described a program intended to improve intelligibility in a learner of Cantonese background by working on vocal resonance in vowels and diphthongs. The results suggest that attention to voice quality has the potential to improve prosody, with a resulting improvement in intelligibility.

◈ CONTRIBUTOR

Joan Kerr works primarily as a speech pathologist in adult rehabilitation. She also works as a sessional ESL teacher for Gordon Technical and Further Education (TAFE) in Geelong, Victoria, Australia, and conducts workshops and seminars on pronunciation teaching for ESL teachers.

◈ APPENDIX A: KEY TO TRANSCRIPT

/   pause
(xxx)   unintelligible

◈ APPENDIX B: VOWEL CHART

Vowels

1. iː   ++ long, spread lips
2. ɪ
3. ɛ
4. æ
5. ɜ   ++ relaxed lips, tongue, jaw
6. ə   ++ short
7. uː   ++ long, rounded lips
8. ʊ
9. ɒ
10. ɔː   ++ long, rounded lips
11. aː   ++ long, relaxed jaw
12. ʌ

Diphthongs

1. ɪə
2. ɛə
3. eɪ
4. ʊə
5. əʊ
6. ɔɪ
7. aɪ
8. aʊ

◈ APPENDIX C: TRANSCRIPTIONS MADE BY OO

OO is a Russian-speaking learner of English, resident in Australia for 2 years. She is a student in an upper intermediate/advanced English course. OO heard each taped sentence twice and was asked to write down what she thought she heard. The tapes were presented in the order shown below, with an interval of at least 3 days between the sessions.

The sections of OO's transcriptions that are accurate are given in bold italic type.

Baseline 1a

1. My home/ er, usually I/ talk the Chinese language

   At ***home usually......Chinese language***

2. Mm, each placement is the three week.

   three week

3. I have learning/ I have been learning the course of the Disability Study

   I happen to ***learning.....***

4. You are/ you can cope with something

   You can *copy* ***with some things***

5. Such as the/ mm, the hostel/ and the/ adults' day/ service and support

   And the house pay ***service and support***

6. Because they got a, a/ a lot of experience about the life

   Because they have a lot of *at parents of own* ***life***

7. Before I/ work as/ as a doctor in Shanghai

   I see ***doctor*** *in same.....*

8. I think this policy not good

   I see polishen

9. Also I got the/ one dog

   Also...

10. Children, they de, develop/ not good for they

    Choose I will ***develop***

Post-CFR

1. But this, I think not only the Hong Kong, is the/ whole world

   ..... the same in ***Hong Kong***, *hold* ***world***

2. Yeah, I got a car.

   Yeah, I've got a car

3. Yeah, go to work/ and go to shopping, and go to visit the friend.

   yes, go to work, go to shopping, go to visit friends

4. And sometimes we go together, go to park

   Sometimes** you go to care, **go to park

5. Mm, I think the/ a lot of Hong Kong people don't like the communists

   ***I think a lot of Hong Kong people don't like** come to....*

6. My house, go to station is the/ ten minutes about

   I how to call...to stay

7. 1985/ I find the people more polite

   *Litely **85 I find the people more polite***

8. He, he/ he know he is wrong

   He know he is wrong

9. Yeah, they use for the, transport the food and the, the/ business

   New to...from

10. Yeah, the, the/ people live in the China is very/ very poor

    *If you **live in the China**.....you are **very poor***

Baseline 1b

1. Usually the half an hour/ for/ each treatment

   ***In you said it how know**.....it*

2. Because at the moment I think more difficult

   Because**.....women **I think it's more difficult

3. You, you/ didn't got the/ too much the/ patient

   You didn't**.....**to much**... **patient

4. Oh, er, go to park/ yeah, go to park/ with my dog

   O**....it coll **your part

5. And the only you/ talk about how to/ about the acupuncture point

   *Your teach you **how to**.....**about acupuncture***

6. Only/ mm, one/ one and two/ years old, very/ children

   One and two years old** when (where) is **children

7. You can give some advice

   *And is only **you can give** somebody*

8. You need more time, maybe forty five minutes/ maybe the one hour

   *.....**more time forty five minutes** may.....**one hour***

9. And the older one, maybe/ the eighty, mm, the ninety

   *...**old one**...eight year, more, nine years*

10. Too much- I don't know the/ where they come from

    to much I didn't know where they come from

◈ APPENDIX D: ENGLISH LANGUAGE ARTICULATION FOR ASIAN LEARNERS

Speaking English Clearly

When you speak, you use your breath, voice, jaw and lips. Different languages use them differently. What do you need to know to speak English with a good accent?

Breath: In English you have to breathe deeply, right down to your stomach, because we speak with a smooth, flowing rhythm and join words together, so a lot of breath is needed to keep speaking smoothly.

Voice: Some languages speak in the throat, some in the nose, and some, like English, at the front of the mouth. When you speak English you should try to bring your voice right to the front of the mouth.

Tongue: Because we speak English at the front of the mouth, we use the front of the tongue a lot. Make sure your tongue isn't held back towards your throat, and try to relax your tongue.

Jaw: English is spoken with a relaxed, open jaw. Make sure you aren't keeping your teeth very close together when you speak.

Lips: Don't make your lips too round when speaking English. Smile a little bit when speaking.

CHAPTER 9

Accessing "D" Discourse: Using Systemic Functional Grammar and Conversation Analysis to Examine Nonnative Speaker Interaction in the Classroom

Judy Cohen

◈ INTRODUCTION

This chapter looks at features of nonnative English speaker (NNS) interaction in order to examine the effectiveness of the interaction and the influence of certain aspects of NNS speech on the power relationships among the participants. In the latter instance, this means identifying those language features that may lead to the marginalization of certain students in language learning situations. If, as Savignon (1991) and Larsen-Freeman and Long (1991) suggest, language learning is facilitated by participation in communicative events, it is particularly important to investigate the implications of language-initiated power relationships in the classroom.

The study that this chapter presents adopted Gee's (1990) Discourse theory to investigate the role of different learners' perceptions of an individual's language ability and looked at the way social marginalization may occur as a result of negative perceptions. The data examined consist of a transcript of a recording of students completing a classroom activity and were analyzed from a systemic functional (Eggins, 1994; Halliday, 1985) and a conversational analysis (Burns, Joyce, & Gollin, 1996) perspective.

◈ CONTEXT

The program discussed in this chapter is an optional course for Swedish university students of engineering and is designed to improve their general English language skills as well as skills specific to their program of study, for example, the use of appropriate technical terms. Classes structured for groups of 20–30 are held over a 2-hour period (including a break) two or three times per week, with teaching sessions being allocated to work on either written or spoken language. The teaching approach adopted is one of problem-based learning through active class participation rather than through lectures.

Students are generally in their early 20s and have Swedish as their first language (L1) although there is a small but significant minority who are of non-Swedish background. Of this minority group, many have English as their third language (L3;

Swedish being the common second language [L2]); some, however, speak more than three languages. This is particularly true of students from Asian or African backgrounds, many of whom speak various dialects of their L1 as well as Swedish, English, and even a third European language. Thus, in the English language classes, there is both a range of English language ability and, interestingly, a noticeable difference in the students' perception of their English abilities. I observed that many of these L3 speakers (including the subject of this study) felt and even stated that they were "no good" at English and were prepared to defer to the L2 (Swedish) students in carrying out English language tasks. The Swedish students, on the other hand, were generally more confident in their English language abilities, a sizeable number having spent some time in an English-speaking environment. However, I further observed that this confidence was not always justified by their actual linguistic performance.

Language use incorporates socially acceptable behaviors and involves users in adopting a certain social identity, a process Gee (1990) terms *Discourse*. He demonstrates that Discourse (as opposed to *discourse,* which he defines as stretches of text) will by its very nature lead to the marginalization of certain groups because a Discourse and its "sub-Discourses" (p. 142) are ways of displaying membership of a particular social group or network. Discourse, in fact, acts as a type of identity kit, and, as Nemetz Robinson's (1985) discussion on schema theory shows, use of such an identity kit may serve to provide a basis from which individuals can evaluate themselves and others within society. This process of evaluation can be seen in this study at points in the interaction where students identify themselves with a particular Discourse and then use this identity kit and other aspects of language use to establish their positions within the interaction, leading to a process of marginalization.

In this specific context, the English spoken by the Swedish (L2) students can be seen in Gee's terminology to be the "dominant Discourse," where "dominant" refers to that Discourse leading to the distribution of social goods in a society (p. 144), whereas the English spoken by the L3 students can be seen as the dominated (marginalized) literacy.

◈ DESCRIPTION

The learner (S), the subject of this study, was a former refugee from Bosnia who had been living in Sweden since the age of 13. She was studying the first year of a combined bachelor and master of science degree in engineering, and she spoke Bosnian and Swedish fluently (plus some German). S was chosen for this study on account of her non-Swedish background and English being her L3. In accordance with the comments above, S often stated that she felt her English was very poor and that she was not as good as the other students. She did not attempt the final exam due to this lack of confidence and was very hesitant about attempting the second exam. (In Sweden, students have the option of choosing whether to attempt an exam at the first or subsequent sittings within a set period.)

1.*

ID	Transcript	Comments
1 M	Sh shall we start with number 1/.. unweel/	
2 S	unweel/ unweel/ what is it..is it umm erm	Trailing off
3 A	(sighs)	
4 S	when you . um	
5 M	when you (whisk) off a cover/	
6 A	*uncover*\/\ something/	query
7 M	Yeah	
8 S	uncover/\ <u>unweal it *isn't*/\ . because it's a *car*</u>\	Mispronunciation of unveil
9 A	but then again . un-veal <u>is very funny because</u> . because if you	Pause after because and
10	say unveal\ we should need we need a word that *doesn't*\ start	continues as if S hasn't
11	with *un*\	spoken
12 S	wh<u>at do you need</u>/	Cut off by A
13 A	<u>if you would say</u> uncover\ with with *revealed* half the answer	
14 M	yeah yeah	backchannelling
15 S	yeah yeah	backchannelling
16 A	if you understand what I *mean*\ .. so ahh .. we need to find a b-	Confirmation
17	better word .. and I guess we <u>should</u>	Falling tone
18 S	<u>unweal what</u> sh .. how how are we gonna *explain*.*unweal*.for dem	Spoken fast, high then
		falling tone
19 A	unveal\ . <u>um</u>	Said definitely
20 S	(<u>I mean</u>) we *don't* need to . we can't say (the) word	
21	unweal\ we can say	Cut off
22 A	uh it's it's pronounced *unveald* with a *v* not a *w* .. not *unweald* .	Note the mispronunciation
23	do you have/ .. do you know the difference/	
24 S	v uh	Attempts pron.-laughs
25 M	(laughs)	
26 A	Uh hu ok anyway	laughs
27 S	but how . how are we gonna *explain*/ that\ for the er	Attempts to refocus
		discussion
28 A	well uncovered\/\ is one word	Exasperated tone
		Pause in speech
29 M	number 10/	Question/suggestion to
		move onto another word
30 S	number 10/\ I really don't know what to say- but we c can *start*	
31	wit ( ) quite easy to explain *power*\/	
32 M	power here\	
33 A	what kind of power/\ is/ it\	
34 M	engine . power perhaps/ . or something like that/ ( )	
35 S	p power mm power wh if you had a mootor/\ den you den you	
36	have\ . where energy *started*/\ and then you can explain how\ .	
37	then you can make\ . ( ) dey they will understand/\	
38 M	I'll see/ .. where this is in the text/	
		Pause while they look in
39 S	( ) unveal/\	the text

*Note: See Appendix for key to transcripts.

40	M	uh yea I think I have it	
41	A	um unveal p . ok (I found power anyway) but there's more than	
42		just the the under*lined* words isn't it\	
43	M	no it's *not*/ them\ .. there are *more* words\ than that\ .. ok and then	
44		they can be taken anywhere . from the text\	
45	A	oh no\	Going quiet
46	S	oh we *got* . so\ (shall) we take this one how how shall we explain	
47		wigor∧	Meaning vigor
48	M	strength/ . maybe/ . or something like that	
49	S	if something is *strength*\ |and . uh it's uh	Attempting to explain
50	A	yeah\	
51	M	strength strength lets use/ that/	Thoughtful then suggesting
52	S	but . *power*∧ is .| *strength* . as well\ |is . that *power*/	querying
53	A	um .. yeah power∧ is strength\	
54	S	it's quite/ <u>de same</u>\	
55	M	<u>(yes but) shall</u> we say the same for ( )	pause
56	A	( ) but anyway∧ . anyway\ um	
57	S	but we can *explain* it\ .. we we can *say* . some sentence so dey	Starts higher
58		can know\ . ( ) in powered . or something and then it's .. but	Trails off
59		shall we take o urban/ orban/ arban/	Trying to pron. urban
60	M	shouldn't couldn't you *say*/ like\ ah that the *engine* has this kind	
61		of strength/ or . something like that\	
62	S	yes b but I I *actually*/ don't/ *know*\ . |when you use *wigour*∧ |and	Starts higher
63		when you use *power*∧ |is it actually∧ the *same word* .| is power∧	
64		<u>some ( )</u>	
65	A	<u>no\ there</u> is a *diff*erence\ I think it's actually ah	Ends with a sigh
66	S	we should have some *explanation* then uh we we can ah . *find*	
67		these words in the text .. and you have .	

The text analyzed (see Example 1) was a recording of three students completing the first part of an information exchange crossword. During this stage, the students were given the opportunity to work in groups with others who had the same crossword-half in order to discuss their words and construct their clues. Although S spoke with a noticeable Bosnian accent, she displayed relatively few noteworthy nonstandard phonological forms, other than "mootor" for *motor* in Line 35 (to rhyme with *scooter* and in line with the Swedish pronunciation of /o/), and the use of /d/ instead of /θ/ in Lines 18, 35, 37, 54, and 57. However, she produced a close approximation to /θ/ in Lines 27, 36, 46, 52, 58, 63, and 66. Because she generally pronounced /θ/ correctly, it is likely that she was acquiring this form and that her variation reflected the notion of variable competence in interlanguage (Ellis, 1990). However, the Swedish for *they, them, the, this,* and *that* all begin with /d/ and have similar forms to the English words (note that /θ/ does not exist in Swedish). Thus S's variation might also have resulted from interference from the Swedish word forms as well as being a pronunciation error. S also had difficulty pronouncing /v/ and said in interview that she could barely distinguish the sound. However, she successfully produced /v/ (with some effort, see Line 24), after A had corrected her. It is interesting to observe that A's attempt to model the correct form for /v/ yielded misinformation because she mispronounced *unveil* as "unveel" (rhyming with *reveal*) and added a /d/ ending (Line 22). In contrast, S showed a nativelike pronunciation of "gonna" (Lines 18 and 27).

In terms of lexicogrammatical features, S showed few major errors, except the form "started" in Line 36 instead of the more appropriate *is created,* and a similar slip with the use of "know" (*understand* would have worked better) in Line 58. In both cases, her intended meaning was quite clear, and there was no interruption to the students' discussion. However, such errors might have put S at a disadvantage if the L2 students had viewed her speech as incomplete Discourse (i.e., as a parody of English), thus serving to reinforce their perception of her as "outside" their Discourse (Gee, 1990, p. 173).

In terms of prosody, S showed good control. In Lines 12, 52, and 59, she used a rising intonation to show a question, whereas in Lines 8, 37, and 54, she used a falling tone to indicate the end of a turn. In Line 18, she used a higher pitch to interrupt A's falling tone and effectively took, or initiated, a turn in the exchange. In Line 8, S displayed several points of control: first, a falling tone to indicate her definite opinion because she was in fact contradicting a misinterpretation by the others of the contextual meaning of *unveil* (here used to mean the first public showing of a prototype rather than the literal *uncover*); second, a rise-fall tone over "isn't"; and, third, emphasis on "car" to highlight and contrast key information in the utterance. Interestingly, although general sentence stress in Swedish is substantially similar to English, S's use of a rise-fall intonation to emphasize a particular word is not common (Håkan Hollqvist, Linköping University, personal communication, November 2000).

Stress and pitch are used in English to differentiate the propositional content in a message hierarchically, with the most important item receiving the most prominent marking (Clennell, 1997). S's intonation demonstrated awareness of this feature. In Line 49, for example, she gave tonic (or nuclear) stress to "strength" as the newsworthy item and placed it at the end of the phrase. (This placement accords also with the systemic functional notion of *Theme* and *Rheme* (Eggins, 1994), whereby the Rheme, generally containing new information, is placed after the Theme.) In Line 52, S placed both "power" and "strength" at the front of the tone group; this marked placement of Theme indicates S's ability to foreground information (McCarthy, 1991). In these ways, S effectively communicated a contrastive query by using prosodic features. Her marking here can be compared with her using neutral tonic stress in Lines 62 and 63, where "vigor" and "power" (the stressed items) are placed in the unmarked newsworthy (or Rheme) position while the (repeated) Theme is *when.*

The pauses S used throughout these lines indicate tone-group boundaries and a certain amount of hesitancy, possibly because she was querying the suggestions of A and M. In accordance with conversation analysis, Burns et al. (1996) show that pauses (particularly between turns, but here, during) may indicate a "dispreferred response" (p. 18). That is, in adjacency pairs, each turn is of a particular type, whereby a speaker's reply is congruent with the first speaker and is either expected (preferred) or in opposition (dispreferred), in which case the reply is often accompanied by a justification or explanation. Thus, in questioning A's and M's proposals, S was actually making a dispreferred response (including pauses) by subtly challenging rather than supporting their ideas with the explanation "I don't actually know…" (Line 62).

S further reinforced her subordinate position in the interaction by explaining hesitantly rather than repositioning herself as the dominant speaker by boldly challenging the validity of A's ideas. In Lines 66 and 67, S suggested the need for a proper explanation because the words could be identified in their context, thus again attempting to introduce contextual information, which had earlier been disregarded (Line 8). In these ways, S showed control over certain discourse strategies, particularly turn taking and topic management (the task being to accurately describe each word). However, the task was not completed successfully owing to A's dominance in the interaction and S's apparent inability to alter this situation.

◈ DISTINGUISHING FEATURES

This study aimed to highlight features of NNS interaction (namely, an L2–L3 interaction) using a functional analysis as well as applying certain aspects of conversation analysis to the transcript to show the power relationships among the participants. It is evident that despite S's attempts to refocus the discussion on the meaning of the words in question (e.g., Lines 12, 18, 27, 46–47, 52, and 62), the other participants did not actively cooperate to construct clues for the crossword task; in effect they marginalized S during the interaction, and she was apparently unable to directly recognize or alter this situation.

Negotiating Knower Status

Although S effectively encouraged interest and perseverance in the task by attempting to focus the discussion, as described in the previous section, and tried to compare results (Lines 52 and 62), her lack of knowledge (in this case, vocabulary) stopped her finding the solution herself, whereas A became sidetracked by a literal interpretation of "unveil" (Line 6). Although A and S used confirmation checks and clarification requests, which are collaborative communication strategies, these strategies did not work collaboratively here because A ignored S's input. A's dominance in this text was evident in her controlling the topic (Line 9), ignoring S's comment (Line 13), answering S's question as "knower" (see Burns et al., 1996, p. 15), and, in particular, in her questioning S's pronunciation (Line 22). On this occasion, the use of a statement followed by a question with no attempt at mitigation signalled superiority rather than conventional politeness. This type of questioning further situated A as the dominant knower in this exchange (i.e., knower and user of the dominant Discourse), with S unable to reposition herself. At this point, through using specific discourse skills (e.g., ignoring A's blunt question and asking A to refocus on the task), S might have become the knower and a more powerful participant in the conversation. S did attempt to return to the topic (Line 27), but A's exasperated tone and pause in speech clearly signalled the end of the discussion about that word, and they moved on to the next item (Number 10).

Topic Control and Speaker Status

In terms of topic, S was unable to bring up the contextual information about the car in Line 8 because A ignored her comment. In fact, A talked over S's contribution and continued with her own incorrect interpretation. Interestingly, when S suggested moving on to "urban" (another word and a new topic), she was again ignored (Lines

59–60) as M continued the discussion about the previous words. This type of behavior was likely linked to the students' mutual perceptions of status (including the status accorded to the particular Discourse) and probably influenced the extent to which the students listened to each other and interacted (see Nemetz Robinson, 1985). Pierce (1995) suggests that the decision of whether or how to interact is quite possibly related to the power between interlocutors and that the ability to claim the right to speak should be considered an integral part of any notion of communicative competence. Because communication was evidently ineffective on this particular occasion, awareness-raising in socializing language and skills, together with training in communication strategies, would have helped S deal more adequately with exclusion in group work.

◈ PRACTICAL IDEAS

Because a Discourse is acquired rather than learned (Gee, 1990), students need to be able to compensate for their varying levels of Discourse competence. Discussions in class should aim to provide students with what Gee calls "mushfake" Discourse (p. 159), by which Gee means "partial acquisition coupled with meta-knowledge and strategies to 'make do'" (p. 159). At the same time, they need to develop appropriate strategies to improve their self-confidence so that they can experience positive outcomes in "gatekeeping encounters" (Fairclough, 1989, p. 47), such as job interviews or information exchanges where the powerful participants have differing cultural and linguistic backgrounds from the nonpowerful. Judging from the above analysis, students like S would benefit from Gee's mushfake Discourse.

Below, I give some practical ideas about how to raise learners' awareness of the issues involved as well as how to introduce the language and strategies needed to cope with these kinds of unequal power interactions.

Collect a Sample of Student Spoken Interaction

From analyzing a recorded interaction, students can become aware of how language use influences personal interactions. Select a suitable language teaching task for your recording. A simple information exchange task may yield a rich supply of conversational interactions and discourse modifications for analysis. Such a task would also have a clear beginning and end; thus, the complete transcript could yield useful material for a systemic functional analysis of genre and register (see, e.g., Burns et al., 1996). Use a male-female pair for your first recording because the voices are much easier to distinguish. Make sure that you reduce the background noise because if other students are nearby, their talk may interfere with your recording.

Make a Transcript

Transcribe the tape and mark any particular intonation or prosodic features you think are important. Pay particular attention to aspects of turn-taking behavior and their intonation patterns. Identify instances of overlapping speech: for example, who takes or yields a turn, who interrupts whom, and what prosodic features are associated with these different turn-taking maneuvers.

Analyze the Recording Using Systemic Functional and Conversation Analysis

Look for noteworthy nonstandard phonological or lexicogrammatical forms. Pay particular attention to the use of prosodic features as well as other communication strategies that may be linked with conversational turn taking. A systemic functional analysis of the transcript can provide precise information about the current state of the learners' interlanguage and the appropriateness of their choice of lexical items or intonation related to the specific language function they wish to fulfill (see, e.g., Eggins, 1994).

Analyze the transcript from an interpersonal (Tenor) perspective (Eggins, 1994, p. 63) because this will clearly identify any ongoing power play and marginalization process. A Tenor analysis will examine the choices of Subject and Finite (initial verb element) in a clause. The Subject element will reveal "who is held responsible," whereas the Finite element serves "to anchor the proposition" (Eggins, 1994, p. 157). The use or absence of modality (e.g., *should, would*) is also important in that it signals a speaker's degree of certainty and obligation or both. Identify and discuss all these features with the students to help them develop the metaknowledge of discourse skills and strategies they require for individual situations such as those as discussed above.

A Textual (Mode) analysis of the transcript will indicate thematically who dominates the interaction. Maynard (1986) points out that an equal contribution of Theme and Rheme between speakers in ordinary conversation indicates a truly equal encounter and that a speaker who constantly inserts new Themes may be "heard as dominant or aggressive" (cited in McCarthy & Carter, 1994, p. 72). The implications of this kind of analysis for NNSs facing marginalization is highly relevant because it may be used both to illustrate marginalization and to provide metaknowledge about conversation management so that students can avoid being dominated (or dominating unintentionally) in this way.

Once you have identified specific communication strategies used in the interaction, have students role-play various taped activities that they have already analyzed or have them act out different social situations they have already encountered or will encounter in the future. The point is for them to practice situating themselves as equal participants in a conversation and encourage them to use effective strategies that will avoid marginalization. This kind of explicit practice of discourse strategies can particularly benefit learners who lack self-confidence or who feel they speak bad English but who, in fact, may display excellent communication strategies. The teacher can point out the skills they do possess, thus encouraging their participation in class. Alternatively, students can be given the recording and asked to make their own analysis, which they can then compare with the teacher's analysis. A valuable discussion could follow from such a comparison, if student numbers permit it.

Identify and Discuss Discourse Strategies

Examine the analysis of your transcript for instances of marginalization and draw your learners' attention to them by highlighting the specific discourse features that create this effect. Students at this point can brainstorm alternative responses (behavioral or verbal), or the teacher can demonstrate new strategies that would enhance the speaker's power in the interaction.

For example, if S had had access to such a strategy when her pronunciation was questioned (Example 1, Line 22), she could have repositioned herself in the interaction either by not complying with A's question or by refocusing the discussion on the actual task. Furthermore, students can be made aware of the different implications that underlie their choice of wording when they make requests or ask questions. This kind of information would be revealed through a textual analysis as discussed above.

For example, using the analysis of the discourse reproduced in Example 1, you could demonstrate to students that when S asked a question and prefacing it with "I don't know," she diminished her power in the interaction (see Line 62), whereas by adopting a bold approach and saying, for example, "Explain what you mean here," not only would she have improved her status in the interaction, but other participants would have been less likely to ignore her. Students need to be supplied with this type of explicit information regarding their conversational behavior and language choices so that they can reposition themselves in interaction and move from a dominated Discourse to that of an equal participant.

◈ CONCLUSION

This chapter has examined the effect of lexical choice and discourse competence on the interpersonal relations between NNSs of English when carrying out an academic task. It identified features of language use that lead to the marginalization of certain students and showed how a specific L3 student was unable to participate equally in the task due to her consistent exclusion by the other L2 speakers. The study showed how a combination of actual, though relatively minor, differences in one student's English language ability were perceived as significant by other students in ways that allowed English to be used as a discriminatory tool among them. In an environment where English is increasingly valued and yet is often the third (or more) learned language for many individuals, the risk of creating a social elite based on English mastery becomes considerable (Phillipson, 1992). Because the English language is considered an important subject of study in Sweden, the need to prevent the marginalization of L3 English speakers becomes that much more of a concern. This particular study has demonstrated the importance of analyzing students' spoken discourse in order to provide accurate, specific information for learners on language use, lexical choice, and effective discourse strategies for different communicative situations. The use of systemic functional grammar as an analytical tool may reveal hidden aspects of English use to NNSs and, in particular, may provide further insights into dealing with unequal power relations or language ability.

◈ CONTRIBUTOR

Judy Cohen began this study as part of the requirements for the master of education degree, specializing in TESOL, offered by the University of South Australia, and while employed by Linköping University, Sweden.

◈ APPENDIX: KEY TO TRANSCRIPT

Underlining	Overlapping speech
Italics	Emphasized speech via tone or lengthened vowel(s)
/ placed AFTER word	Rising tone
\ placed AFTER word	Falling tone
| |	Tone group boundaries (only certain lines marked)
. after word	Pause
..	Longer pause
(brackets) parentheses	Unclear speech; "guessed" transcription
( ) empty parentheses	Unintelligible speech; unable to transcribe

PART 3

Interaction as Course Input

CHAPTER 10

Looking at Spoken Interaction Through a New Lens: Researchers and Teachers Working Together

Anne Burns

◈ INTRODUCTION

In this chapter, I reflect on a teacher education project that took spoken interaction outside the classroom as its starting point. In this project, the teacher educators and the teachers with whom I worked focused on developing skills in discourse analysis and applying the insights gained to teaching speaking in adult immigrant ESL classrooms. Our specific focus was on collecting, analyzing, and using natural data from native English speaker (NS) interactions produced in settings outside the classroom. I describe the project briefly, and consider what issues and new directions emerged, as well as what further work needs to be undertaken. I draw this discussion together by offering practical suggestions for teacher educators wishing to adopt a similar approach.

◈ CONTEXT

My role at the time of the project was professional development coordinator in the National Centre for English Language Teaching and Research (NCELTR). The Centre is funded by the Federal Department of Immigration and Multicultural Affairs (DIMA) to undertake research and teacher education nationally for the Adult Migrant English Program (AMEP), a settlement English program for new immigrants to Australia.[1]

One of the challenges facing researchers at NCELTR was to conduct research in such a way that teachers in the AMEP felt involved in its research areas, processes, and findings, and would see the potential for classroom applications (Brindley, 1990; Burns, 1999; Burton, 1998a). As a teacher educator, I was also interested in how collaborative involvement with teachers in research could contribute to professional

---

[1] Since the beginning of 2000, the Centre has been reconfigured as the AMEP Research Centre, involving a consortium of NCELTR at Macquarie University, Sydney, and the Institute for Education at La Trobe University, Melbourne.

growth and strengthen teaching practice (Brindley, 1991). My interest was in line with the research agenda operating in the Centre, namely, that research and practice should be integrated so that research could "support and be supported by professional development and materials development" (Brindley, 1990, p. 10). Brindley summarized the rationale for the Centre's approach in terms of the influence of three factors: (a) the move to learner-centered education and decentralized curriculum planning; (b) the increasing professionalization of AMEP teachers; and (c) the increasing influence of research on AMEP policy formation.

To try to meet these challenges, we designed the project so that the teachers and academics involved became joint researchers. We each took different but complementary roles in that our respective expertise as classroom practitioners and academic researchers merged and shifted according to our goals at different phases of the project (see Hammond, 1989).

The Spoken Discourse Project, as the program came to be known, continued from 1990 to 1993. Approximately 16 AMEP teachers from New South Wales and 7 from South Australia participated at different phases of the project during the 3 years. In addition, three academic researchers from NCELTR advised and supported me in my role as project coordinator. Other Sydney-based researchers with expertise in the area of discourse analysis and spoken English also delivered workshops and provided input to data analysis (see Burns, Joyce, & Gollin, 1996).[2]

We incorporated three dimensions of research progressively into the project as it unfolded. The first two occurred simultaneously during 1990–1991 as project meetings were held monthly in each state; the third was a follow-up phase between 1992 and 1993.

Phase 1: Theoretical Research and Literature Reviews

In this first phase, the project organizers aimed to develop participants' knowledge about discourse analysis through theoretical input. The teachers read selected texts (Atkinson & Heritage, 1984; Cook, 1989; Hammond, 1990; Thomas, 1983) and attended three workshops held at various times over the first year at NCELTR. During this phase, various speakers with specialist knowledge (Suzanne Eggins, Diana Slade, Ken Willing, Chris Candlin, and Clare Painter) presented a range of approaches to discourse analysis, and participants had opportunities to practice applying these approaches to samples of spoken text (see Burns, 2001, for a detailed overview of these various approaches). During this phase, a number of theoretical principles and assumptions were drawn out as underpinnings for the project:

- Speech is socially and culturally motivated and is highly sensitive to context.

- Speech occurs through extended forms of discourse or *text,* and grammatical patterns of language are mediated by the topic or setting (*Field*), relationships between speakers (*Tenor*) and the channel of communication and distance in time and space from events (*Mode*).

---

[2] Funding for the project was provided through the DIMA as part of the annual NCELTR Special Project Program for the AMEP (1990–1992).

- Speech can be categorized in two major forms of functional interaction: interactional (or interpersonal) and transactional (or pragmatic). *Interactional* genres focus primarily on creating and maintaining interpersonal social relationships (e.g., casual conversation). *Transactional* genres focus primarily on achieving pragmatic outcomes (e.g., service encounters).

- Speech genres that have their own overall structure and purpose (e.g., narrative, personal recount, service encounter, interview) can be identified.

- Social relationships and context are significant in spoken interactions and interact with the speech roles speakers adopt, the turn-by-turn linguistic choices they make, and the discourse strategies they use.

Phase 2: Ethnographically Oriented Research

In this second phase, we collected and analyzed samples of spoken discourse from outside the classroom. Despite the different focus, we were able to interrelate what we did with the first phase of the project.

Soon after the first of the theoretical workshops described above, the teachers began collecting samples of natural spoken language (issues relating to natural or authentic data and the classroom context are taken up later). The research orientation we took during this phase was ethnographic, based on the idea that to teach communicatively, language professionals need to be strongly aware of how spoken language is used in a variety of natural settings, and that to develop this awareness, they will need to observe and analyze actual language use closely.

Our purpose in this phase was to begin assembling a database of spoken texts that could be analyzed from different discourse perspectives and function as a potential source for classroom activities.

Phase 3: Action Research

In the third phase, conducted in 1991–1992, we adopted a collaborative action research approach (Burns, 1999; Kemmis & McTaggart, 1988), which focused on applying what we learned in the first two phases to classroom practice. Put simply, action research involves addressing a practical teaching issue or problem, applying a plan of action to implement change, and observing and reflecting on the results of the action through systematic data collection and analysis (see Burns, 1999, for an extensive discussion of action research). Having collected and analyzed their discourse samples, the teachers experimented with activities that could be used in the classroom. They monitored the use of these activities, looking especially at how they could be used to extend their students' understanding of discourse features, and discussed the activities they had developed during workshop discussions, which again were held approximately monthly in each of the participating states.

◈ DESCRIPTION

The immediate period before the early 1990s, when the project began, was a time of considerable and growing interest in classroom discourse. Breen (1985) argued convincingly that the classroom was a social context with its own particular register.

His view was reflected in the publication of several studies outlining developments in classroom observation and investigating features of classroom interaction and behavior (e.g., Allwright, 1988; Chaudron, 1988; van Lier, 1988). Other writers (e.g., Edmondson & House, 1981; Sinclair & Brazil, 1982) had already provided useful procedures and categories for analyzing classroom language. Clearly, this trend offered teacher educators a major route for engaging teachers in recording classroom interaction to gain detailed insights into classroom discourse. This was the direction taken in the very early stages of the project before my direct involvement in it: Teachers were asked to record their classroom interactions with the intention that these would be used for analysis.

Example 1 is taken from one of the early recordings. The teacher's workplace class, located in a steel factory, consisted of a group of mostly southeast Asian male process workers, all within 3 years of arriving in Australia. The workers were intermediate-level speakers of English and, conscious that they were underemployed, were attending the course to improve their interaction in the workplace and their understanding of Australian English. Having discussed their learning needs with them, the teacher focused on listening and speaking development. The recorded lesson derived from a video extract (from *Hello Australia*; Department of Immigration and Ethnic Affairs, 1986), the topic of which was the Melbourne Cup, a major, national horse-racing event in which many Australians take a high level of interest and join in workplace sweepstakes. From the video, the teacher had picked out various expressions listed in the order in which they were heard (see Example 1). Each expression was then replayed several times and analyzed for four elements:

- words and meaning, noting structure and context
- pronunciation
- sentence stress
- intonation and related attitude, feeling or meaning

1. *

(*Video plays*)
S1: Got your $2 ready, Bronwyn?
S2: Here's hoping
T: What is she doing?
S: She sell ticket
S: She pick up the ticket
T: Uh-uh
S: and...ah...she hope to win
T: ah...good...she's hoping to win, isn't she?
     She's hoping to win
     How many parts [syllables] are there?
SS: Three...four
T: You don't have to worry about that
S: Four
T: OK, where's the stress?
SS: Here...hope...number three hoping...
T: Have a listen again

---

*Note: See Appendix for key to transcripts.

(Video is replayed)
SS: Here...hope
T: This is stronger, isn't it?
S: Yeah
T: Here's hoping. Here's hoping
      Where does her voice go up?
SS: Here...up...

(Video replayed and students repeat phrase)
T: Here's hoping. In fact she almost says this one, doesn't she?
      Here's hoping
SS: Here's hoping
T: Make your voice go up a little at this point.
      See how we go. Try again

(Short drill develops)

(from *Hello Australia*; Department of Immigration and Ethnic Affairs, 1986, p. 42) Reprinted with permission from National Centre for English Language Teaching and Research (NCELTR).

We felt that examples such as this proved problematic as a focus for the research. For a start, they highlighted the initiation–response–feedback (IRF) patterns (Sinclair & Coulthard, 1975) of traditional classroom interaction and focused attention on mechanical aspects of teaching such as drills and pronunciation practice, as well as the teacher-centered nature of the interaction. Although the teachers had expressed interest in the learner-centered and communicative pedagogies espoused by the AMEP (e.g., Nunan, 1988), the tasks seemed to draw mainly on *pedagogic* materials developed specifically for the classroom, such as the video materials used in the lesson extract, rather than *authentic* text samples that exist in their own right outside the classroom. Given that teachers were volunteering their time in workshops as well as undertaking data collection, we felt that it would be difficult to dwell on features of classroom interaction that appeared to criticize the teachers' classroom practices.

Such concerns no doubt seem overly cautious and sensitive now. However, the tremendous interest in reflective practice that characterized second language (L2) teacher development in the 1990s (e.g., Edge & Richards, 1993; Gebhard & Oprandy, 1999; Nunan & Lamb, 1996; Richards & Lockhart, 1994) was still then in its infancy and relatively unfamiliar in most teacher education settings. At the beginning of the 21st century, given these publications, teachers would probably find critically analyzing interactional patterns in their classrooms much more acceptable.

Also, in the early 1990s, because several of the researchers had previously been involved in a national literacy project (Hammond, Burns, Joyce, Gerot, & Brosnan, 1992), they were interested in natural spoken and written texts that existed outside the classroom. Furthermore, as many of the teachers were mainly interested in learners' everyday communication needs, we all felt we needed to change direction to collecting and transcribing nonclassroom discourse from which we could learn more about the features of natural speech. By the end of the project, we had collected 38 samples of spoken texts taken from a range of interactional and transactional settings including

- social or interpersonal interactions (e.g., conversations between family, friends, and acquaintances)

- service encounters (e.g., telephone interactions to obtain information or to make and confirm appointments)

- vocational interactions (e.g., workplace or study discussions)

As a result, we were able to concentrate more specifically on developing new approaches to classroom interaction and discourse-related tasks. We became more aware of the function and structure of natural nonclassroom spoken discourse and learned more about textual and linguistic features. Inevitably, however, this change of direction raised its own problems and challenges. I will discuss three of the major issues we needed to address as the project progressed:

1. collecting and transcribing data

2. developing a framework for analysis

3. using natural data with learners

I will take up some of the ways in which we tackled these problems in the Practical Ideas section of this chapter.

Collecting and Transcribing Data

As the project participants soon discovered, recording and transcribing spoken data is time-consuming and often problematic. One immediate issue was the need to inform people, for ethical reasons, that they were being recorded, thereby possibly influencing the language they used as a result. The teachers also reported that the presence of the recording equipment intimidated some speakers and prevented them from speaking naturally (this phenomenon is well known in ethnographic research; Labov, 1972, refers to it as *the observer's paradox*). Some speakers questioned the teachers' requests to record them, wondering why their conversations could possibly be of interest. Several of our workshop discussions revolved around the issue of the objectivity and authenticity of the data; several participants found the issue questionable. In other words, having been subjected to recording and transcription processes that involve the researcher's own forms of selection and interpretation, to what extent could such data be seen as authentic?

Preparing and setting up recording equipment presented an added task in an already busy teaching program, and the quality of the recordings was also sometimes poor because of background noise or inadequate recording equipment. Having obtained the data, participants were faced with the task of transcribing them. Clearly this was a time-consuming business that depended on the delicacy of the transcription required, so, at this point, it was important to reach agreement about common conventions that would result in usable transcripts for analysis and possibly teaching purposes. In turn, the process of transcription itself focused our attention on the highly contextualized nature of some of the interactions. This resulted in discussion on the best ways to include contextual information, especially as we aimed to use the data with learners.

The overall difficulties of collecting and transcribing natural samples are reflected in the relatively small number of texts (38) collected during the project. These samples were of great interest and provided a basic database for the project, but the question of how representative they could be of different types of interaction was also an issue. Additionally, we could not be sure that the interactions were of the type in which learners themselves might be involved outside the classroom.

Developing a Framework for Analysis

The theoretical approaches presented in the project workshops included genre and register analysis, conversation analysis, pragmatics, and critical discourse theory. We felt it was important to adopt a range of approaches, rather than a single approach, that allowed for analysis at the macrolevel (e.g., genre analysis) as well as at the microlevel of interaction (e.g., conversation analysis). Macrolevel analysis allowed us to highlight

- in which kind of interaction speakers are involved and its social purpose and topic
- how language varies in different situations according to the topic, the relationships among speakers, and the channel of communication
- how the interaction unfolds from stage to stage and the kind of grammar and vocabulary that can be anticipated by the topic

Microlevel analysis enabled us to consider conversational features, such as

- how people open and close interactions
- how turns are negotiated and what implicit rules underlie turn-taking behavior
- how listeners mark and acknowledge the interactive development of the interaction
- what strategies are used to repair and clarify meaning
- what kinds of responses can be anticipated in turn-by-turn exchanges

As the project unfolded and we became more familiar with these theoretical ideas and how we could apply them to the spoken samples we had collected, we developed an overall framework for teachers to use as a reference point to guide their teaching and the aims they had for various learning tasks (see Practical Ideas). A major advantage of working with the samples we had collected was that we could focus on the regularities and patterns we saw emerging from the data, rather than on grammatical rules or prescriptions.

Using Natural Data With Learners

Lively discussion arose throughout the project about whether and how to use natural data samples with learners. Some participants felt that working with natural speech samples was too difficult for most learners. Others felt that expecting learners to use NS samples as the basis for language learning was unrealistic because transcribed raw data look too fragmented and disorganized. The question of how to amend or simplify transcripts for some learners permeated these discussions, as well as some of the decisions teachers made about classroom tasks. Others argued that natural data brought into the classroom could no longer be considered authentic because they then became decontextualized and static.

Against these arguments, others took the view that to withhold insights about spoken language choices and use that could be gained from working with natural data was disempowering for learners. This restriction denied them the opportunity not only of developing greater awareness about the grammatical features of spoken language and how it differs from written language, but also of experiencing how cultural understandings are embedded in spoken interactions, and observing what strategies NSs use to handle unpredictability and negotiate meaning.

So far I have focused on the thinking and the processes that accompanied and characterized a project that took place in the early 1990s. What impact has this project had more generally in the AMEP, and where has it led me as a teacher educator? Over the past decade, the project with its underpinnings in discourse analysis has complemented further AMEP curriculum development, professional development, research, and materials publication. In the early 1990s, the project was not isolated from other developments occurring in the AMEP. A discourse-based approach, which takes (extended) text samples that are meaningful in their contexts of use (see Burns & Seidlhofer, 2002) as the basis for language analysis and learning, became shortly afterwards the major theoretical base for a curriculum framework, The Certificates in Spoken and Written English, adopted nationally by the AMEP from 1993. This framework took language competencies needed for the production of various written and spoken text types as its starting point. Teachers select social contexts or topics related to their learners' needs and identify the text types associated with them. They then develop their own syllabus specifications—tasks, learning strategies, materials, teaching methods and techniques—to address different aspects of the text types. Learners are assessed on various criteria that indicate their ability to produce the text types (see Burns & McPherson, 2001, for an example of the curriculum in classroom use; Feez, 1998, for an extended discussion of text-based syllabus design).

As a researcher and teacher educator working with the AMEP, I have been greatly influenced by the notions of *sustainability* and *collaboration* between researchers and teachers in much of my subsequent work (see the Teachers' Voices Series published by NCELTR, 1995–2001). In my thinking about teacher education, I have come to see these factors as essential if research processes and findings are to have any real impact on classroom practice—and this applies not just to a specific project such as the Spoken Discourse Project, but to many other related professional development processes and how they combine to form an integrated professional development program (see Burton, 1998c). Sustainability and collaboration need to be facilitated in practical and professional ways.

In my situation, the practical ways have been through

- continuing AMEP Special Project research funding from the Australian Commonwealth Government

- system-level support for teachers to move in and out of action research projects through a sustained research program

- managerial involvement from the teachers' organizations through the provision of local support and coordination (see Burns, 2000, for further discussion)

Professional ways have included

- the production of professional development publications disseminating research findings in forms accessible to teachers (e.g., Burns et al., 1996; Burns & de Silva Joyce, 1997; Burns & Gardner, 1997)

- production of teaching materials and videos (e.g., de Silva Joyce & Hilton, 1999)

- continuing seminars and workshops where teachers bring along for analysis their own discourse samples or use those collected in previous projects (e.g., Burns & de Silva Joyce, 2000)

- further action research projects taking up and developing the findings of the original Spoken Discourse project (e.g., in the area of casual conversation, de Silva Joyce, 2000; McKay, Bowyer, & Commins, 2000)

- conference presentations, often with teacher colleagues discussing their action research

Such activities have carried forward the processes and findings of the project explicitly, but my assumption is that there have also been more implicit effects, in that AMEP teachers have been offered opportunities for professional growth and networking as both researchers and consumers of this research.

The overall point here—one that has had a major impact on me as a researcher and teacher educator—is that a program of integrated and networked professional processes in which teachers can take active research roles as well as teaching roles is ultimately more likely to be a catalyst for change and have a lasting influence than a smorgasbord of isolated or loosely related information-based sessions.

◈ DISTINGUISHING FEATURES

Different Starting Points for Teaching

McCarthy and Carter (1994) argue that "the moment one starts to think of language as discourse, the entire landscape changes, usually forever" (p. 201). This sentiment is one that captures my own responses to the project as well as those of many of the participants (cf. Gollin, 1994). Seeing the raw material of language learning from the point of view of how language is used in different social contexts seriously challenged my thinking and that of my coresearchers about how to assist our learners to develop speaking skills that better reflected their lives outside the classroom. It moved us to think beyond conventionally used approaches—such as the presentation and practice of particular language structures or speech acts, the learning of isolated items of vocabulary, or the selection of series of communicative tasks—to consider different starting points for teaching. These involved asking questions such as

- How can different texts (spoken and written) be categorized?

- What social and cultural purposes do they have?

- What impact does the situational context have on language roles, structures, and patterns?

- How are spoken texts constructed by speakers?

- How do speakers negotiate spoken interactions?

- What are some of the characteristic features of spoken grammar, and how do they differ from the grammar of written texts?

- What aspects of spoken language use are highlighted that do not conform to the conventionally accepted descriptions often used in language teaching?

In the course of wrestling with these questions, it was necessary to come to terms with some uncomfortable realizations. Although many of us had spent years as language teachers, teacher educators, and researchers, clearly our knowledge about natural spoken discourse was rudimentary. With the greater insights we had gained while grappling with spoken data analysis, many of us were led to reevaluate our teaching practice, especially in relation to teaching structure and grammar. Taking language (What is the nature of spoken discourse?), rather than methods (What classroom activities shall we use?) as a starting point provided—as one teacher put it—"a new lens" through which to focus on our learners' language needs.

This perspective gave us a way to link their learning needs to different social contexts in which they may wish to interact; to clarify what text types, grammatical structures, vocabulary, and discourse strategies could be required in such contexts; and to analyze the language the learners themselves produced in order to diagnose further needs. Using this perspective, we could then attempt to design integrated classroom tasks with a view to supporting and developing spoken language knowledge and skills.

Authentic Use of Language in the Classroom

One of our major aims in this project was to introduce authentic discourse samples into the classroom. Taking this perspective meant deliberately moving away from the introspected or scripted dialogues very common in current classroom textbooks and other materials. Our new insights enabled us to evaluate more critically the differences between textbook dialogues—usually idealized, neat, symmetrical, and polite interactions, focused on practicing specific syntactical structures—and natural interactions—usually unpredictable; asymmetrical in terms of power and ideology; often competitive rather than cooperative; with syntactical structures embedded in cultural and situational contexts; and also fragmented, with incomplete utterances, ellipsis, clarification checks, follow-up moves, and so on.

Although our intentions in the project were to introduce greater spoken-language authenticity into the classroom, the question of how authentic such data can be deserves consideration. I have already referred to the questions that arise about the naturalness of data that is collected when speakers are aware of the processes of video- or audiotaping. Others factors also intervene.

Transforming spoken data into written text poses its own challenge to authenticity. Problems of reliability (the transcriber is removed from the original context and sources of the data) as well as validity (the transcribed information is a product of the transcriber's own interpretations and decisions—some data are highlighted and others are lost) all affect the final written version (cf. Riggenbach, 1999). Transcribed data cannot reflect the subtle meanings exchanged among speakers through intonational features, such as changes in pitch and volume, or through facial expressions, gestures or posture (cf. Burns & Seidlhofer, 2002). Presenting the accompanying video- or audiotapes in the classroom may be able to compensate for some of these transcription limitations (given a reasonable quality of recording and the level of the learner) and should, in my view, be used whenever possible to strengthen the authenticity of the data presented to learners. It is important to realize, however, that classroom representations of authentic discourse will always rely to a greater or lesser extent on the researcher's interpretations.

A further point needs to be raised here in relation to classroom discourse. As I have already explained, our project moved away from collecting the discourse of classroom interactions. However, classroom discourse is, of course, authentic discourse in its own right. As with the discourse of other social contexts, it has its own generic structures, lexical and grammatical features and patterns of usage, reflecting the (power and status) relationships among teachers and learners, and learners and learners, and the modes of communication (spoken, written, audio-/videotaped, computer-mediated) incorporated in its interactional processes. In this project, classroom interaction was not explored in depth (although see, e.g., Kebir, 1994, on the classroom strategies used by her postbeginning learners to negotiate information gap tasks), though the teachers collected some classroom interaction data during the trialing of the activities. Instead, in this phase, workshop discussion focused on the kind of discourse-based activities teachers could use. Further limitations lay in the extent to which classroom data based on the trialing of discourse-based teaching activities by the project teachers were systematically collected in the action research phase, as this phase focused more on workshop discussion of the kind of activities teachers had used, or could use. In a future project of this nature, it would be very interesting to explore in much greater detail the nature of classroom interaction when using a discourse-based approach (indeed, we need to know much more about what such an approach may be like), or to trial the use of classroom data with learners as a way of assisting them to develop autonomous language awareness skills (see van Lier, 1996).

◈ PRACTICAL IDEAS

Some of the suggestions presented in this section arise from the issues and questions that the participants faced in the project. Others are drawn from aspects of the subsequent thinking and professional development work I referred to earlier. To some extent, they are also a personal wish list—what I wish I had known then that I know now. The suggestions, based on my own experience of working with language teachers over time, are made from the perspective of the teacher educator who wishes to work with teachers to enhance awareness of spoken discourse.

Consider Working With Spoken Data

Spoken data collection and transcription take considerable time and effort. Pooling your time and resources with other teacher educators and teachers is a valuable way to build up a usable collection of texts (see Burns et al., 1996, for extended discussion on spoken data collection and transcription).

Collecting Spoken Data

- Ensure that participants request speakers' permission to video- or audio-tape them (you may also need to check your organization's ethical guidelines on conducting research). The effects of what is often called *the observer's paradox* can be reduced by letting speakers get used to the presence of recording equipment or informing them that they will be recorded only from time to time. They can also be assured that their anonymity will be respected (for an example of a simple information and consent form, see Burns, 1999, p. 74).

- Emphasize the importance of collecting verbatim spoken data, that is, what is actually said rather than what participants assume is said in a particular context. This should be done either by using recording equipment or alternatively closely shadowing (i.e., unobtrusively observing and listening to) speakers and recording exact samples of their speech.

- Encourage participants to include contextual information at the time of recording: for example, to note the social context, the participants and their relationships, the tasks they are performing, and related written or multimedia texts or symbols. If possible, interview speakers for their own responses to these aspects to help clarify any misinterpretations.

- Remind participants of the advantages of recording in quiet surroundings. Although this is not always possible, it is a distinct advantage to have a collection of relatively clear recordings (for possible use in the classroom) rather than ones affected by background noise.

- Develop with participants some practical guidelines for recording (e.g., test equipment beforehand; keep a supply of spare tapes; place the microphone as close as possible to speakers; remember to turn on the recorder).

Transcribing Spoken Data

- Agree with participants early in the professional development process on conventions to be used for transcription (e.g., names or initials of speakers, "..." to indicate gaps in conversation, "[" for overlapping speech).

- Draw attention to the fact that the (time-consuming) transcription process can be used to develop initial awareness of spoken data features, and encourage participants to note and discuss their immediate observations.

- Encourage participants to envisage ways that recordings and transcripts can be used for classroom activities as they transcribe their data.

- Include workshop discussions about the advantages and disadvantages of using transcripts with learners.

Analyzing Spoken Data

Analysis requires engaging closely with the data to observe emerging features and patterns. Workshops where teachers can work together to use their own observational and intuitive insights are valuable. However, it is also very useful to help participants develop a working knowledge of some of the major approaches to discourse analysis that have developed from recent research.

- Develop your own set of relevant professional references using print and Internet resources. References that link discourse analysis with pedagogical applications (as in this volume) are becoming much easier to find than they were a decade ago and provide useful pointers both for analyzing texts and developing teaching strategies (see, e.g., Burns, 2001).

- Select some key readings that participants can discuss during workshop sessions. Even better, set up a local reading circle where teachers also exchange relevant theoretical materials they have found helpful in teaching. In my experience, participants prefer a limited number of up-to-date, overview readings, particularly in the initial stages, rather than large amounts that make them feel overloaded. As the research progresses, other readings can be added as required.

- Use theoretical ideas from the readings to develop your own frameworks for analysis. Figure 1 contains a framework developed for the NCELTR Spoken Discourse Project.

- Remember that analysis can be focused at different levels of delicacy from macro to micro—a bit like refocusing a microscope lens to see things in greater detail. Focus in workshops on looking specifically at different aspects of analysis (as in Figure 1) rather than attempting to analyze many features of the text at the same time.

- If possible, invite local or visiting speakers skilled in discourse analysis to address teacher workshops and assist in data analysis. Professional associations (e.g., the local TESOL affiliate), particularly if they are organizing a program of seminars or conferences, may be able to help provide names and contact details.

Consider Using Natural Data With Learners

The question of whether spoken data should be used with learners is an interesting one to discuss as part of a teacher education project on spoken interaction. My own view is that just as we are interested in developing our learners' learning strategies, we can also encourage them to develop language awareness strategies through personal observation and analysis. This is particularly the case for learners at the postbeginning level onwards. Some of the areas that could become possible topics for workshop discussion about the use of authentic data follow. However, in presenting these ideas, I am not necessarily suggesting that authentic data must always, or inevitably, be the best source of classroom material (see Owen, 1993).

- Explore and discuss the notion of a continuum of spoken language awareness starting with beginning learners. Introduce such questions as: Is it true that beginning learners have no awareness of authentic spoken English? What authentic expressions do your beginning learners already know? Can you collect examples from your learners of contexts where they use these expressions? Encourage participants to explore these ideas in the classroom.

1. Transcribe the Recording.
   - Give the text a title.
   - Leave a line between each speaker, and number lines for easy reference.
   - Label each speaker using letters, first names or positions (e.g. A, Jo).
   - Insert contextual information.
   - Retain the wording of the discourse as accurately as possible.

2. Analyze the Transcript.
   - Complete a general analysis on a page facing the transcript.
   - Use the following headings to complete the general analysis:
     (a) Background to the text:
        - Identify when, how, and why the text was produced.
        - Include relevant social and cultural information.
     (b) General comments:
        - Make relevant general comments that will help students.
        - Understand overall features of the text.
     (c) Type of interaction:
        - Identify whether the text is transactional or interactional.

3. Analyze the Discourse and Linguistic Features of the Text.
   - Select the focus of the analysis from the following areas:
     (a) Generic structure analysis:
        - Identify the social purpose of the text.
        - Label the stages of the text with functional labels.
        - Indicate which stages are obligatory and which are optional.
     (b) Register analysis:
        - Identify the field (topic) of the text.
        - Identify the tenor (speakers' interpersonal relationships).
        - Identify the mode (channel of communication).
     (c) Conversation analysis:
        - Identify significant adjacency pairs (e.g., question-answer).
        - Analyze turn-taking patterns and related discourse signals, and markers.
        - Analyze turn types and related strategies.
     (d) Pragmatic analysis:
        - Identify speech functions.
        - Analyze how speakers conform to conversational strategies.
        - Analyze any cross-cultural aspects that may be significant.
     (e) Critical discourse analysis:
        - Identify any significant aspects of the text in terms of ideology or social power (e.g., bureaucratic gatekeeping)

4. Implications for Teaching
   - Identify significant teaching points arising from the analysis.

FIGURE 1. Framework for Discourse Analysis (Based on Burns et al., 1996, pp. 64–67) Reprinted with permission from National Centre for English Language Teaching and Research (NCELTR).

- Consider why and how learners could be gradually exposed to authentic data. Think about the range of texts that could be used in this process (e.g., interim texts, such as dialogues from plays, soap operas, and so on, that are tidier and less fragmented than many natural samples; or semi-scripted texts that are simplified and planned by the speakers).

- Discuss the profiles (e.g., level, age, language background, goals) of the learners taught by the participants and develop a set of criteria for introducing authentic data to these different groups of learners.

- Consider the type of program in which learners are being taught and the opportunities within the program to include authentic data: for example,

  — the program's aims and objectives (if any) for spoken language development

  — the different types of spoken texts that could be introduced (interactional/transactional)

  — the aspects of spoken language to be focused on in class

  — the nature of the tasks and methods used to teach spoken language

- Encourage teachers to work in groups or pairs to develop classroom texts modeled on real data. This process can include simplifying or modifying aspects of the data (e.g., ellipsis, complex or technical vocabulary).

- Work together to develop a teaching bank of authentic texts that all participants can use. If possible, include ideas for teaching that have already been trialed by participants.

- Workshop and trial activities that encourage learners, especially at more advanced levels, to become ethnographers of spoken interactions through out-of-class activities and projects (see Clennell, 1999a; Riggenbach, 1999, for some excellent ideas).

◈ CONCLUSION

During the 1990s, the analysis of natural spoken discourse became something of a hot topic in research (e.g., Biber, Conrad, & Reppen, 1998; Cook, 1989; McCarthy, 1991; McCarthy & Carter, 1994). One interesting aspect of this research is that it has begun to address applications of a discourse-based perspective of language to language teaching.

In this chapter, I have tried to give a sense of how my own interest in and knowledge about discourse analysis have developed as a result of being a researcher and teacher educator working closely with teachers. In particular, I have attempted to explore ways in which developments in knowledge and understanding of spoken discourse analysis can be linked to teaching practice through action research and to offer practical suggestions for others who may wish to follow suit.

Research and practice in this area still have a long way to go. As Carter (1997) points out, "Such work is in its infancy and more than any other domain demands a new paradigm for applied linguistics research in which descriptive linguist, materials writer and classroom teacher work together in a process of refinement" (p. 9). My own sense is that there is a growing interest among many language teachers in learning more about natural spoken (and written) data and their potential use in the classroom. The arguments for attempting to draw pedagogically on natural data are increasing, reflected through a general move in this direction in some of the more recent literature on English language teaching. However, there is still a general paucity of material available to teachers. In the meantime, teacher education opportunities, such as those I have outlined here, that focus on collecting, transcribing, and analyzing spoken discourse can provide teachers with relevant and practically oriented ways of learning more about this approach to teaching spoken interaction.

◈ CONTRIBUTOR

Anne Burns is associate professor in the Department of Linguistics, associate director of the National Centre for English Language Teaching and Research (NCELTR), and dean of the Division of Linguistics and Psychology at Macquarie University, in Sydney, Australia. She has published extensively on action research, spoken discourse, and literacy. Her recent books include *Collaborative Action Research for English Language Teachers* (Cambridge University Press, 1999) and *Analysing English in a Global Context* (edited with Coffin; Routledge, 2001).

◈ APPENDIX: KEY TO TRANSCRIPT

T = Teacher
S = unidentified student
SS = students speaking simultaneously

CHAPTER 11

Constructing English as a Foreign Language Curriculum From Learner Discourse

Jill Burton and Yoopayao Daroon

◈ INTRODUCTION

Communication in a foreign language is complex, influenced by factors such as prior knowledge and experiences and motivation to communicate, as well as by the communicative context or situation. From an EFL teaching perspective, creating favorable learning circumstances is not only essential but challenging. When learners can use contextual clues to work out meaning, such as their learning environment and existing knowledge of the target language, acquisition is generally enhanced (Krashen, 1982; Long, 1983b; Pica, 1994a, 1994b).

Research now suggests that teacher and learner studies of their own interaction (e.g., Burton & Rusek, 1994; Carter & McCarthy, 1997; Riggenbach, 1999), and teachers' use of pedagogical questions (e.g., Banbrook & Skehan, 1989; Tsui, 1995) and other scaffolding devices (e.g., Bruner, 1984; Iwashita, 1999; Mackay, 1995; Mercer, 1994; Wells, 1981) encourage learning and effective classroom interaction. Furthermore, courses that use students' knowledge, experiences, and needs can provide naturally motivating input for language learning activities (Nunan, 1988; Tarone & Yule, 1989; van Lier, 1996; West, 1994).

This chapter documents how we, a Thai teacher of EFL and a native-English-speaking (NS) teacher educator, worked with a group of EFL learners. Yoopayao aimed to have her students explain in English to Jill, who had no technical knowledge of their field of study, what they were learning as food science students. Our study suggests that tasks requiring language learners to reflect on, however indirectly, the strategies they use to communicate can be an effective means of developing language awareness and discourse competence. Vygotsky (1962) points out that as learners progress, they can increasingly reflect on their discourse ability and use reflection as a learning tool in different situations. We were interested, therefore, to initiate language teaching processes that encouraged learners to learn from their own language use. We believed that the process of classroom interaction itself could generate such learning opportunities more naturally and effectively than specially designed teaching material. Our belief is supported by language curriculum research, which suggests that such task-based learning approaches can create genuine purposes for language use and acquisition (Burton, 1998b; Long & Crookes, 1992; McCarthy & Carter, 1994; van Lier, 1996; Willis, 1996, 1998).

We draw here on data from one unit of work that centered on a video recording of an extended encounter between the Thai EFL students in Yoopayao's class and Jill as the NS. We show how task-based curriculum planning led into the interaction and was exploited afterwards in classroom activities.

◈ CONTEXT

The group of adult EFL students with whom we worked were studying in an English for specific purposes (ESP) program at Rajamangala Institute of Technology (RIT), on its Lampang campus, in northern Thailand. RIT is a national education and research institute with many regional campuses. The Lampang Campus offers two degree programs: a vocational diploma and a bachelor's degree in various fields of vocational study, including food technology. The philosophy of RIT is to develop qualified personnel to utilize, apply, and develop technology for the socioeconomic development of Thailand. English is therefore a necessity for RIT students in their education and careers.

Unfortunately, most RIT students do not really believe they need English, and this increases the challenge of teaching English in this environment. A typical RIT student only encounters English once or twice a week in the language classroom, or about 48 hours over 6 months. The environment, therefore, is one that creates little or no motivation to learn a new language. Students typically have studied English for 8 years before coming to RIT and feel limited by their inability, feel intimidated by English, or are simply uninterested. RIT students' abilities in English in the four macroskills range from very low—some students are unable to read even simple English—to exceptionally advanced.

Preparation

Yoopayao prepared the 15 nonnative-English-speaking (NNS) preintermediate students, enrolled in the bachelor degree program in food science and technology, and aged 19–23 years, for Jill's visit as follows:

- A NNS specialist teacher who had graduated abroad was invited to describe the work of her department in English. Her talk was videotaped.

- The students viewed and analyzed the videotape of this talk as an example of how they could introduce a visitor to their own department in English.

- Each student then prepared presentations in which they were required to role-play telling a visitor in English what was happening in each section of the food laboratory. Their performances were videotaped and used for classroom discussion. As they had not previously spoken English with anyone other than Yoopayao, the role plays and their analyses were important preparation for Jill's visit.

◈ DESCRIPTION

In the videotaped communicative episodes, the students explained food processes, equipment, and technical concepts in English to Jill. Each episode gave the EFL learners the opportunity of a genuine conversation with a NS, and Yoopayao as their

Table 1. Numbers of Turns Generated by the Ns and Nnss

Episode settings	Number of turns generated by the NS	Number of turns generated by the NNSs
1. At the round table	23	28
2. Fish fermentation	9	11
3. In the bakery	13	19
4. Bread slicer	8	10
5. Sausage maker	26	26
6. Emulsifier	6	9
7. Vacuum seal	13	15
8. Ice cream maker	12	12
9. Viscosity meter	8	9
10. Incubation	11	11
11. Desiccator	5	6
12. Hot air oven	5	9
13. Titration	5	10
14. Distilled water machine	12	11

teacher was able to observe how they negotiated the conversation. Talk developed spontaneously. The number of turns per episode (see Table 1) indicates the number of opportunities NS and NNSs had to speak in each episode. As Table 1 and examples in this chapter show, turns were relatively equally distributed between NS and NNSs. Jill's role as an uninformed NS interactant was to ask questions about the students' work to encourage explanation. Even though some students were more reluctant to speak up than usual, working together they managed overall to negotiate meaning by using communication strategies.

Using the recorded data, we identified moments of miscommunication for teaching purposes, interpreting miscommunication as moments in the interaction with the potential for sustained communication breakdown. These were indicated by inappropriate uptake (verbal or nonverbal) by other speakers in succeeding turns. Thus, we labeled turns *C* for communication or *M* for miscommunication, depending on uptake in the following turn. For example, Turn 185 was labeled *C* because Turn 186 indicated understanding:

Turn

185   J   So what do you use it [a vacuum seal] for? What products? C
186   SS   er er (Thai powdered milk] powder milk powder milk sausage and
              meat product and dry product

whereas Turn 342 was labeled *M* because of the ensuing lack of comprehension in Turn 343:

Turn

342 J   It's good So you test nitrogen for how much? M
343 SS er

We examined the moments we identified according to their level of impact on the ensuing communication. The moments ranged from potential communication breakdown being immediately averted, to delayed effects, to miscommunication becoming evident on reflection. Although the miscommunications—ranging from mispronunciation and mishearing to misunderstanding of meaning (technical and nontechnical)—were mainly overcome, there were some occasions when complete understanding proved impossible. Some examples are described below to demonstrate some of the points Yoopayao hoped to bring out in teaching.

We then describe how a couple of transcriptions were used in classroom teaching with the same students.

Miscommunication of Technical or Nontechnical Information

Communication in Examples 1–3 could have foundered at a number of points through Jill's lack of technical knowledge, the students' imprecise description, or a mixture of both factors. The temporary miscommunication that did occur at these points in each of these examples had cumulative potential at each occurrence to jeopardize the unfolding conversation. Communication did not break down, however, in any of the three examples. Throughout them, the students and Jill worked constantly to repair communication, the students often collaborating over their contributions.

These and the other episodes show the speakers' desire to achieve shared understanding—evident in their flexibility and adaptability during the negotiation of meaning. The interaction in Example 3 is assisted by a demonstration. Showing how the sausage-making machine worked provided a natural scaffold for the students' talk and reduced the need for detailed explanation, although Jill tried to model appropriate language and structure the students' explanation in some of her turns (somewhat teacherly strategies!).

1.*

18 J   [end of turn] what do you make from soybean?
19 S1 [Thai: what product]
20 S2 Miso miso
21 J   So that's like a sauce? No No?
22 SS No no
23 J   No more like in consistency like tofu?
24 SS More like [Thai: soya bean paste]
25 S2 Sorry can you speak slowly?
26 J   Ah ah OK ((laugh)) you have soya bean you ferment it and you make miso er can you tell me what miso is? Can you tell me?
27 S2 ( )
28 J   Speak up A bit louder
29 S2 ((louder)) We mix powder er and er we put aspergillus oryzae
30 S1 Aspergillus oryzae

---

*Note: See Appendix for key to transcripts.

31	J	Is that a chemical?
32	S1	A fungae
33	S2	A chemical?
34	Y	Is it a fungae or chemical?
35	J	Fungus?
36	SS	Fungae
37	J	Fungus One fungus Two fungi ((students echo)) yes because the word the word is not English it's um Latin an old word A lot of scientific terms come from Latin from Latin From Latin we have Italian and English we have a lot of Italian words so it is not really English
		OK ( ) so you added a fungus and then finish?
38	S2	We er we wait [Thai: fermentation] er growth? The er when the fungae growth we put the fungae in jar and fer ferment it

2.

54	J	Why do you ferment fish?
55	Sx	er fish rice garlic salt er mix ()
56	J	Is this what you call what I would call fish sauce?
57	SS	No
58	J	Maybe this is a farang term in a lot of Thai cooking you use fermented fish like a sauce or a paste?
59	SS	No no
60	J	No? so the fish is preserved you keep it whole?
61	S1	Ah [Thai: Where do you keep?] It is a fish
62	J	Is it a liquid?
63	SS	No
64	J	It is a fish?
65	SS	No it is a whole <u>body</u> of the fish
66	J	So when you ferment it it is a way of pre<u>serv</u>ing so that you keep it OK OK and it gives it a special taste
67	SS	Yes Salty salty
68	J	OK
69	SS	((laugh))

3.

139	J	Tell me what you do
140	SS	((demonstrate how to use the equipment))
141	SS	We put the meat and ingredients and er
142	J	Yes and then
143	S1	Roll roll ((demonstrates))
144	J	And then you turn the handle
145	SS	Yes
146	S3	and plastic er er
147	J	Where did it come out?
148	SS	((demonstrate how it works)) here
149	J	OK
150	S2	Put artificial plastic in here
151	J	And that's a skin skin for the sausages
152	SS	Yes
153	J	And until you get one <u>long</u> sausage
154	SS	Yes and we ((demonstrate)) er

155	J	And then you twist?
156	SS	Yes
157	S2	Yes er twist about er
158	J	How long of ( )
159	S2	Five er
160	J	Five centimetres
161	S3	And then er
162	J	And how fat? How fat? Are they thin or are they fat?
163	SS	Fat? Thin?
164	J	You can have this is this is thin this is fat ((demonstrates))
165	S3	Ah about this ((demonstrates))
166	J	So what happens next?
167	SS	Twist
168	J	Twist?
169	SS	Yes

With hindsight, the communication in Example 4 concerning emulsification was not completely successful. When Jill suggested a cleansing additive, the students disagreed. The students appeared not to recognize "detergent" as a chemical. Did this matter? In a sense it did not, given that Jill understood "chemical." However, misunderstanding had actually occurred even though on the surface it seemed resolved. That this can happen is, we believe, a salutary learning point for students.

4.

180	J	and just <u>pure</u> water or do you have to put detergent in the water?
181	SS	No
182	S4	We use chemical in water
183	J	You use chemical in water
184	SS	Yes

Review of the whole recording confirms that there is no simple rationale for a technical or common-use term. For example, in Example 5, Jill questions the students' technical explanation only once (Turn 189), and the students appear confident, finishing or polishing each other's turns, for example, in Turns 191, 198, and 205. In Example 6, the students and Jill managed to understand each other despite no common technical language. So the interaction in this example cannot be labeled unsuccessful. However, without a bystander's interjections in Turns 238 and 240, negotiation of meaning might have completely broken down early on. Communication was finally fully back on course in Turn 247 with Jill's introduction of "honey." All interactants understood what honey was and that one of its chief attributes was stickiness. However, communication was not complete because Jill could not fully understand the students' technical explanation. In Examples 5 and 6 then, both Jill's lack of scientific knowledge and the students' lack of English contributed to incomplete negotiation of meaning.

5.

187	J	...and why do you seal [vacuum seal]?
188	S2	Er why why er because er the oxygen is er oxygen is brown browning

189 J   Browning?
190 S2   In meat product
191 S3   Ran er rancidity of meat product
192 J   Can you just tell me once more something about the oxygen You
            you take out the oxygen?
193 SS   Yeah
194 J   You ex<u>tract</u> the oxygen?
195 SS   Without oxygen
196 J   OK why do you ex<u>tract</u> the oxygen?
197 S2   Because it causes er the oxygen is making the browning reaction
198 S3   And rancidity rancidity of the product
199 J   Right it turns the products bad
200 S3   Yes
201 J   And you you said it makes some of the products rancid?
202 SS   Yes
203 J   Like the milk products when they go bad they go rancid
204 S2   And when we we we have the oxygen in the product we the mi
            micro er
205 SS   Micro organism micro-organism can er growth in the product
206 J   Yes and you said before it turns brown so you just (   )
207 S2   We can keep a long time when we loss the oxygen

6.

236 J   Can you explain?
237 S4   [Thai: What is this machine?]
238 Sx   [a student working in the laboratory, and not part of the group]
            vicos vicos
239 J   This is a viscosity meter? What does that mean? I don't understand
240 Sx   [Thai: Find out viscosity of the food sample] viscosity of liquid er
241 J   Right and if it's yoghurt you want high viscosity or low viscosity?
242 S1   Low
243 J   What does viscous mean? What does viscous mean?
244 SS   [Thai: viscosity force] force [Thai: force Is it force]? (   )
245 J   What kind of liquid if it it's viscous?
246 SS   It force that against er the way of er moving in er liquid
247 J   Is it like honey? or is it like water?
248 SS   Viscosity? honey have ((laugh))
249 J   Yes viscosity is the em describe a kind of liquid something is
            viscous or not and I want to know what it means does water have
            viscosity? Viscosity Does water? Does that have is water does milk
            have viscosity? and honey? which is more viscous honey or milk?
250 SS   Honey
251 J   OK I understand I understand

Potential communication breakdown is displayed at its most acute in Example
7. Turns 356–384 show the strategies Jill attempted to achieve mutual understanding: confirmation checks (Turns 358 and 361), questions (Turns 356, 366, and 372),
repetitions (Turns 368, 376, and 378), suggestions (Turns 370 and 376), and
indications of uncertainty (Turns 380, 382, and 384). Though these strategies
encouraged the students to explain the fiber test, the students and Jill had insufficient
shared language, technical and lay, to understand one another.

7.

352	J	Can you tell me come on what is this machine?
353	S5	Use for analysis er ash ash
354	SS	and fibre ash
355	S1	and fine ash
356	J	and fine ash I thought you said ash but I didn't ( ) ((laugh)) OK and what do you do with the ash?
357	S5	Open the door <<[Thai: Don't do that] They are afraid there might be some samples inside>>
358	J	You open the door?
359	S2	High temperature
360	S5	Food sample in the crucible
361	J	In the crucible OK
362	S2	And er put in hot air [Thai: first evaporated?]
363	SS	( ) burn evaporate evap evap
364	S1	And then put it crucible in and close the door
365	S5	We can control the temperature
366	J	Yes em very very hot why do you do all of this? What are you testing for?
367	S2	Want to find the fibre
368	J	Want to find the fibres
369	S6	Ash ash centrifuse [centrifuge] centrifuse
370	J	Then you put you take the ash
371	SS	No no
372	J	It is very complicated can you tell me what this is?
373	S6	It is centrifuse help the er
374	S3	Help er
375	S6	Analyse fat from milk
376	J	To analyse fat from milk OK so the milk you heat The milk separates and and then you analyse the ( )
377	S3	OK the titration er the titration evaporate the burette
378	J	Ah the burette
379	S3	You can find acid er if example solution 10 ml and you check titration and check [Thai: if] and the end point is pink colour
380	J	Em Mhm
381	S3	You stop titration
382	J	Em
383	S3	OK?
384	J	I think so
385	SS	((laugh))

Follow-Up Teaching

After the videotaped session, teaching with Yoopayao continued over several sessions, as described below.

Analysis

1. The students examined and transcribed parts of the videotape searching for specific language features.

2. The students asked questions about additional discourse features they had discovered during the first task.

3. Yoopayao continued to use the videotape, together with student transcripts and their questions, in activities such as the following.

Practice

Yoopayao designed tasks that enabled the students to practice the language items and communication strategies identified in the recording, and then recorded their task work for further analysis, discussion, and practice.

Sessions tended to begin with students immediately watching—often at their own request—the videotapes of their language work. To encourage their awareness of language use, Yoopayao asked them to choose at least one language point for discussion. The points they identified often included lexis, such as items from Turns 147–152 (see Example 3). On this occasion, the students explained that they had learned "skin for the sausages" from Jill. They said that they had already known the word *skin* but not that it was used with sausages, nor that they need not always use special words to describe things. On this occasion and others, the students commented that the interaction with Jill and follow-up classroom work had helped them learn such items, saying, for example, "I won't forget that way of speaking English again."

In more extended classroom discussion, Yoopayao used another episode that contained several types of communication strategies (transcribed in Example 8): questions and prompts to check understanding of information provided (Turns 75, 86, 90, and 94); conversation structuring (Turns 73, 82, 88, 92, and 95), including display questions to ensure that the students told Jill necessary information; and elaboration of input to check understanding (Turns 97 and 99). Additionally, students used Thai to help each other (Turns 77 and 78), and Jill's and Yoopayao's uptake gave the students a continuing, strengthening scaffold to follow.

8.

71	J	OK
72	S1	It is the moulder moulder
73	J	It's the moulder for yes er so what would you make here?
74	S2	Put the dough in
75	J	For noodle? Pastry?
76	SS	No No
77	S1	[Thai: to knead the dough for making bread]
78	S2	[Thai: to flatten the dough]
79	J	Now try telling me in English come on don't make him do all the work
80	SS	((laugh))
81	J	Come on
82	Y	What's that?
83	S3	Drum dryer
84	SS	No No
85	S4	Put er the dough in here
86	J	In here?
87	S4	Yes
88	J	And what do you do next?
89	S2	[Thai: turn it here] roll roll
90	J	Turn you turn
91	SS	Yes yes

92	J	What do you do next?
93	S3	[Thai: adjust the thickness and thinness]
94	J	It comes out here
95	Y	This is for what?
96	S2	[Thai: enlarge] thin thin
97	J	To thin thin to thin so you can adjust that? So you can have thicker and thinner
98	SS	Yes yes
99	J	So you adjust it and then you put that on
100	SS	Yes yes
101	S2	Start start ((i.e. the engine))

Yoopayao's teaching journal records that she introduced analysis of this episode through discussion of some general characteristics of spoken discourse, including how to exploit the fact that it is face-to-face. For instance, in this example, students exchanged signals of noncomprehension when they spoke in their first language (Turns 77 and 78), and drew on the context in which it occurred (the bakery room). The context and the events in this episode provided a natural discourse structure. Classroom analysis ended with collaborative construction of a diagram (see Figure 1).

The analysis led to the students writing about how to use bakery equipment. Doing this reinforced the students' growing awareness of differences between written and spoken discourse and also led to continued discussion of lexical and structural items. Because making pastry is not part of Thai culture, the vocabulary, uses of baking equipment, and the way dough and pastry are used all stimulated discussion. Whereas the students were predisposed to see vocabulary as the make or break of information exchange, the classroom discussion of how conversation could be progressed through questions, prompts, checks, and so forth made them more aware of how they could make communication work.

Yoopayao used Example 7 in similar ways. As with Example 8, this example contained a range of communication strategies: instances of language switch by

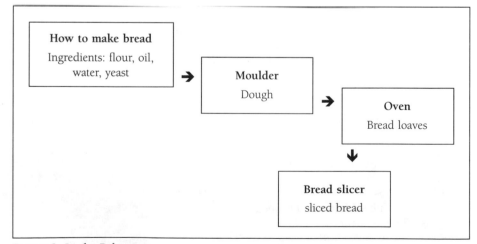

Figure 1. In the Bakery

students (Turns 357, 362, and 379); student collaboration (Turns 354 and 355, and 374 and 375); and circumlocution, approximation, or both (Turns 355, 359, 363, and 379). Jill's speech provided examples of clarification bids (Turns 356, 358, 366, and 370), confirmation checks (Turn 376), and repetition (Turns 376 and 378). The students' and Jill's communication strategies utilized the situational (food laboratory) and informational (task discourse) contexts (Bialystok, 1990). Classroom analysis of this episode focused on systemic functional grammar (as in Halliday, 1994). For example, students considered whether their use of modality was caused more by Jill's ignorance (her lack of technical Field) or by their own nervousness in front of a NS (interpersonal language, or Tenor).

Since this first teaching experience, we have begun to pilot other ways of increasing students' awareness of discourse strategies. These include giving students communication prompts in the form of turns based on recordings of their interaction, asking each of them to respond, playing the actual response from the recordings, and having them compare all the different versions, including the developments these versions might prompt in any ensuing conversations. Activities such as this will, we hope, offset the overwhelming importance that students traditionally place on vocabulary and grammatical form. We think most EFL students need to be more aware of how effectively they can make talk work for them even when their language competence is quite limited.

Yoopayao frequently asked the students in this study to collaborate on transcriptions of small parts (up to a minute) of any interactions recorded in class. They were not expected to transcribe everything, but were asked to lay out sections in turns of talk, identify speakers, and transcribe what they could. If they came upon something they could not understand, they were asked to represent it as ( ) (see Appendix for key to transcripts) and go on with what they could work out. Initially, the students needed teacher help, but they soon developed independence. Seeing that they could communicate and understand at least small stretches of English pleased them enormously. Moreover, transcription and analysis increased their language awareness and made them more open to talking and to self-correcting.

This readiness became evident in an unexpected way when we found that students had begun attempting to correct rather than transcribing talk, as in Examples 9 and 10 from the original recording with Jill show. The two transcripts represent the same short stretch of discourse, though the turns are differently interpreted. In the students' own transcription (Example 10), they have transcribed Turn 7 differently from the equivalent Turn 246, in Example 9. On questioning, they admitted that they had begun to correct what they actually heard.

9.

241	J	Right and if it's yogurt you want high viscosity or low viscosity?
242	S1	Low
243	J	What does viscous mean? What does viscous mean?
244	SS	[Thai: viscosity force] force [Thai: force Is it force]? ( )
245	J	What kind of liquid if it it's viscous?
246	SS	**It force that against er the way of er moving in er liquid**
247	J	Is it like honey? or is it like water?
248	SS	Viscosity? honey have ((laugh))
249	J	Yes viscosity is the em describe a kind of liquid something is

viscous or not and I want to know what it means does water have viscosity? Viscosity Does water? Does that have is water does milk have viscosity? and honey? which is more viscous honey or milk?

| 250 | SS | Honey |
| 251 | J | OK I understand I understand |

10.

4	J	And in yoghurt you want high viscosity or low viscosity
5	S1	Low
6	J	What viscosity mean what kind of the liquid?
7	SS	**It's a force that against the way of moving in liquid**
8	J	Is it like honey? Or is it like water?
9	SS	Honey
10	J	Is the water has viscosity? Just milk honey or milk OK I think I'm understand

Learner Feedback

The 15 students completed a questionnaire at the end of the unit providing feedback on learning English through discourse-based tasks drawing on their professional knowledge and language output. The results indicated (Figure 2) that the students had found the approach enjoyable and interesting, and that they felt the unit of work had increased their ability and confidence to use English.

They commented as follows:

- Using English can be fun or enjoyable. (7)
- We have developed confidence in our English ability. (6)
- The session with the NS was useful. (5)

One student summed up their views: "At first I am very scared to speak in English but later on I feel more confident while talking." Though they had all found the session with a NS challenging, as another of them wrote, it had reassured him that he could "speak some English." From the learners' perspective, the teaching approach appeared to have been motivational.

Class:	Bachelor of Food Science (1st Year)		
Date:	31 January 2000		
The tasks were:			
1.	Fun	or	Boring
	15		**0**
2.	Good for me	or	No use to me
	15		**0**
3.	Appropriate	or	Too difficult
	11		**4**

FIGURE 2. Students' Questionnaire Data

◈ DISTINGUISHING FEATURES

The data and teaching approach we adopted with these students interested us for a number of reasons.

All Speakers Worked at Communicating

As the data demonstrate, miscommunication may equally well be the responsibility of a NS as of NNSs. In these data, the NS lacked technical knowledge whereas the NNSs were learning English, the medium of communication. These gaps on both sides had the potential to seriously disrupt communication. Overall, however, all participants judged the interaction successful. There is, for example, no evidence in the data of avoidance strategies. Instead, the interactants worked turn by turn to communicate, through, for example, confirmation and clarification checks, questions, repetitions, rephrasing, collaborative talk, and scaffolded turns. Ultimately, it is the moment-to-moment interaction that affects overall understanding (Rampton, 1997), and in the recording discussed in this chapter, participants stayed on task throughout what proved to be a lengthy interaction (2 hours).

What kept the NNSs on task? We believe it was a conviction that what they were doing was useful and interesting. For them, the interaction was an opportunity to test their English. At the finish, the sense of achievement seemed to come from the work the participants had done together rather than from what they had actually learned individually (cf. Aston, 1993). The initial mutual incompetence had created a stimulus to communicate and a means of solidarity. The NS's lack of technical knowledge offset her English teaching background, and the NNSs' technical knowledge redeemed their lack of English. So for all speakers, there was challenge and a genuine interest in communicating.

Although the high level of concentration was gratifying, its presence also revealed something else: Communicating is hard work. In addition to language competence, it requires concentration, attention to detail, and planning and reflecting as well as improvising. All these skills need experience and practice, which tasks like the one in this study can provide.

The Nature of the Interaction

The students interacted with the NS using what they had first developed and practiced in a classroom setting. The students' pushed output (Iwashita, 1999; Mackay, 1995) in the initial videotaping became a new classroom text for transcribing, analyzing, rerecording, and reanalyzing. Regular transcription and analysis gave them opportunity for detailed study of their own language use and that of their peers in ways that aided and motivated their learning. Although the interaction had a pedagogic focus, it was professional in context and mode, and unforced in that all interactants had compatible communicative goals.

Communication was achieved despite the potential for breakdown. In addition to the strategies we have already discussed, each shift to a different set of equipment offered a new location and the chance to restart communication, maybe with someone different taking a lead. At the same time, interactants could build on information exchanged in previous episodes if they wished. Because the talk frequently accompanied demonstration of technical processes, often involving chronological sequences of actions, it also frequently had an inbuilt scaffold. Thus, in a number of ways, the interactants were able to address the task of communication in manageable chunks. Chunking, like teacher scaffolding, is a conservative strategy (see Williams, Inscoe, & Tasker, 1997). It enables interactants to concentrate on what they can manage at any one time, thus reducing concern about communication's unpredictable nature.

The students were not aware at the time, but studying the recording and transcribing sections of the data afterwards brought these features to their attention. Interaction that seemed unpredictable retrospectively gained reason and order, and thus could help students prepare for future communicative tasks. Analyzing their interaction, therefore, made these students more aware of how they could manage interaction.

Being a NNS of English Does Not Have to Be an Issue

The further realization that a NS was more interested in what they knew than how they expressed it was reassuring for the students. The fact that they were the primary knowers (see Berry, 1981) proved more useful than knowledge of English. In any case, the structure of the tasks meant that they were still able to focus on discourse structure in later classroom activity. This combination of factors strengthened these students' desire to use and learn English.

From the teaching that followed the recording with Jill, the students perceived that a different NS would have communicated with them differently and that all output, in fact, is constantly subject to reinterpretation. Although these realizations removed some of their feelings of responsibility for successful communication, it made them more aware of what they could each contribute. These students had experienced a genuine desire, or need, to explain their work to an outsider; this factor had overcome their inexperience and lack of confidence in English.

◈ PRACTICAL IDEAS

In this section, we outline some ways in which EFL teaching can make use of learner discourse as course content and structure, and we briefly discuss their implications for EFL teacher education.

Suggestions for EFL Teaching

Prioritize the Identification of Learning Activities

In a task-based syllabus, the teacher's role and course content can derive from the learning activities themselves because the context in which language forms are used can be a means of teaching in itself.

Create Tasks That Encourage Authentic Communication

This case study documents how a teacher designed tasks that motivated the students to use English in a TEFL context. The students were able to use their learning environment as subject matter, and the communicative objective, to explain how they used food science equipment to a NS of English, required them to use English. These two factors created a genuine motivation for using EFL. Further, the teacher's presence and the videotaping meant that the interaction could be easily integrated in later classroom study. We call such a task-based program—that is, one based on tasks with information gaps that genuinely encourage EFL students to focus on their own language output as course content—*a discourse-based approach to language learning.*

Be Flexible and Learn From Your Own Teaching

Though the course described here involved the teacher in conventional ESP teaching, the preparation of her students for interaction with a NS—its recording and its analysis with students—also involved Yoopayao in new activities.

First, as the discourse analyst, she had to train her students to transcribe and conduct simple analyses. Second, she became a teacher researcher. Because she had not taught in this way before, Yoopayao designed the course as action research. Studying classroom interaction is as useful for teachers as for their students (Burton, 2000) because it can lead teachers to discover the effect of their own communication patterns on others and suggest ways for them to exploit or modify them (Sato, 1990).

Focus on Making Input Comprehensible

Teaching an EFL ESP course designed around discourse-based tasks means that students are not merely involved in making input comprehensible (Ellis, 1986; Jenkins, this volume), they also have to study interaction and find out how comprehensibility has been achieved.

In addition to the teaching strategies used here, having students write simple protocols on transcripts of their interaction is another way of focusing their attention on their use of communication strategies and negotiation of meaning. Students can share their accounts and analyze any differences among them. In the interaction recorded for this case study, contrary to expectation (e.g., Long, 1996), students as well as the NS used communication strategies to make input comprehensible.

Create Opportunities for Negotiation of Meaning and Feedback

The interaction with the NS worked for these students because all participants had to negotiate meaning. Recording and analyzing the negotiation gave the students useful feedback on their performance. Although in Example 7, the students did not successfully communicate what they intended to Jill, all interactants realized the limits of their understanding. Later in the classroom, the students were ready to analyze what had happened and work on their output (Glew, 1998; Lyster, 1998; Swain, 1985; Swain & Lapkin, 1995, 1998).

Utilize Nonteachers and NSs When Possible

Opportunities to use speakers other than the language teacher vary from teaching context to teaching context. However, most EFL ESP teachers have some opportunity to use outsiders in their classrooms (e.g., see Lynch & Anderson, this volume). For example, visitors might be specialists in the students' fields of study, nonteaching NSs of English, or other teachers of English. Whatever the visitors' English backgrounds, their visits can provide a stimulus for genuine communication. Because many EFL learners' future use of English will be with other NNSs in situations where English is the lingua franca, providing these kinds of learning and practice opportunities is invaluable. As in this study, the EFL teacher can exploit the teaching potential of such situations.

Suggestions for EFL Teacher Education

We have suggested a close focus on student language use in the classroom and study-related contexts. This means that EFL teachers would find it helpful to do the following.

Investigate Classroom Language

Through recording classroom interaction, and transcribing and studying it with students, practicing teachers can learn about discourse functions and second language acquisition while they train their students in learner-language analysis (see Burton, 2000; Carter & McCarthy, 1997; Riggenbach, 1999). For example, recorded classroom interaction can be simultaneously used as course content and needs negotiation.

Investigate Alternative Syllabus Designs

Increasingly, language teachers involve students in needs negotiation and as language resources. Burns, Joyce, and Gollin (1996), Feez (1998), McCarthy and Carter (1994), and Riggenbach (1999) offer some examples of how discourse analysis can be integrated in syllabus design and implementation.

Investigate Strategies That Learners Can Use to Help Them Learn Language

Most speakers some of the time rely on communication strategies to negotiate understanding. Most language learners, therefore, are already skilled strategists in at least one language. Willing's (1987) work is still a useful overview of how language learners can harness strategic skills to assist communication and suggests a range of classroom learning activities.

Become an Action Researcher

Many preservice teacher education programs now teach teacher learners how to become reflective practitioners. Action research, a tool of reflective practice, is an investigative process that has been widely successful in keeping teachers informed about their practice (e.g., the potential of curriculum innovations). There are many useful manuals and resources available, including Edge (2001), Freeman (1998), and McNiff, Lomax, and Whitehead (1996).

Teach Collaboratively

We each brought different perspectives (e.g., TEFL, teacher education, discourse study, ESP, materials development, curriculum theory) to this study that the other could share or learn from. The value of teachers collaborating in professional development and curriculum renewal is strongly endorsed in the literature (e.g., Bailey, Curtis, & Nunan, 1998; Burns, 1999; Burton, 1997; Freeman, 1998) as a means in pre- and in-service education of providing supportive frameworks for classroom teachers (see Edge, 2001, for some recent examples).

◈ CONCLUSION

Task-based language teaching that uses student knowledge and classroom language as learning resources is an authentic means of communicative language teaching. The approach is particularly suitable in global contexts in which NNSs of English increasingly outnumber NSs. In this study, because the teacher was still able to fine-tune content and activities to meet external work requirements, the approach also proved very flexible. But the approach worked most of all because it developed out of a natural reason and context for using English. Thus, the students were motivated to study the target language.

Equally clearly, involving both teacher and students in the study of learner language can aid research into second language learning processes (see Allwright, 1998; Burton, 2000; Samuda & Rounds, 1993). This case study has made us increasingly conscious of the extent to which analyses of EFL classroom transcripts need to be accompanied by the contextual observations that can only be made by the participants, the teachers, and the students who are the focus of study. That such involvement in research can also be a means of teaching language is a very important bonus.

◈ CONTRIBUTORS

Jill Burton is associate professor of applied linguistics at the University of South Australia, in Adelaide, where she teaches and supervises postgraduate work in discourse analysis and language curriculum. She has published on these topics and edited a number of publications on TESOL. Her current research interests include how learners can, as analysts of their own discourse, become more effective language users.

Yoopayao Daroon is completing a doctorate on language curriculum for EFL learners in professional contexts. A widely experienced teacher, she is interested in task-based learning and discourse-based curricula, and works for the Rajamangala Institute of Technology, in Lampang, Northern Thailand.

◈ APPENDIX: KEY TO TRANSCRIPTS

<< >>	Enclose an aside	
[ ]	Contain transcriber-added information (e.g., translation of Thai phrase)	
( )	Contain unintelligible wording	
(( ))	Contain nonverbal information	
...	Indicate a pause (each dot represents 5 seconds)	
pre<u>ser</u>ving	Underlining indicates a stressed syllable or word	
S1, S2, etc.	Individual students in order of occurrence	
SS	More than one student speaking at a time	
Sx	Unidentifiable students	
J	The native speaker, Jill	
Y	The EFL teacher, Yoopayao	

Turns are numbered on the left.

CHAPTER 12

Students as Discourse Analysts in the Conversation Class

Ann Wennerstrom

◈ INTRODUCTION

A general-purpose course in spoken communication, or conversation class, has traditionally been a component of many ESOL programs. Ideally, a conversation class should be practical and applicable to real-life situations. It should offer students a chance to build speaking, listening, vocabulary, fluency, and other social skills for the purpose of interacting in informal settings in the host country. This chapter describes the use of a set of materials designed for a conversation class in which ESOL students work on their own interactions as texts.

Under this discourse-analytic approach, students audiotape samples of their own conversations, transcribe the actual language used, and analyze the interactions. Rather than hypothetical dialogues, the class texts consist of language that has occurred in context. Students, in a sense, become researchers of their own language development, as advocated by Nunan (1989a). This makes for a student-centered class, with the instructor taking the role of a facilitator and informant. The discourse-centered approach is highly motivating as students become emotionally invested in their transcripts. Riggenbach (1999) describes a similar approach, justifying it as follows:

> For many learners, involvement in their own language-learning processes helps to empower them in the sense that they are able to gain a measure of control over their own position in the target culture . . . . Students develop the ability to come up with their own discoveries and need not always rely on pat answers prescribed from textbooks or on "expert" opinions provided by instructors. (p. 15)

Furthermore, by sharing their findings in the classroom, the class as a whole can build a repertoire of conversational strategies. They can also attain a more sophisticated understanding of the greater sociocultural forces that contribute to discourse organization in the host country and the range of interactional behaviors to expect.

◈ CONTEXT

The conversation course for which the materials in this case study were designed is offered in an intensive ESOL program at a major university in the United States. The students are mostly young adults of mixed nationalities, the majority being from Asian countries. Their purpose for studying English ranges from a general one of personal enrichment, to a more specific one of working or attending a university in the United States in the future. The proficiency level of the students in the program ranges in six levels, from beginning to advanced. Although most students have already studied English in their home countries, and many have completed other 10-week terms in the same ESOL program, few have lived in an English-speaking country for more than 1 year. For the average full-time student, this conversation course is taken as an elective in addition to three other courses in grammar, reading, writing, and other subjects. Each class meets 5 days a week, 1 hour a day, for 10 weeks—a total of 50 hours.

Course evaluation surveys make evident that students view this course as a practical choice for improving their spoken English. Living in dormitories on a U.S. university campus, students are faced with speaking English frequently in order to negotiate their daily affairs. In addition, the ESOL program provides other opportunities to interact with native English speakers (NSs) through field trips, home stays with U.S. families, and a conversation partners program. The materials described here are part of a permanent collection of pedagogical options available to future teachers of the conversation course. Teacher education workshops demonstrating the approach have also been presented at local conferences and the TESOL convention, in Vancouver, Canada (Wennerstrom & Riggenbach, 2000).

◈ DESCRIPTION

The course is organized around what Harshbarger (1985) refers to as *conversation management* skills, with each week devoted to a different skill or set of skills. Harshbarger's conversational skills, drawn from conversation analysis research (based on Sacks, Schegloff, & Jefferson, 1974, and many subsequent analyses) include both steering and supporting functions of conversation. The list in Table 1 is a modified version of Harshbarger's. Each of these conversational skills becomes a departure point for a series of activities:

- a brainstorming session to introduce the skill
- data collection of real-world conversations
- transcription of the data; analysis of the data with regard to both conversation management and linguistic accuracy
- follow-up activities incorporating what the students have learned

Students are also required to keep journals in which they track their experiences, monitor their linguistic development, and record new conversational gambits and strategies. What follows is an account of how these activities were used over a period of time with several groups of students. Sample transcripts from students are included.[1]

---

[1] Additional discourse analysis activities for the classroom are suggested in Riggenbach (1999) and Wennerstrom (in press).

TABLE 1. OUTLINE OF CONVERSATION MANAGEMENT SKILLS

Steering / Controlling	Following/Supporting/Developing
Starting a conversation	**Listening cues**
Getting attention	Attending signals
Greetings	Encouragement signals
Topic nomination	
	Volunteering information
Turn taking	
Taking the floor	**Volunteering opinions**
Pause control	
Hesitating	**Volunteering assumptions**
Changing topics	
	Clarifying
Ending a conversation	Questioning
Sequencing end signals	Restating
Reinforcing relationships	
	Agreeing
Repairing conversation breakdowns	
	Disagreeing
	Contributing anecdotes
	Joking, kidding, poking fun, etc.

Brainstorming

The initial brainstorming activity serves as an introduction to the conversational skill(s) of the week. It is a way of focusing attention on the skill, predicting what NSs might say, and assembling a collection of any conversational gambits that students already know. The brainstorming session is also a good forum for a discussion of appropriate topics for conversation and social norms that may differ from culture to culture. Prior to the in-class brainstorming session, students are generally given a journal assignment to encourage them to think about such questions in advance.

Data Collection

Next, students audiotape themselves in conversation with NSs outside of class. Ideally, taping should be done in a quiet place to ensure good sound quality. Conversations can be short—even a 3-minute conversation can yield a wealth of data. If tape recorders are scarce, students work in teams, sharing equipment. After taping the conversation, students listen to the tape and select certain portions for transcription and analysis. For some conversational skills, there may be specific targets, such as the opening or closing of the conversation, or a segment where a joke was told. Another approach, suggested by Riggenbach (1999), is to ask students to select two segments, one in which they felt that the conversation went smoothly with respect to the skill(s) of the week, and the other in which they felt the conversation was problematic.

Data Transcription

After choosing the relevant portions of the tape, students transcribe their selections and bring several photocopies of their transcripts to class. Before the first transcription assignment, one or more class sessions are usually spent demonstrating and justifying the process of transcription. This step is crucial as some students may show an initial resistance to the detailed work of transcription. If ample class time is allowed for small-group transcription work with guided instruction, and initial transcription assignments are kept short, students are more likely to accept the process as an interesting challenge. Once the process is understood, the level of student interest is usually high: Some students routinely transcribe entire 10- to 15-minute conversations instead of my more manageable 2- to 3-minute assignments.

Coding sheets with transcription symbols are provided to the class. A good system for conversation coding is available from Jefferson (1984), a simplified version of which is given in the Appendix and used for the transcription that is contained in this chapter.

Because students are sometimes embarrassed about what they consider to be errors in their speech, I point out some common characteristics of naturally occurring conversational speech. Even NSs use sentence fragments, hesitations, noises, overlapping speech, and other features that would not seem grammatical in writing, but are perfectly appropriate in casual speech. It is essential for the activities that follow that students learn to transcribe all the little details of their speech—including the hesitation sounds and other so-called errors. To illustrate what natural speech is really like and the level of detail needed for subsequent exercises, preexisting transcripts can be shown and their tapes played. Example 1 is a short sample of naturally occurring speech from NSs that I have used as an illustration for ESOL students. In the transcript, Dan has recently had a serious illness.

1.*

```
       Jan:   So are you gaining weight? (.4)
              I mean- (.3)
              y- you lost a lotta weight, right?=
       Dan:   =yeah. We:::ll I think I am, (.8)
   5          Uhh — it's hard to tell. (1.0)
              I feel- I mean- I feel like I'm eating full meals, (.4)
       Pam:   You ⌈ will gain weight.
       Dan:        ⌊ Now I'm just stuffing myself you know. (.8)
       Ray:   Want some ice cream? (.3)
  10   Dan:   Uh ha ha    ⌈ ha ha ha no, I don't think so. (.9)
       Ray:               ⌊ ha ha ha.
```

Example 1 features false starts in Lines 3 and 6; a direct latch (=) from Jan to Dan in Lines 3 and 4; a hesitation noise in Line 5; overlapping speech in Lines 7 and 8; a slang expression ("stuffing myself") in Line 8; a joking sequence, including laughter,

---

*Note: See Appendix for key to transcripts.

in Lines 9–11; and various pauses and intonation patterns throughout. If students have never seen a transcript of natural speech before, examples such as this can familiarize them with transcription conventions and save them from being too self-critical when they begin to transcribe their own speech.

Data Analysis: Conversation Management

The first analysis activity takes place in class as students take turns discussing their data in small groups. Students pass out photocopies of their transcripts to the others, explaining the circumstances surrounding the conversation and why the particular segment was chosen. They can then either play the taped conversation while others in the group follow along, or have group members take parts and read the transcript. Other group members ask questions and provide feedback and suggestions with respect to the conversation management skill of the week. This is also a time to share useful vocabulary and conversational gambits.

After the group analysis work, the class as a whole pools its findings. I use questions such as the following to stimulate discussion about the conversation management issue of the week:

- What strategies were effective in managing this issue of conversation?
- What vocabulary or conversational gambits have you learned?
- How did age, ethnicity, education, or gender affect the way the speakers used language in conversation?
- Were certain conversations more or less formal, and if so, why?
- What was frustrating, pleasing, surprising, and so forth in your conversation?

Such a discussion can increase awareness of the structure and vocabulary of the conversation, the cultural norms underlying the interaction, and the sociolinguistic variables that may affect it. To illustrate how such a discussion might proceed, Examples 2 and 3 provide segments that some of my students actually chose for analysis. Example 2 illustrates the skill of supporting the conversation. The nonnative-English-speaking (NNS) student was Italian, and his partner, a NS from the United States, was a close friend from the university, his own age. Both speakers were male. The conversation centered on a recent phone call that the NNS made to his family, the "they" of Line 1.

2.

    NS: How are they?
    NNS: nn — They are — <u>fine</u>.
          <u>Actually</u> they are pretty <u>busy</u>.
    NS: Doing <u>what</u>?
5 NNS: Doi::::::ng — all the stuff that they <u>usually</u> do.
    NS: ha ha Which is <u>WHAT</u>?! ha ha
    NNS: ha ha ha
          um they are organize-
          <u>organizing</u> different things for —
10   uh keep the <u>business</u> going.
    NS: They're <u>organizing</u> things?

NNS: to keep the <u>business</u> going.
NS: to keep the <u>business</u> going.
NNS: Yeah.
15 And uh my <u>mother</u> was- wasn't <u>feeling- feeling</u> well.
She has a <u>cold</u> — <u>bad</u> cold, yuh. An' she can't get <u>rid</u> of it.
So — and — I spoke with my brother <u>Eduardo,</u>
NS: How is <u>he</u>?
NNS: Oh he's he's <u>crazy.</u>
20 NS: He's <u>CRAZY</u>?!
NNS: Ha ha ha
NS: What's he <u>doing</u>?
NNS: Oh he's- he's studying <u>hard.</u>
hnn studying —
25 He's <u>happy</u> because there y- are just <u>three</u> of them in class.
NS: What? Three people?
NNS: <u>Three</u> <u>people</u> in <u>class.</u>
yeah, so it's=
NS: =very <u>nice</u>!
30 NNS: Oh yes.

In this sequence, the student focused on a strategy of repetition that the NS used to keep the conversation moving; this occurs in Lines 11, 13, 20, and 26. This strategy, along with personal questions, served to draw the NNS out on the topic of his family. Other students agreed that this would also be an easy strategy for a NNS to use because it involves repeating the language of the NS at the moment it occurs. At the same time, there was some tension in this conversation, which led to a discussion of the appropriateness of personal questions in U.S. culture. Here, the American seemed to expect more personal details than the Italian was comfortable giving. This was evidenced by his reply in Line 6, which was received with laughter by the NS for being so general.

Example 3 involves a common complaint from a NNS about turn taking—that of how to break into a conversation when the NS is dominating the floor. The transcript was provided by a Korean man in conversation with a U.S. male friend. The topic is U.S. football.

3.

NNS: Did you-
did you go to Hus- ah <u>Huskis</u> suh ah <u>Stadium</u> <u>today</u>?
NS: <u>Yeah</u>, I went to Husky Stadium —
and I saw the <u>Husky</u> <u>football</u> team play the <u>Arizona</u> <u>State</u> <u>Sundevils</u>
5 NNS: Yeah.
How's the <u>game</u>?
NS: It was really <u>exciting</u> an um —
but the Huskies did so <u>well</u> that they just completely <u>beat</u> ASU=
NNS: =ahh.
10 NS: yeah <u>ASU</u> came out at the <u>start</u> of the game they had their- their <u>flag</u> and everything, but the <u>Huskies,</u> the all the people in Husky Stadium <u>booed</u> their <u>flag.</u>
NNS: yeah ha ha uh uh
<u>Can</u> you imagine —
ahh —

15		how many <u>people</u> was there today?
	NS:	Ahh, I think <u>seventy</u> <u>thousand</u>.
	NNS:	WOW!
		goohhd ((xxx))
		Uhh, do you think <u>who</u> is the uh <u>best</u> player today?
20	NS:	Well, I think they <u>all</u> played well —
		um, like the <u>de</u>fensive <u>backs</u>, <u>Reggie</u> <u>Reeser</u> and uh <u>Kairstin</u>, uh, numbers
		<u>26</u> and <u>4</u>, played very good <u>de</u>fensive <u>coverage</u> and the uh inside <u>line</u>
		backers, uh <u>Dink</u> <u>Aliaga</u> and <u>Dave</u> <u>Kilpatrick</u> also did very well.
	NNS:	uh huh,
25	NS:	But that that meant the <u>de</u>fensive tackles were playing well <u>too</u>. The defensive
		tackles opened up some <u>real</u> <u>nice</u> <u>holes</u>.
	NNS:	huh.
	NS:	<u>Dink</u> <u>Aliaga</u> and <u>Kilpatrick</u> got in and got a lotta good <u>sacks</u> on the <u>quarterback</u> and
		they got some of the <u>running</u> backs and <u>losses</u>
30	NNS:	yaaah. ha
	NS:	and <u>Reggie</u> <u>Reeser</u> and uh <u>Kairstin</u> did most of the time really <u>well</u> on <u>pass</u> coverage
		they really <u>held</u> Arizona <u>down</u>.
	NNS:	yeah, uh — but uh — I don't know about the ahh —
		football football game's <u>rules</u>,
35		so that's why I don't like <u>football</u>. haha
		but uh —
		I'm gonna le- uh <u>learn</u> about the <u>rules</u>.

Not being a fan of football myself, I can heartily sympathize with the Korean man's lack of understanding of this jargon-filled monologue. One student pointed out that sometimes it is easiest and most polite just to feign understanding in such situations. However, we also discussed ways that he might break in and slow the NS down. For example, in Lines 24, 27, and 30, the NNS offers what could be taken as encouraging sounds ("uh huh," "huh") as if he understands. If he had instead displayed his confusion at these points by saying "Wait!", "Hold on!", or simply "Huh?" with a rising intonation, he might have obtained a bigger opening in which to ask for further clarification.

Data Analysis: Linguistic Accuracy

An additional dimension of the transcript analysis can be to focus on linguistic accuracy. Depending on the goals of the instructor and the students, this may be done at the time of the initial analysis, in later class activities, or individually in journals. There are many possible ways to encourage the development of grammar, pronunciation, intonation, and vocabulary for each individual. Transcripts offer a kind of window into the mind of the students, displaying the current state of their interlanguage development.

Grammar

It may be useful to pick a target structure and scan the transcripts for that structure. For example, the NNS in the football transcript in Example 3 shows some inconsistency in his formation of questions. A list of them looks like this:

Did you go to Husky Stadium today?

How's the game?

Can you imagine how many people was there today?

Do you think who is the best player today?

The student studying the transcript could then be encouraged to review verb phrase structure and to correct any errors in the above questions. If many students had similar problems, the instructor could review the pertinent grammatical structures with the class as a whole.

Pronunciation

Similarly, for pronunciation, students can target a particularly troublesome sound and then search their transcripts for all instances of that sound. This can then become the focus of pronunciation practice activities. Another approach is to have students identify places where a NS misunderstood them due to unclear pronunciation. The conversation in Example 4 between a Japanese woman and a U.S. man illustrates this. Here the NS missed the word *life* twice in Lines 1 and 2 before finally catching it in Line 4 when the NNS rephrased it as "life-style." This problem could be traced to an /l/ versus /r/ pronunciation problem, for which the student could be directed toward self-practice materials.

4.

NNS: But <u>they</u> <u>don't</u> <u>know</u> the ah uh <u>actual</u> <u>Japanese</u> <u>life</u>.
So I wanted to <u>say</u> the ah <u>Japanese</u> <u>life</u> is <u>similar</u> to <u>yours</u>.
NS: The Japanese <u>what</u>?
NNS: <u>Japanese</u> — <u>life</u> — <u>sty</u>   ⌈ <u>le</u>.
5 NS: ⌊ <u>LIFESTYLE!</u> <u>LIFESTYLE!</u>

Intonation

Students can also use their transcripts to study intonation, an important and meaningful component of discourse that can pose difficulty for NNSs (Clennell, 1997; Wennerstrom, 1994). I usually explain to students that speech is divided into short thought groups or *intonational phrases* that are often followed by a pause and are likely to coincide with points of turn shift. Each intonational phrase typically has one main idea that bears the *focus* of the phrase.[2] The focus is the most prominent syllable of the phrase, tending to be louder, longer, and higher in pitch than other syllables in the same phrase. With this in mind, students replay their own tapes to determine how they have divided their speech into intonational phrases and where they have placed the focus in each phrase.

The transcript in Example 5 from a Japanese woman shows a fairly typical problem of pausing very frequently and focusing almost every word (intonational phrases are indicated with slash marks). Such word-by-word phrasing can obscure a NNS's turn-taking intentions because to the NS ear, every word sounds like a complete intonational phrase and thus a potential turn completion point. In this case,

---

[2] The notion of *focus* has been discussed by various intonation theorists, though with differing terminology. Halliday (1967) and Brazil (1985) use the term *tonic*, Cruttendon (1987) the term *nucleus*, and Pierrehumbert (1980) the term *nuclear pitch accent*, all referring to the most prominent syllable in an intonational phrase.

the NNS was actually interrupted by the NS in the middle of her turn in Line 1 (data from Wennerstrom, 2000).

5.

    NNS: <u>but</u> / <u>not</u> / <u>only</u> / <u>words.</u> / <u>If</u> / <u>I</u> /   ⎡ <u>showed</u>
    NS: ⎣ You not only wear the tra-
    ditional Japanese clothing but you wear modern
    NNS: <u>Yeah</u>
  5 NS: Jap- modern clothing
    NNS: <u>Yeah</u>
    NS: like in western ah America
    NNS: <u>Yeah</u>

(pp. 122–123). Reprinted with permission.

Students can instead be encouraged to group words together into longer intonational phrases, linking the end of one word to the beginning of the next wherever possible within each phrase. If the speaker needs to hesitate, a good strategy is to elongate the final vowel prior to the hesitation into a long plateau shape or to insert an elongated hesitation sound such as *ummm* or *uhhh*. This can be seen in the transcript in Example 6 where the NNS, another Japanese woman at a more advanced level, used longer intonational phrases while indicating her intention to continue her turns by extending her intonation before pauses and using hesitation sounds (data from Wennerstrom, 2000):

6.

  1 NNS: And <u>actually</u> / <u>Kobe</u> doesn't ha:::::ve nnnn <u>art</u> school
  2 NS: Really?   That surprises me.
  3 NNS: ⎡ mm hmm / annnn just <u>design</u> school / and <u>two</u> years school

(pp. 120–121). Reprinted with permission.

Another common intonation problem is to place the focus of a phrase on a function word. As noted above, the focus of an intonational phrase should coincide with the main idea of that phrase, usually a new or contrasting piece of information in the discourse. If the focus is misplaced, the meaning of an utterance can change considerably. The conversation transcript in Example 7 shows a complex episode of teasing that stems in part from placing the focus on the function word *one* in Line 6. It involves a NNS, a woman from Korea, being teased by a U.S. male friend on the topic of her TOEFL score. In Line 6, the NNS said, "I got <u>one</u>" in response to the question of whether she had taken the TOEFL test. The verb *got* instead of *took* plus the focus on the word *one* could be taken to convey the meaning that she received a score of one point on the test—instead of which, she had meant to convey that she had taken the TOEFL test one time. The NS decided to tease her about the error by pretending to take the "one point" meaning seriously and then criticizing her for getting such a low score. She did not catch onto the joke until Line 25. Although I personally would have decked the guy, she appeared to take the joke in stride. Others admired her graceful exit from the episode: her good humor and laughter in Lines 25–32 and the amused comment "Funny" in Line 33.

This segment provided the opportunity to teach the students more about the placement of focus. It also opened up the whole question of the pragmatics of teasing—when it is appropriate, who can tease whom, how far one can go, which topics are taboo, and what the options are if one is uncomfortable. Although an excerpt like this one may not lead to any clear-cut generalizations about the language of teasing, the analysis did help the student to understand how she had missed the NS's initiation of the joke and how her own word choice and intonation might have led to the possible dual meaning (data from Wennerstrom, 2000).

7.

	NNS:	Today we're gonna talk abou:::::t —
		I don't know.
	NS:	The TOEFL test.
	NNS:	Ohhh! My TOEFL test!
5	NS:	Yeah.
	NNS:	I got one.
	NS:	Just one? That's really low.
	NNS:	No, it's not low.
		It's ⌈ not low.
10	NS:	⌊ 's a low score.
	NNS:	Who say that?
	NS:	A one? —
	NNS:	hhh
	NS:	Out of six hundred or something?
15		That's really ⌈ low
	NNS:	⌊ Six hundred,
	NS:	uh huh=
	NNS:	=is REALLY HIGH SCORE!
	NS:	Yeah but ⌈ you got
20	NNS:	⌊ If I got six hundred
		I can get into HARVARD UNI- UNIVERSITY
	NS:	Well you said you just got a one.
	NNS:	I just got a one?
	NS:	Yeah.
25	NNS:	⌈ One point? huh huh huh
	NS:	⌊ One point?
	NNS:	hahahaha Hey!!
	NS:	OHHHH! You mean you took one of the tests.
	NNS:	Yes, I just took ⌈ just once. heeheeheehee
30	NS:	⌊ OHHHHH!! I understand now.
		⌈ oh, I thought you spoke English better.
	NNS:	⌊ hahahahahahaha —
		Funny.

(pp. 115, 119). Reprinted with permission.

Vocabulary

Transcripts are an excellent source of data for vocabulary development because the words are always embedded in context. New words and expressions are often discovered during the transcription of the NS's part of the conversation. Students can be encouraged to keep ongoing journal entries of new vocabulary from the transcripts along with the contexts in which they occurred. If some language cannot be deciphered at all, students can leave blanks in their transcripts so that others in their group or the instructor can catch the missing words.

Another outcome of the transcription process is that students may be motivated to find alternatives to their own word choices. This can be seen in the transcript in Example 8 from a conversation between a Chinese woman (a NNS) and a U.S. man (a NS) who had just returned from San Francisco. From the transcript, it is clear that this NNS liked to inject positive exclamations into her conversation. However, she felt that she overused the word *great*, which occurred in Lines 6, 15, 18, and 34. By adding a few alternatives to her repertoire—*Wonderful!, Cool!, Interesting!*—she could make her contributions more varied in the future.

8.

```
      NS:   . . . no I just came back from there today.
      NNS:  mm hmm. How was the weather?
      NS:   Oh, the weather was beautiful!
      NNS:  Really?
  5   NS:   Really really nice.
      NNS:  ah hah. That's great.
      NS:   but — I don't know — uh Chinatown was nice —
            I went to Chinatown.
      NNS:  ah huh
 10   NS:   It's really big.
      NNS:  mm hmm
      NS:   It's a lot bigger than Seattle's Chinatown.
      NNS:  Did you eat something?
      NS:   Yeah, I ate some      ⎡ Taiwanese food
 15   NNS:                        ⎣ Wow that's grea-
            Chinese food?
      NS:   Taiwanese.
      NNS:  Uh huh that's great.
            What kind of food.
 20   NS:   oh I- just some Mongolian beef and rice
      NNS:  ah huh. Hch
            May-maybe my roommate?
            she can make it.
      NS:   ⎡ oh
 25   NNS:  ⎣ hhh
            She's a good cook but I'm not good — about cooking so
      NS:   yeah.
      NNS:  yeah
      NS:   How about that movie.
 30   NNS:  movie?
      NS:   um
      NNS:  Aah! hh
      NS:   ((xxx)) sick
      NNS:  Yeah, that looks great!
 35         but uh   we cannot understand very well because —
            they y- speak kind of British English?
      NS:   yeah?
      NNS:  yeah, so its really hard to catch the word.
```

Follow-Up Activities

At the end of each unit, follow-up activities give students the opportunity to practice interactive language skills and build self-confidence for future encounters:

- Instructors or students can develop role-play situations for others to perform spontaneously. It can be interesting to vary the situation of the role plays in order to practice the corresponding language variation. For example, the language one uses in a brief encounter with a taxi driver is quite different from that of meeting a friend's parents for the first time.

- A further extension of this activity is for students to write and perform short skits incorporating new conversational strategies and gambits.

- Another option is for instructors to develop follow-up activities using recycled transcripts from previous classes. Certain lines or segments can be left missing in the transcripts and students, working individually or in groups, can be asked to supply appropriate contributions.

- Students may also be assigned to revisit previous skills in their own future transcripts, so that skill building becomes a cumulative process.

- Finally, in their journals, students can reflect on what they have learned, making generalizations and conclusions about conversation management, linguistic accuracy, and their own role in the interaction.

◈ DISTINGUISHING FEATURES

Students Choosing Texts

What distinguishes this approach from that of more traditional conversation classes is that it is the students who choose the texts for the class, based on their own real-life interactions. As can be seen from the sample transcripts, there is a wide gap between the hypothetical dialogues found in many textbooks and the actual dynamics of interaction captured by these students. By using their own texts in class, students bridge the gap between classroom and real-world language. Encounters in the outside world that may be uncomfortable and difficult to control can be better understood, and alternative approaches can be designed. By sharing their experience with others, students can feel support for their progress. The process of self-analysis is highly motivating, resulting in a stronger feeling of competence and self-confidence.

Learner Autonomy and Individualization

The approach also allows for a high degree of individualized learning because each transcript reflects its creator's own stage of development. Thus, conversation management skills, grammar, pronunciation, intonation, and vocabulary can be studied at an appropriate level for a particular individual's current language proficiency. By keeping individual journals, students can record their ongoing progress, and monitor particular aspects of their language development from one transcript to the next throughout the course.

Pragmatic Focus

Beyond linguistic development, the conversation-analysis approach offers students the opportunity to improve their sociolinguistic competence. Pragmatic issues are bound to arise—personal questions, teasing, and jargon, for example, as the sample transcripts have demonstrated. However, it is also possible for students to pursue other cultural issues that they deem interesting or relevant to their lives. By varying the conversation topic and by choosing conversation partners of different ages, genders, dialect groups, and so on, students can actively explore the cultures of their host countries.

◈ PRACTICAL IDEAS

Adapt the Approach to Different Student Populations

Although I have applied this approach to a general conversation class, it is easily adaptable to the needs of different student populations. English for specific purposes (ESP) courses can be designed with a data collection component within the target discourse communities (cf. Swales, 1990). For example, a course in business communication can involve the audiotaping of encounters at the workplace.[3] If an employee is required to give a business presentation, he or she can record and transcribe it for analysis. Similarly, in an ESP course of academic English, students can be directed to collect data from those discourse genres most prevalent in the academic setting—study group meetings, class discussions, meetings with advisers, and the like. Such speech analysis assignments can be interspersed with other activities in the ESP context.

Target a Variety of Skill Areas

Another adaptation is to slant the course toward particular language skill areas by assigning conversation topics to target certain constructions. The result of such targeting can be a kind of content-based grammar or pronunciation class (cf. Wennerstrom, 1992). For example, in a grammar class, a story-swapping topic can be introduced requiring the use of various past tenses. I have asked students to audiotape stories from their lives and then draw timelines to illustrate the sequence of events in order to study the use of various verb tenses in combination. Such adaptations can also be made for level of proficiency in English. Lower level students can be encouraged to audiotape brief service encounters, rather than longer conversations, while more advanced students can engage in more demanding types of encounters.

Adapt the Approach to Local Constraints

If the logistics of audiotaping is difficult in some settings, it is possible to adapt the assignments to take this into account. In countries where the cost of equipment is

---

[3] Slade and Norris (1986) provide an interesting source of data with ESOL activities in the area of workplace discourse.

prohibitive, students can work in teams with a single tape recorder. Riggenbach (1999) cites an instance in her own teaching in Zimbabwe: 40 students developed a rotation system to share a single tape recorder in small teams. It is also possible to use preexisting scripts from movies, television shows, or radio talk shows, or to use a combination of these along with a small number of student transcripts. At the other end of the economic spectrum, some students have access to video recorders, which are excellent data collection devices, allowing for discussion of body language, eye contact, and other nonverbal behaviors.

Emphasize the Ethics of Recording Speech

Whatever the technology, it is important to discuss the etiquette and legal aspects of audiotaping and to stress the importance of obtaining permission before taping the speech of others. Instructors can provide information sheets explaining the assignment; students can then present these sheets, or variations, to potential conversation partners and obtain their permission to be taped. If students make it clear that the spirit of the assignment is to improve their language skills, it is usually possible to obtain cooperation.

◈ CONCLUSION

The program described here engages students and instructors in the active process of discourse analysis research. By focusing on naturally occurring conversations, ESOL learners acquire an awareness of the linguistic and cultural norms of social interaction in their host country. Within the relatively safe community of the classroom, students are able to analyze the details of their real-world social encounters, sharing and developing strategies of conversation management. Each individual can discover facts about his or her own language development and study grammar, pronunciation, and intonation at an appropriate level of difficulty. Conversation analysis allows students to become more flexible in their use of language and more self-reliant in facing the interactions of their daily lives. Indeed, course evaluations from the students attest to the success of this approach: The first time I used these materials, the course was rated 3.7 out of a maximum of 4 on a series of questions about student satisfaction. In the words of one student, "Discourse analysis is difficult, but it is so very interesting."

Finally, although the emphasis of this chapter has been on what the learners can achieve through conversation analysis, the field of TESOL as a whole could undoubtedly benefit from a better understanding of interactive interlanguage data as well. Therefore, I recommend that instructors and researchers continue to compile excerpts of language learners' conversations. A corpus of such data could ultimately lead to the development of more comprehensive models of language acquisition in interactive settings and the pragmatics of cross-cultural communication.

◈ CONTRIBUTOR

Ann Wennerstrom teaches applied linguistics and ESL at the University of Washington, in the United States. She is the author of *The Music of Everyday Speech: Prosody for*

Discourse Analysts (2001), *Techniques for Teachers: A Guide for Nonnative Speakers of English* (1991), and several articles on intonation and discourse.

◈ APPENDIX: KEY TO TRANSCRIPT

Overlapping utterances	[	A:	I used to smoke [a lot
		B:	⌞ I see
One speaker latches onto the next	=	A:	I used to smoke=
		B:	=I see
Timed pause	(time)	When I was (.6) oh nine or ten
Short untimed pause	—	Umm — my mother will be right in
Thought group division	/	I was so upset / and I was so embarrassed.
Prolonged vowel	:::	I'm so::: sorry
Abrupt cutoff	-	I just- don't know
Final, falling intonation	.	That's great.
Continuing intonation	,	Thanks, but I can't come.
Rising intonation	?	He was late?
Prominence/focus	word	It happens to be <u>mine</u>.
Louder speech	WORD	And the winner i::s (1.4) RACHAEL ROBERTS
Other comments	((text))	I used to ((cough)) smoke a lot.
		((loud bang)) What was that?
Can't decipher	((xxx))	That was ((xxx))

(Many of these conventions are typically used in conversation analysis research, e.g., Jefferson, 1984)

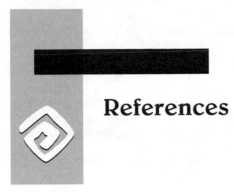

References

Abercrombie, D. (1967). *Elements of general phonetics*. Edinburgh, Scotland: University of Edinburgh.

Allwright, D. (1988). *Observation in the language classroom*. London: Longman.

Allwright, D. (1998). Contextual factors in classroom language learning: An overview. In K. Malmkaer & J. Williams (Eds.), *Context in language learning and language understanding*. Cambridge: Cambridge University Press.

Allwright, D., & Bailey, K. (1991). *Focus on the language learner*. Cambridge: Cambridge University Press.

Anderson-Hsieh, J. (1990). Teaching suprasegmentals to international teaching assistants using field-specific materials. *English for Specific Purposes, 9,* 195–214.

Andrews, M. (1995). *Manual of voice treatment*. San Diego, CA: Singular Press.

Arslan, L., & Hansen, J. (1997). A study of temporal features and frequency characteristics in American English foreign accent. *Journal of the Acoustical Society of America, 102*(1), 28–40.

Aston, G. (1993). Notes on the interlanguage of comity. In G. Kasper & S. Blum-Kulka (Eds.), *Interlanguage pragmatics* (pp. 224–250). New York: Oxford University Press.

Atkinson, J. M., & Heritage, J. (1984). *Structures of social action*. Cambridge: Cambridge University Press.

Bailey, K. M., Curtis, A., & Nunan, D. (1998). Undeniable insights: The collaborative use of three professional development practices. *TESOL Quarterly, 32,* 546–556.

Banbrook, L., & Skehan, P. (1989). Classrooms and display questions. In C. Brumfit & R. Mitchell (Eds.), *Research in the language classroom* (MEP Documents 33). London: Modern English Publications & The British Council.

BBC World Service. (n.d.). Retrieved December 16, 2002, from http://www.bbc.co.uk/worldservice/index.shtml

Beddor, P. (1991). Predicting the structure of phonological systems. *Phonetica, 48,* 83–107.

Berry, M. (1981). Systemic linguistics and discourse analysis: A multilayered approach to exchange structure (Class handout). Abridged version published in M. Coulthard & M. Montgomery (Eds.), *Studies in discourse analysis*. London: Routledge & Kegan Paul.

Bialystok, E. (1990). *Communication strategies: A psychological analysis of second-language use*. Oxford: Basil Blackwell.

Biber, D., Conrad, S., & Reppen, R. (1998). *Corpus linguistics: Investigating language structure and use*. Cambridge: Cambridge University Press.

Brazil, D. (1985). *The communicative value of intonation* (Discourse Analysis Monograph 8). Birmingham, England: University of Birmingham English Language Research.

Breen, M. P. (1985). The social context for language learning—A neglected situation? *Studies in Second Language Acquisition, 7,* 136–158.

Brindley, G. (1990). Towards a research agenda for TESOL. *Prospect, 6*(1), 7–26.

Brindley, G. (1991). Becoming a researcher: Teacher conducted research and professional growth. In E. Sadtono (Ed.), *Issues in language teacher education* (pp. 89–105). Singapore: SEAMEO Regional English Language Centre.

Brown, A. (1997). *Use of English in teaching.* Singapore: Prentice Hall.

Brown, H. D. (1994). *Teaching by principles.* Upper Saddle River, NJ: Prentice Hall Regents.

Brown, K., & Hood, S. (1989). *Writing matters.* Cambridge: Cambridge University Press.

Bruner, J. S. (1984). Vygotsky's zone of proximal development: The hidden agenda. In B. Rugoff & J. V. Wertson (Eds.), *Children's learning in the "zone of proximal development"* (pp. 93–97). San Francisco: Jossey Bass.

Burns, A. (1999). *Collaborative action research for English language teachers.* Cambridge: Cambridge University Press.

Burns, A. (2000). Facilitating collaborative research: Some insights from the AMEP. *Prospect, 15,* 23–34.

Burns, A. (2001). Analysing spoken discourse: Implications for TESOL . In A. Burns & C. Coffin (Eds.), *Analysing English in a global context* (pp. 143–148). London: Routledge.

Burns, A., & de Silva Joyce, H. (1997). *Focus on speaking.* Sydney, Australia: National Centre for English Language Teaching and Research.

Burns, A., & de Silva Joyce, H. (2000, June). *Teaching speaking.* Workshop presented to National Centre for English Language Teaching and Research and New South Wales. Adult Migrant Education Service, Sydney, Australia.

Burns, A., & Gardner, R. (Eds.). (1997). Spoken discourse [Special issue]. *Prospect, 12*(2).

Burns, A., Joyce, H., & Gollin, S. (1996). *"I see what you mean". Using spoken discourse in the classroom: A handbook for teachers.* Sydney, Australia: National Centre for English Language Teaching and Research.

Burns, A., & McPherson, P. (2001). An Australian adult ESL settlement classroom. In P. Byrd & J. Murphy (Eds.), *Understanding the courses we teach: Local perspectives on English language teaching* (pp. 155–176). Ann Arbor: University of Michigan Press.

Burns, A., & Seidlhofer, B. (2002). Teaching speaking and pronunciation. In N. Schmitt (Ed.), *An introduction to applied linguistics* (pp. 211–232). London: Edward Arnold.

Burton, J. I. (1997). Sustaining language teachers as researchers of their own practice. *The Canadian Modern Language Review/La Revue Canadienne de Langues Vivantes, 54,* 84–109.

Burton, J. I. (1998a). A cross-case analysis of teacher involvement in TESOL research. *TESOL Quarterly, 32,* 419–446.

Burton, J. I. (1998b). Current developments in language curriculum design: An Australian perspective. *Annual Review of Applied Linguistics, 18,* 287–303.

Burton, J. I. (1998c). Professionalism in language teaching. *Prospect, 13*(3), 24–34.

Burton, J. I. (2000). Learning from discourse analysis in the ESOL classroom. *TESOL Journal, 9*(4), 24–27.

Burton, J. I., & Rusek, W. (1994). The learner as curriculum resource in English for professional employment courses. *Prospect, 9*(3), 30–46.

Carter, R. (1997). Speaking Englishes, speaking cultures, using CANCODE. *Prospect, 12*(2), 4–11.

Carter, R., & McCarthy, M. (1995). Grammar and spoken language. *Applied Linguistics, 16,* 141–158.

Carter, R., & McCarthy, M. (1997). *Exploring spoken English.* Cambridge: Cambridge University Press.

Chaudron, C. (1988). *Second language classrooms: Research on teaching and learning.* Cambridge: Cambridge University Press.

Clark, H. (1996). *Using language.* Cambridge: Cambridge University Press.

Clennell, C. (1995). Communication strategies of adult ESL learners: A discourse perspective. *Prospect, 10*(3), 4–20.

Clennell, C. (1997). Raising the pedagogic status of discourse intonation teaching. *ELT Journal, 51*(2), 117–125.

Clennell, C. (1999a). Metalinguistic features as message enhancers in learner discourse. *Prospect, 14*(1), 20–27.

Clennell, C. (1999b). Promoting pragmatic awareness and spoken discourse skills with EAP classes. *ELT Journal, 53*(2), 83–91.

Cook, G. (1989). *Discourse.* Oxford: Oxford University Press.

Corder, S. P. (1974). The significance of learners' errors. In J. Richards (Ed.), *Error analysis: Perspectives on second language acquisition* (pp. 19–27). London: Longman.

Coulthard, M. (1979). *Exchange structure.* Birmingham, England: University of Birmingham English Language Research.

Coulthard, M. (1981). *An introduction to discourse analysis.* Hong Kong: Longman.

Crookes, G. (1986). *Task classification: A cross-disciplinary review* (Technical Report No. 4). Honolulu: Centre for Second Language Classroom Research, Social Science Research Institute, University of Hawai'i.

Cruttendon, A. (1997). *Intonation* (2nd ed.). Cambridge: Cambridge University Press.

Crystal, D. (1995). *The Cambridge encyclopaedia of the English language.* Cambridge: Cambridge University Press.

Crystal, D. (1997). *English as a global language.* Cambridge: Cambridge University Press.

da Silva, R. (1999). A small-scale investigation into the intelligibility of the pronunciation of Brazilian intermediate students. *Speak Out! Newsletter of the IATEFL Pronunciation Special Interest Group, 23,* 19–25.

David, M. K. (1992). Consciousness raising of communicative strategies—A springboard to language proficiency? In B. Wijasuria & H. Gaudart (Eds.), *Teaching and learning English in challenging situations, Proceedings of the First MELTA Conference, Kuala Lumpur, Malaysian English Language Teaching Association* (pp. 45–49). Kuala Lumpur: Malaysian English Language Teaching Association.

David, M. K. (1994). Building self esteem by utilizing learner knowledge. *Thai TESOL Bulletin, 6*(2), 46–48.

David, M. K. (2000). Status and role of English in Malaysia: Ramifications for English language teaching. *English Australia, 18*(1), 41–50.

David, M. K., Tan, S. Y., Lim, S. L., Cheah, S. W. (1990). *Cockles.* Unpublished manuscript, University of Malaya, Kuala Lumpur.

Department of Immigration and Ethnic Affairs. (1986). *Hello Australia.* Canberra: Author.

de Silva Joyce, H. (Ed.). (2000). *Teachers' voices 6: Teaching casual conversation.* Sydney, Australia: National Centre for English Language Teaching and Research.

de Silva Joyce, H., & Hilton, D. (1999). *We are what we talk* (Video and workbook). Sydney, Australia: Darrell Hilton Productions.

Di Pietro, R. (1987). *Strategic interaction.* Cambridge: Cambridge University Press.

Edge, J. (Ed.). (2001). *Action research.* Alexandria, VA: TESOL.

Edge, J., & Richards, K. (Eds.) (1993). *Teachers develop teachers research 2.* Oxford: Heinemann.

Edmondson, W., & House, J. (1981). *Let's talk and talk about it.* Munich, Germany: Urban und Schwarzenberg.

Eggins, S. (1994). *An introduction to systemic functional linguistics.* London: Pinter.

Ellis, R. (1986). *Understanding second language acquisition.* Oxford: Oxford University Press.

Ellis, R. (1990). *Instructed second language acquisition.* Oxford: Basil Blackwell.

Ellis, R. (1994). *The study of second language acquisition.* Oxford: Oxford University Press.

Ellis, R. (1997). *Second language acquisition.* Oxford: Oxford University Press.

Esling, J. (1987). Methodology for voice setting awareness and the teaching of pronunciation. *Revue de Phonétique Appliquée, 89,* 449–472.

Esling, J. (1994). Some perspectives on accent: Range of voice quality variation, the periphery, and focusing. In J. Morley (Ed.), *Pronunciation pedagogy and theory: New views, new directions* (pp. 44–63). Alexandria, VA: TESOL.

Esling, J., & Wong, R. (1983). Voice quality settings and the teaching of pronunciation. *TESOL Quarterly, 17,* 89–95.

Faerch, C., & Kasper, G. (Eds.). (1983). *Strategies in interlanguage communication.* London: Longman.

Fairclough, N. (1989). *Language and power.* London: Longman.

Fawcus, M. (1986). *Voice disorders and their management.* London: Chapman & Hall.

Feez, S. (1998). *Text-based syllabus design.* Sydney, Australia: National Centre for English Language Teaching and Research.

Flowerdew, J., & Miller, L. (1996). Lectures in a second language: Notes towards a cultural grammar. *ESP Journal, 15*(2), 121–140.

Freeman, D. (1998). *Doing teacher-research: From inquiry to understanding.* Boston: Heinle & Heinle.

Fry, D. (1979). *The physics of speech.* Cambridge: Cambridge University Press.

Gass, S., & Varonis, E. (1985). Task variation and nonnative/nonnative negotiation of meaning. In S. Gass & C. Madden (Eds.), *Input in second language acquisition* (pp. 149–161). Rowley, MA: Newbury House.

Gebhard, J. G., & Oprandy, R. (1999). *Language teaching awareness: A guide to exploring beliefs and practices.* New York: Cambridge University Press.

Gee, J. (1990). *Social linguistics and literacies: Ideologies in discourses.* London: Falmer.

Gilbert, J. (2001). *Clear speech from the start.* Cambridge: Cambridge University Press.

Giles, H., & Coupland, N. (1991). *Language: Contexts and consequences.* Milton Keynes, England: Open University Press.

Giles, H., & St. Clair, R. (1979). *Language and social psychology.* Oxford: Basil Blackwell.

Giles, H., & Saint-Jacques, B. (1979). *Language and ethnic relations.* New York: Pergamon Press.

Glew, P. J. (1998). Verbal interaction and English second language acquisition in the classroom context. *Issues in Educational Research, 8*(2), 83–94.

Gnutzmann, C. (Ed.). (1999). *Teaching and learning English as a global language.* Tubingen, Germany: Stauffenburg Verlag.

Goffman, E. (1974). *Frame analysis: An essay on the organization of experience.* New York: Harper & Row.

Gollin, S. (1994). Some insights from the NCELTR Spoken Discourse Project. *Interchange, 23,* 28–31.

Graddol, D. (1997). *The future of English?* London: The British Council.

Hadfield, J. (1990). *Intermediate communication games.* Surrey, England: Thomas Nelson & Sons.

Haines, S., & Stewart, B. (1996). *New first certificate masterclass.* Oxford: Oxford University Press.

Halliday, M. A. K. (1967). *Intonation and grammar in British English.* The Hague: Mouton.

Halliday, M. A. K. (1985). *Spoken and written language.* Melbourne, Australia: Deakin University Press.

Halliday, M. A. K. (1991). The notion of "context" in language education. In T. Le & M. McCausland (Eds.), *Language education: Interaction and development* (pp. 39–61). Launceston: University of Tasmania.

Halliday, M. A. K. (1994). *An introduction to functional grammar* (2nd ed.). London: Edward Arnold.

Hammond, J. (1989). The NCELTR Literacy Project. *Prospect, 5*(1), 23–30.

Hammond, J. (1990). Is learning to read and write the same as learning to speak? In F. Christie (Ed.), *Literacy for a changing world* (pp. 26–53). Hawthorn, Victoria: Australian Council for Educational Research.

Hammond, J., Burns, A., Joyce, H., Gerot, L., & Brosnan, D. (1992). *English for social purposes.* Sydney, Australia: National Centre for English Language Teaching and Research.

Hancock, M. (1995). *Pronunciation games.* Cambridge: Cambridge University Press.

Hancock, M. (1997). Behind classroom code switching: Layering and language choice in L2 learner interaction. *TESOL Quarterly, 31,* 217–235.

Harshbarger, W. (1985). Teaching conversation management. *WAESOL Newsletter, 15*(2), 4–7.

Hashimoto, O.-K.Y. (1972). *Phonology of Cantonese.* Cambridge: Cambridge University Press.

Hatch, E. (1992). *Discourse and language education.* Cambridge: Cambridge University Press.

Honikman, B. (1964). Articulatory settings. In D. Abercrombie, D. Fry, P. MacCarthy, N. Scott, & J. Trim (Eds.), *In honour of Daniel Jones* (pp. 73–84). London: Longman.

House, J. (1999). Misunderstanding in intercultural communication: Interactions in English as *lingua franca* and the myth of mutual intelligibility. In C. Gnutzmann (Ed.), *Teaching and learning English as a global language.* Tubingen, Germany: Stauffenburg Verlag.

Iwashita, N. (1999). *The role of task-based conversation in the acquisition of Japanese grammar and vocabulary.* Unpublished doctoral dissertation, University of Melbourne, Australia.

Jariah Mohd, J., & David, M. K. (1996). Oral skills—A need for acceptance of L1 cultural norms. *Pertanika Journal of Social Science and Humanities, 4*(1), 11–19.

Jefferson, G. (1984). Transcript notation. In J. M. Atkinson & J. Heritage (Eds.), *Structures of social action: Studies in conversation analysis* (pp. ix–xvi). Cambridge: Cambridge University Press.

Jenkins, J. (2000). *The phonology of English as an international language: New models, new norms, new goals.* Oxford: Oxford University Press.

Johnson, K. (1982). *Communicative syllabus design and methodology.* London: Pergamon.

Johnson, K. (1996). *Language teaching and skill learning.* Oxford: Blackwell.

Johnson, K., & Morrow, K. (1981). *Communication in the classroom.* London: Longman.

Jones, J. (1999). From silence to talk: Cross-cultural ideas on students' participation in academic group discussion. *English for Specific Purposes, 18,* 243–259.

Kao, D. (1971). *Structure of the syllable in Cantonese.* The Hague: Mouton.

Kasper, G. (1998). A bilingual perspective on interlanguage pragmatics. In J. H. O'Mealy & L.E. Lyons (Eds.), *Language, linguistics and leadership. Essays in honor of Carol M. K. Eastman.* Honolulu: University of Hawai'i Press.

Kebir, C. (1994). An action research look at the communication strategies of adult learners. *TESOL Journal, 4*(1), 28–31.

Kellerman, E. (1991). Compensatory strategies in second language research: A critique, a revision and some (non-) implications for the classroom. In R. Phillipson, E. Kellerman, L. Selinker, M. Sharwood Smith, & M. Swain (Eds.), *Foreign pedagogy research.* Clevedon, England: Multilingual Matters.

Kemmis, S., & McTaggart, R. (Eds.). (1988). *The action research planner.* Geelong, Victoria, Australia: Deakin University Press.

Kerr, J. (1998). *Changing focus of resonance: Effects on intelligibility in a Cantonese speaker.* Unpublished master's thesis, Deakin University, Geelong, Victoria, Australia.

Kerr, J. (2000). Articulatory setting and voice production: Issues in accent modification. *Prospect, 15*(2), 4–15.

Kingston, J. (1991). Integrating articulations in the perception of vowel height. *Phonetica, 48,* 149–179.

Knowles, G. (1987). *Patterns of spoken English: An introduction to English phonetics.* London: Longman.

Kow, Y. C. (1995). It is a tag question, isn't it? *The English Teacher, 1*(24), 42–55.

Kow, Y. C. (2000). *Strategies employed by pre-school children in communicating meaning.* Unpublished doctoral dissertation. University of Malaya, Kuala Lumpur.

Kramsch, C. (1985). Classroom interaction and discourse options. *Studies in Second Language Acquisition, 7,* 169–183.

Krashen, S. D. (1982). *Principles and practice in second language acquisition.* Oxford: Pergamon Press.

Labov, W. (1972). *Sociolinguistic patterns.* Philadelphia: University of Pennsylvania Press.

Ladefoged, P., & Maddieson, I. (1990). Vowels of the world's languages. *Journal of Phonetics, 18,* 93–122.

Laroy, C. (1996). *Pronunciation.* Oxford: Oxford University Press.

Larsen-Freeman, D., & Long, M. (1991). *An introduction to second language acquisition research.* London: Longman.

Laver, J. (1980). *The phonetic description of voice quality.* Cambridge: Cambridge University Press.

Lippi-Green, R. (1997). *English with an accent.* New York: Routledge.

Long, M. H. (1983a). Linguistic and conversational adjustments to non-native speakers. *Studies in Second Language Acquisition, 5,* 177–194.

Long, M. H. (1983b). Native speaker/nonnative speaker conversation and the negotiation of comprehensible input. *Applied Linguistics, 4,* 126–141.

Long, M. H. (1985). Input and second language acquisition theory. In S. Gass & C. Madden (Eds.), *Input in second language acquisition* (pp. 377–393). Rowley, MA: Newbury House.

Long, M. H. (1996). The role of the linguistic environment in second language acquisition. In W. C. Ritchie & V. S. Bhatia (Eds.), *Handbook of research on language acquisition: Vol. 2. Second language acquisition* (pp. 413–468). New York: Academic Press.

Long, M. H., & Crookes, G. (1992). Three approaches to task-based syllabus design. *TESOL Quarterly, 26,* 27–56.

Long, M. H., & Robinson, P. (1998). Focus on form: Theory, research and practice. In C. Doughty & J. Williams (Eds.), *Focus on form in classroom second language acquisition* (pp. 15–41). Cambridge: Cambridge University Press.

Lynch, T. (2001). Seeing what they meant: Transcribing as a route to noticing. *ELT Journal, 55* (2), 124–132.

Lynch, T., & Anderson, K. (1992). *Study speaking.* Cambridge: Cambridge University Press.

Lyster, R. (1998). Recasts, repetition, and ambiguity in L2 classroom discourse. *Studies in Second Language Acquisition, 20,* 51–81.

Mackay, A. (1995). *Stepping up the pace: Input, interaction, and interlanguage development: An empirical study of questions in ESL.* Unpublished doctoral dissertation, University of Sydney, Australia.

Macneil, D. (1987). Some characteristic aspects of Vietnamese English pronunciation. *Prospect, 3*(1), 61–72.

Maynard, S. (1986). Interactional aspects of thematic progression in English casual conversations. *Text, 6*(1), 73–106.

McCarthy, M. (1991). *Discourse analysis for language teachers.* Cambridge: Cambridge University Press.

McCarthy, M., & Carter, R. (1994). *Language as discourse: Perspectives for language teaching.* London: Longman.

McKay, P., Bowyer, L., & Commins, L. (2000). *Towards informal work talk: Investigating the teaching of casual conversation in workplace English.* Unpublished project report, National Centre for English Language Teaching and Research, Macquarie University, Sydney, Australia.

McNiff, J., Lomax, P., & Whitehead, J. (1996). *You and your action research project*. London: Routledge.

Mercer, N. (1994). Neo-Vygotskian theory and classroom education. In B. Stierer & J.Maybin (Eds.), *Language, literacy, and learning in educational practice* (pp. 92–110). Clevedon, England: Multilingual Matters.

Moncur, J., & Brackett, I. (1974). *Modifying vocal behaviour.* New York: Harper & Row.

Murphy, J. (1992). Preparing ESL students for the basic speech course: Approach, design and procedure. *English for Specific Purposes, 11,* 51–70.

Neil, D. (1996). *Collaboration in intercultural discourse*. Bern, Switzerland: Peter Lang Verlag.

Nemetz Robinson, G. (1985). *Crosscultural understanding: Processes and approaches for foreign language, English as a second language and bilingual instructors*. Oxford: Pergamon Press.

Nichols, S. (1998). Current issues in oral literacy. In P. Cormack, P. Wignell, & S. Nichols (Eds.), *Classroom discourse in the upper primary and early secondary years: What kind of school-based activities allow students to demonstrate achievement of outcomes in talking and listening?* (Vol. 1; pp. 8–29). Canberra, Australia: Department of Employment, Education, Training and Youth Affairs.

Nichols, S. (2001). *Mapping the literacies of young adulthood: A review of literature.* Adelaide, Australia: Senior Secondary Assessment Board of South Australia/Centre for Studies in Literacy, Policy and Learning Cultures.

Nichols, S., & Najar, R. (2000). Making knowledge claims: Assisting international students to formulate and authorise topics. In C. Beasley (Ed.), *Making the critical connection. Proceedings of the Third Biennial Communication Skills in University Education Conference, 28–29 September*, Fremantle, Western Australia (pp. 142-151). Murdoch, Australia: Murdoch University Teaching and Learning Centre.

Nolan, F. (1983). *The phonetic bases of speaker recognition*. Cambridge: Cambridge University Press.

Nunan, D. (1988). *The learner-centred curriculum*. Cambridge: Cambridge University Press.

Nunan, D. (1989a). *Designing tasks for the communicative classroom*. Cambridge: Cambridge University Press.

Nunan, D. (1989b). *Understanding language classrooms: A guide for teacher-initiated action*. London: Prentice Hall.

Nunan, D. (1992). *Research methods in language learning*. Cambridge: Cambridge University Press.

Nunan, D. (1995). *Language teaching methodology*. New York: Prentice Hall.

Nunan, D., & Lamb, C. (1996). *The self-directed teacher.* Cambridge: Cambridge University Press.

Omar, A. (1995). Indirectness as a rule of speaking among the Malays. In Z. A. Majid & L. M. Baskaran (Eds.), *Rules of speaking* (pp. 47–60). Kuala Lumpur, Malayasia: Pelanduk Publications, Malaysian Association of Modern Languages.

Owen, C. (1993). Corpus-based grammar and the Heineken effect: Lexico-grammatical description for language learners. *Applied Linguistics, 14,* 167–187.

Pennington, M. (1996). *Phonology in English language teaching*. New York: Longman.

Pennycook, A. (1996). Borrowing others' words: Text, ownership, memory and plagiarism. *TESOL Quarterly, 30,* 201–330.

Pennycook, A. (1999). Introduction: Critical approaches to TESOL. *TESOL Quarterly, 33,* 329–347.

Pennycook, A. (2000). The social politics and the cultural politics of language classrooms. In J. K. Hall & W. G. Eggington (Eds.), *The sociopolitics of English language teaching*. Clevedon, England: Multilingual Matters.

Phillipson, R. (1992). *Linguistic imperialism*. Oxford: Oxford University Press.

Pica, T. (1994a). Questions from the language classroom: Research perspectives. *TESOL Quarterly, 28,* 49–79.

Pica, T. (1994b). Research on negotiation: What does it reveal about second language learning conditions, processes, and outcomes? *Language Learning, 44,* 493–527.

Pica, T., & Doughty, C. (1985). Input and interaction in the communicative language classroom: A comparison of teacher-fronted and group activities. In S. Gass & C. Madden (Eds.), *Input in second language acquisition* (pp. 115–136). Rowley, MA: Newbury House.

Pica, T., Lincoln-Porter, F., Paninos, D., & Linnell, J. (1996). Language learners' interaction: How does it address the input, output and feedback needs of L2 learners? *TESOL Quarterly, 30,* 59–84.

Pierce, B. N. (1995). Social identity, investment and language learning. *TESOL Quarterly, 29,* 9–31.

Pierrehumbert, J. (1980). *The phonology and phonetics of English intonation.* Unpublished doctoral dissertation, Massachusetts Institute of Technology, Cambridge, MA.

Prabhu, N. (1987). *Second language pedagogy.* Oxford: Oxford University Press.

Rampton, B. (1997). A sociolinguistic perspective on L2 communication strategies. In G. Kasper & E. Kellerman (Eds.), *Communication strategies: Psycholinguistic and sociolinguistic perspectives* (pp. 279–303). London: Longman.

Ramsey, R. (1987). *The languages of China.* Princeton, NJ: Princeton University Press.

Richards, J. C., & Lockhart, C. (1994). *Reflective teaching in second language classrooms.* Cambridge: Cambridge University Press.

Riggenbach, H. (1999). *Discourse analysis in the language classroom: Vol. 1. The spoken language.* Ann Arbor: University of Michigan Press.

Rivers, W. M. (1978). *Practical guide to the teaching of English as a second or foreign language.* New York: Oxford University Press.

Rutherford, W. (1987). *Second language grammar: Learning and teaching.* London: Longman.

Sacks, H., Schegloff, E., & Jefferson, G. (1974). A simplest systematics for the organization of turntaking for conversation. *Language, 50,* 696–735.

Samuda, V., & Rounds, P. L. (1993). Critical episodes: Reference points for analyzing a task in action. In G. Crookes & S. Gass (Eds.), *Tasks in language learning: Integrating theory and practice* (pp. 125–138). Clevedon, England: Multilingual Matters.

Sato, C. J. (1990). Ethnic styles in classroom discourse. In R.C. Scarcella, E. S. Anderson, & S. D. Krashen (Eds.), *Developing communicative competence in a second language: Series on issues in second language research* (pp. 107–119). Boston: Heinle & Heinle.

Savignon, S. (1991). Communicative language teaching: State of the art. *TESOL Quarterly, 25,* 261–278.

Scarcella, R. (1990). Communicative difficulties in second language production, development and instruction. In R. Scarcella, E. Anderson, & S. Krashen (Eds.), *Developing communicative competence in a second language.* Rowley, MA: Newbury House.

Schiffrin, D. (1996). Interactional sociolinguistics. In S. L. McKay & N. H. Hornberger (Eds.), *Sociolinguistics and language teaching* (pp. 307–328). New York: Cambridge University Press.

Seidlhofer, B. (2000). Mind the gap: English as a mother tongue vs English as a *lingua franca. Vienna English Working Papers, 9*(1), 51–68.

Seidlhofer, B. (2001). Closing a conceptual gap: The case for a description of English as a *lingua franca. International Journal of Applied Linguistics, 11,* 133–158.

Selinker, L. (1974). Interlanguage. In J. Richards (Ed.), *Error analysis: Perspectives on second language acquisition* (pp. 31–54). London: Longman.

Selinker, L. (1988). *Papers in interlanguage.* Singapore: RELC.

Sinclair, J., & Brazil, D. (1982). *Teacher talk.* Oxford: Oxford University Press.

Sinclair, J., & Coulthard, M. (1975). *Towards an analysis of discourse.* Oxford: Oxford University Press.

Slade, D., & Norris, L. (1986). *Teaching casual conversation: Topics, strategies, and interactional skills.* Sydney, Australia: National Centre for English Language Teaching and Research.

So, L., & Dodd, B. (1995). The acquisition of phonology by Cantonese-speaking children. *Journal of Child Language, 22,* 473–495.

Stake, R. E. (1995). *The art of case study research.* Thousand Oaks, CA: Sage.

Stierer, B., & Maybin, J. (1994). *Language, literacy and learning in educational practice.* Clevedon, England: Multilingual Matters.

Swain, M. (1985). Communicative competence: Some roles of comprehensible input and comprehensible output in its development. In S. Gass & C. M. Madden (Eds.), *Input in second language acquisition* (pp. 235–253). Rowley, MA: Newbury House.

Swain, M. (1995). Three functions of output in second language learning. In G. Cook & B. Seidlhofer (Eds.), *Principle and practice in applied linguistics* (pp. 125–144). Oxford: Oxford University Press.

Swain, M. (1998). Focus on form through conscious reflection. In C. Doughty & J. Williams (Eds.), *Focus on form in classroom second language acquisition* (pp. 64–81). Cambridge: Cambridge University Press.

Swain, M. (2000). The output hypothesis and beyond: Mediating acquisition through collaborative dialogue. In J. Lantolf (Ed.), *Sociocultural theory and second language learning* (pp. 97–114). Oxford: Oxford University Press.

Swain, M., & Lapkin, S. (1995). Problems in output and the cognitive processes they generate: A step towards second language learning. *Applied Linguistics, 16,* 371–391.

Swain, M., & Lapkin, S. (1998). Interaction in second language learning: Two adolescent French immersion students working together. *Modern Language Teaching, 82,* 321–337.

Swales, J. (1990). *Genre analysis.* Cambridge: Cambridge University Press.

Tarone, E. (1980). Communication strategies: Foreigner talk and repair in intercommunication. *Language Learning, 30,* 417–431.

Tarone, E., & Yule, G. (1989). *Focus on the language learner.* Oxford: Oxford University Press.

Taylor, B. (1987). Teaching ESL: Incorporating a communicative, student-centred component. *TESOL Quarterly, 17,* 69–89.

Thomas, J. (1983). Cross-cultural pragmatic failure. *Applied Linguistics, 4,* 92–112.

Tsui, A. B. M. (1995). *Introducing classroom interaction.* London: Penguin English.

van Lier, L. (1988). *The classroom and the language learner: Ethnography of second language research.* London: Longman.

van Lier, L. (1996). *Interaction in the language curriculum: Awareness, autonomy and authenticity.* New York: Longman.

Vygotsky, L. S. (1962). *Thought and language.* Cambridge, MA: MIT Press.

Vygotsky, L. S. (1978). *Mind in society: The development of higher psychological processes.* Cambridge, MA: Harvard University Press.

Vygotsky, L. (1986). *Language and thought.* Cambridge, MA: MIT Press.

Walker, R. (2001). International intelligibility. *English Teaching Professional, 21,* 10–13.

Weiss, C. (1978). *Weiss Comprehensive Articulation Test.* Chicago: Riverside.

Wells, G. (1981). *Learning through interaction: The study of language development.* New York: Cambridge University Press.

Wennerstrom, A. (1992). Content-based pronunciation. *TESOL Journal, 1*(3), 15–18.

Wennerstrom, A. (1994). Intonational meaning in English discourse: A study of nonnative speakers. *Applied Linguistics, 15,* 399–420.

Wennerstrom, A. (2000). The role of intonation in second language fluency. In H. Riggenbach (Ed.), *Perspectives on fluency* (pp. 102–127). Ann Arbor: University of Michigan Press.

Wennerstrom, A. (in press). *Discourse analysis in the language Classroom: Vol. 2. Genres of writing.* Ann Arbor: University of Michigan Press.

Wennerstrom, A., & Riggenbach, H. (2000, March). *Discourse analysis activities in the language classroom.* Workshop presented at the 34th Annual TESOL Convention, Vancouver, BC, Canada.

West, R. (1994). Needs analysis in language teaching. *Language Teaching, 27,* 1–9.

Williams, J., Inscoe, R., & Tasker, T. (1997). Communication strategies in an interactional context: The mutual achievement of comprehension. In G. Kasper & E. Kellerman (Eds.), *Communication strategies: Psycholinguistic and sociolinguistic perspectives* (pp. 304–322). New York: Addison Wesley Longman.

Willing, K. (1987). Learning strategies as information management. *Prospect, 2,* 273–291.

Willis, J. D. (1996). *A framework for task-based learning.* Edinburgh Gate, Essex, England: Addison Wesley Longman.

Willis, J. D. (1998). *Task-based learning: What kind of adventure?* Retrieved March 10, 1998, from http://langue.hyper.chubu.ac.jp/jalt/pub/tlt/98/jul/willis/html

Wood, D., Bruner, J., & Ross, G. (1976). The role of tutoring in problem solving. *Journal of Child Psychology and Psychiatry, 17,* 89–100.

Yin, R. K. (1994). *Case study research: Design and methods* (2nd ed.). Thousand Oaks, CA: Sage.

Yong, J., & David, M. K. (1996). The effect of topic on oral performance. *The English Teacher, 25,* 87–95.

Index

Page references followed by *f, t,* and *n* refer to figures, tables, and notes respectively.

A

Abercrombie, D., 99, 103
Accent variation, as sociolinguistic right, 93
Accommodation
  definition of, 65–66
  in pronunciation, 86–91, 92–93
    teaching of, 95–97
  in TESOL education, 76–77
Action research, 129, 157, 158
Adjacency pairs, in student group
  interaction, 56–57
Adult Migrant English Program (AMEP),
  127, 131, 134
Allwright, D., 30, 130, 159
AMEP. *See* Adult Migrant English Program
Analysis of recorded discourse, value of,
  2–3
Anderson, Kenneth, 7, 8, 20, 157
Anderson-Hsieh, J., 105
Andrews, M., 103, 104
Appeals, as communication strategy, 49, 60
Approximation
  as communication strategy, 30
  teaching of, 33
Arslan, L., 103
Articles, use of, 29, 29*t*
Articulatory setting
  altering
    case study of, 105–107
    difficulty of, 99–100, 104
  in Asian languages, 102–103
  definition of, 99
  and intelligibility, 99–110

reflective practice in, 109
and vocal resonance, 100, 101–102, 102*f*
Asian language speakers
  articulatory setting of, 102–103
  pronunciation difficulties of, 100
  pronunciation program for, 100–105,
    108, 114
  vocal resonance of, 101–102, 102*f*
Aston, G., 155
Atkinson, J. M., 128
Avoidance, as communication strategy, 49,
  60

B

Bailey, K., 30
Bailey, K. M., 158
Banbrook, L., 143
BBC World Service, for pronunciation
  research, 96–97
Beddor, P., 103
Benson, Cathy, 20
Berry, M., 156
Bialystok, E., 49
Biber, D., 141
Bowyer, L., 135
Brackett, I., 104
Brainstorming, about conversational skills,
  163
Brazil, D., 130, 168*n*
Breakdown point. *See* Communication
  breakdown point
Breen, M. P., 129–130
Brindley, G., 127, 128
Brosnan, D., 131
Brown, A., 94, 95
Brown, H. D., 42

Also Available From TESOL

Academic Writing Programs
Ilona Leki, Editor

Action Research
Julian Edge, Editor

Bilingual Education
Donna Christian and Fred Genesee, Editors

Community Partnerships
Elsa Auerbach, Editor

Content-Based Instruction in Higher Education Settings
JoAnn Crandell and Dorit Kaufman, Editors

Distance-Learning Programs
Lynn E. Henrichsen, Editor

Grammar Teaching in Teacher Education
Dilin Liu and Peter Master, Editors

Implementing the ESL Standards for Pre-K-12 Students Through Teacher Education
Marguerite Ann Snow, Editor

Integrating the ESL Standards Into Classroom Practice: Grades Pre-K–2
Betty Ansin Smallwood, Editor

Integrating the ESL Standards Into Classroom Practice: Grades 3–5
Katharine Davies Samway, Editor

Integrating the ESL Standards Into Classroom Practice: Grades 6–8
Suzanne Irujo, Editor

Integrating the ESL Standards Into Classroom Practice: Grades 9–12
Barbara Agor, Editor

Intensive English Programs in Postsecondary Settings
Nicholas Dimmit and Maria Dantas-Whitney, Editors

Internet for English Teaching
Mark Warschauer, Heidi Shetzer, and Christine Meloni

Journal Writing
Jill Burton and Michael Carroll, Editors

Mainstreaming
Effie Cochran, Editor

Teacher Education
Karen E. Johnson, Editor

Technology-Enhanced Learning Environments
Elizabeth Hanson-Smith, Editor

For more information, contact
Teachers of English to Speakers of Other Languages, Inc.
700 South Washington Street, Suite 200
Alexandria, Virginia 22314 USA
Tel 703-836-0774 • Fax 703-836-6447 • publications@tesol.org •
http://www.tesol.org/